Ideology, Censorship and Translation

This volume invites us to revisit ideology, censorship and translation by adopting a variety of perspectives. It presents case studies and theoretical analyses from different chronological periods and focuses on a variety of genres, themes and audiences. Focusing on issues that have thus far not been addressed in a sufficiently connected way and from a variety of disciplines, they analyse authentic translation work, procedures and strategies.

The book considers the ethical and ideological implications for the translator, re-examines the role of the ideologist or the censor—as a stand-alone individual, as representative of a group or as part of a larger apparatus—and establishes the translator's scope of action. The chapters presented here contribute new ideas that help to elucidate both the role of the translator throughout history, and current practices. Collectively, in demonstrating the role that ideology and censorship play in the act of translation, the authors help to establish a connection between the past and the present across different genres, cultural traditions and audiences.

The chapters in this book were originally published as a special issue of *Perspectives: Studies in Translation Theory and Practice*.

Martin McLaughlin was Agnelli-Serena Professor of Italian at the University of Oxford, UK, and Director of the European Humanities Research Centre (EHRC).

Javier Muñoz-Basols is Senior Instructor in Spanish at the University of Oxford, UK, and Research Fellow at the European Humanities Research Centre (EHRC).

Ideology, Censorship and Translation

Edited by
Martin McLaughlin and Javier Muñoz-Basols

LONDON AND NEW YORK

First published 2021
by Routledge
2 Park Square, Milton Park, Abingdon, Oxon, OX14 4RN

and by Routledge
52 Vanderbilt Avenue, New York, NY 10017

Routledge is an imprint of the Taylor & Francis Group, an informa business

© 2021 Taylor & Francis

All rights reserved. No part of this book may be reprinted or reproduced or utilised in any form or by any electronic, mechanical, or other means, now known or hereafter invented, including photocopying and recording, or in any information storage or retrieval system, without permission in writing from the publishers.

Trademark notice: Product or corporate names may be trademarks or registered trademarks, and are used only for identification and explanation without intent to infringe.

British Library Cataloguing-in-Publication Data
A catalogue record for this book is available from the British Library

ISBN13: 978-0-367-60989-4

Typeset in Minion Pro
by codeMantra

Publisher's Note
The publisher accepts responsibility for any inconsistencies that may have arisen during the conversion of this book from journal articles to book chapters, namely the inclusion of journal terminology.

Disclaimer
Every effort has been made to contact copyright holders for their permission to reprint material in this book. The publishers would be grateful to hear from any copyright holder who is not here acknowledged and will undertake to rectify any errors or omissions in future editions of this book.

 Printed in the United Kingdom
by Henry Ling Limited

Contents

Citation Information vi
Notes on Contributors viii

Introduction: Ideology, censorship and translation across genres: past and present 1
Martin McLaughlin and Javier Muñoz-Basols

1 Notes on Charles Darwin's thoughts on translation and the publishing history of the European versions of [On] The Origin of Species 7
Carmen Acuña-Partal

2 "¡No Pasarán!": Translators under siege and ideological control in the Spanish Civil War 22
Marcos Rodríguez-Espinosa

3 The censorship of theatre translations under Franco: the 1960s 36
Raquel Merino-Álvarez

4 Between ideology and literature: Translation in the USSR during the Brezhnev period 48
Emily Lygo

5 Censorship and the Catalan translations of Jean-Paul Sartre 59
Pilar Godayol

6 What is an author, indeed: Michel Foucault in translation 76
Jeroen Vandaele

7 Censoring Lolita's sense of humor: when translation affects the audience's perception 93
Patrick Zabalbeascoa

8 The crooked timber of self-reflexivity: translation and ideology in the end times 115
Stefan Baumgarten

Index 131

Citation Information

The chapters in this book were originally published in the *Perspectives: Studies in Translation Theory and Practice*, volume 24, issue 1 (2016). When citing this material, please use the original page numbering for each article, as follows:

Introduction
Ideology, censorship and translation across genres: past and present
Martin McLaughlin and Javier Muñoz-Basols
Perspectives: Studies in Translation Theory and Practice, volume 24, issue 1 (2016) pp. 1–6

Chapter 1
Notes on Charles Darwin's thoughts on translation and the publishing history of the European versions of [On] The Origin of Species
Carmen Acuña-Partal
Perspectives: Studies in Translation Theory and Practice, volume 24, issue 1 (2016) pp. 7–21

Chapter 2
"¡No Pasarán!": Translators under siege and ideological control in the Spanish Civil War
Marcos Rodríguez-Espinosa
Perspectives: Studies in Translation Theory and Practice, volume 24, issue 1 (2016) pp. 22–35

Chapter 3
The censorship of theatre translations under Franco: the 1960s
Raquel Merino-Álvarez
Perspectives: Studies in Translation Theory and Practice, volume 24, issue 1 (2016) pp. 36–47

Chapter 4
Between ideology and literature: Translation in the USSR during the Brezhnev period
Emily Lygo
Perspectives: Studies in Translation Theory and Practice, volume 24, issue 1 (2016) pp. 48–58

Chapter 5
Censorship and the Catalan translations of Jean-Paul Sartre
Pilar Godayol
Perspectives: Studies in Translation Theory and Practice, volume 24, issue 1 (2016) pp. 59–75

Chapter 6
What is an author, indeed: Michel Foucault in translation
Jeroen Vandaele
Perspectives: Studies in Translation Theory and Practice, volume 24, issue 1 (2016) pp. 76–92

Chapter 7
Censoring Lolita's sense of humor: when translation affects the audience's perception
Patrick Zabalbeascoa
Perspectives: Studies in Translation Theory and Practice, volume 24, issue 1 (2016) pp. 93–114

Chapter 8
The crooked timber of self-reflexivity: translation and ideology in the end times
Stefan Baumgarten
Perspectives: Studies in Translation Theory and Practice, volume 24, issue 1 (2016) pp. 115–129

For any permission-related enquiries please visit:
http://www.tandfonline.com/page/help/permissions

Contributors

Carmen Acuña-Partal Department of Translation and Interpreting Studies, University of Malaga, Spain.

Stefan Baumgarten Department of Translation Studies, University of Graz, Austria.

Pilar Godayol Translation, Interpretation and Applied Languages; University of Vic – Central University of Catalonia, Spain.

Emily Lygo Department of Modern Languages (Russian), University of Exeter, UK.

Martin McLaughlin Sub-Faculty of Italian, Faculty of Medieval and Modern Languages, University of Oxford, UK.

Raquel Merino-Álvarez English and German Philology and Translation & Interpretation; UPV/EHU University of the Basque Country, Vitoria-Gasteiz, Spain.

Javier Muñoz-Basols Sub-Faculty of Spanish, Faculty of Medieval and Modern Languages, University of Oxford, UK.

Marcos Rodríguez-Espinosa Department of Translation and Interpreting Studies, University of Malaga, Spain.

Jeroen Vandaele Faculty of Arts and Philosophy, Ghent University, Belgium.

Patrick Zabalbeascoa Department of Translation and Language Sciences, Universitat Pompeu Fabra, Barcelona, Spain.

INTRODUCTION

Ideology, censorship and translation across genres: past and present

Martin McLaughlin and Javier Muñoz-Basols

History demonstrates that ideology and censorship are two concepts that appear to be inextricably linked to the translation process. Who translates, under what circumstances, and for what purposes are only some of the questions that come to mind as we attempt to examine the activity of translation, cognizant of the notion that 'the ideology of a translation resides not simply in the text translated, but in the voicing and stance of the translator, and in its relevance to the receiving audience' (Tymoczko 2003, p. 183).

There are numerous examples where transformations of historical accounts and literary texts have resulted in the omission or distortion of information for ideological and political purposes. In his preface to the Ukrainian translation (1947) of *Animal Farm*, George Orwell conveyed his awareness that a translation may not always be understood in the way the writer of the work intended it to be. Perhaps it is for this reason that, in addressing Ukrainian prisoners of war outside the Soviet Union, Orwell felt compelled to explain his background as a world traveller and avid reader, all the while recognizing his own lack of first-hand experience of that country: 'And here I must pause to describe my attitude to the Soviet régime. I have never visited Russia and my knowledge of it consists only of what can be learned by reading books and newspapers' (1945/1989, p. 117).

Much like Orwell, who was able to view with remarkable insight and perspicacity a political apparatus he had never experienced up close, we today are able to gather information about places unknown to us, talk about them, form opinions and question the viability of their leaders and governments, bombarded as we are by news and information that come to us through different media from diverse corners of the planet, either in the original language or, more frequently, in translation. The difference between our time and Orwell's, as regards the ability to absorb and process information, is not so much the nature of the information itself since, in the main, the problem of its transmission – be it faithful, pseudo-faithful, or distorted – remains constant. What has changed, however, is the overwhelming quantity of sources and immediateness of the data we receive, with the result that the discipline of Translation, functioning as a vehicle for making information accessible from one culture to another, has had to adapt to this plethora of different sources and voices.

It goes without saying that today's technology offers increasingly sophisticated and efficient mechanisms for communicating both historical and current events, disseminating ideological agendas, and censoring and manipulating ideas in translation. Within the media landscape, digital platforms such as WikiLeaks, Youtube, Twitter, etc., as well as new and old television channels like *Al-Jazeera, Russia Today* or *Fox*, reach ever-widening audiences. In so doing, they serve as conduits for instant broadcasts of independent and contrasting viewpoints, which more often than not serve the purposes of political and ideological manipulation, addressed to speakers of different languages.

A case in point is the Russian TV channel *Russia Today*, a mass medium through which pro-government commentators spout pre-packaged narratives. This relative newcomer to the global media landscape – broadcasting in English, Spanish and Arabic – is said to be an instrument designed to 'foster a sense of shared identity among "brotherly peoples" as well as to punish political enemies' (Pomerantsev 2013, p. 17). Not surprisingly, as Peter Pomerantsev has observed, *Russia Today* characterized the 2013 demonstration against the Ukrainian government, when Kiev refused to sign a free trade treaty with the European Union, as a 'pogrom' fomented by 'foreign forces'. Such scenarios are, in many cases, 'social and ideological conflicts rooted in psychological models and manifested in speech and word usage that are in need of airing and decoding' (David and Muñoz-Basols 2011, xviii). Clearly, notwithstanding our high-speed access to information – previously available almost exclusively through newspapers and books – translation remains the key vehicle for disseminating, sifting and understanding cultural and social phenomena that come to us from foreign countries and languages.

It is for this very reason that our present special issue on 'Ideology, censorship and translation across genres: past and present', is premised on the idea that an integrated perception of both ideology and censorship in conjunction with translation across a variety of genres and contexts, and drawing on past and present examples, can be instructive for analyzing the role translation has played, and is able to play, both in disseminating information as well as in manipulating and distorting it. Accordingly, this special issue presents case studies and theoretical analyses from different chronological periods. In so doing, it considers the ethical and ideological implications for the translator, re-examines the role of the ideologist or the censor – as a stand-alone individual, as representative of a group, or as part of a larger apparatus – and establishes the translator's scope of action.

Indeed, the articles in this issue invite us to revisit these important communication issues by adopting a variety of perspectives. Organized chronologically, these various articles focus on ideology, censorship and translation across a variety of genres, themes and audiences. These include: scientific writing, the publishing industry, propaganda, theatre, translated literature, the philosophical and critical essay, the history of ideas, literary theory and cultural studies, cinema and film adaptation, the theory of translation and power relations.

In the first article, Carmen Acuña Partal studies the history of European translations of Charles Darwin's [*On*] *The Origin of Species* to demonstrate how ideological manipulation, censorship and publishing strategies affected the reception of the translated text. As she explains, the worldwide publishing success of the book only came after Darwin's death, even though manipulated, fragmented and illegal editions in English and in other languages seem to have proliferated, within what was already an increasingly complex book market not exempt from the havoc wreaked by censorship or spurious commercial interests. The author's analysis sheds considerable light on certain issues regarding the reception of classical science texts, an area which to date has remained largely unexamined in Translation Studies.

The second essay, by Marcos Rodríguez-Espinosa, traces the biographies of a group of women (Paulina and Adelina Abramson, Irene Falcón, Maria Fortus, Ilse Kulcsar, Constancia de la Mora, Lise Ricol and Lydia Kúper), who worked as translators during the Spanish Civil War. Eventually travelling to the USSR, where they received political indoctrination and linguistic training as translators, these women were recruited by the Comintern (the Communist International), founded in 1919 following the radical political changes of the Bolshevik Revolution of 1917, to promote revolution throughout the world. Rodríguez-Espinosa explains how the Spanish Civil War was, for these translators, a unique opportunity to put translation at the service of 'the last great cause'. However, for most of them, the end of the Spanish conflict ultimately meant the beginning of a long exile, not just because of the defeat of the Republic, but also on account of their dissidence from Soviet orthodoxy. The article reminds us of the fact that translators always work in a political dimension, and when they have to deal with dictators such as Franco and Stalin, translation is literally a question of life and death.

In the third contribution, Raquel Merino-Álvarez analyzes the translation of imported theatre into Franco's Spain during the 1960s, a period which, interestingly enough, was characterized by political openness within the Ministry in charge of theatre censorship, as well as a time of intense activity on the Spanish stage. Paying particular attention to the changes undergone by foreign plays, such as those by Edward Albee and Tennessee Williams, as they were rendered into Spanish, the author notes that the censorship archives are virtually the only source of information we have available for researching the history of theatre translations in Spain. Merino-Álvarez shows how texts of plays were treated when submitted to the censors' ideologically biased scrutiny; armed with such evidence, she illustrates the extent to which foreign plays were integrated into Spanish theatre even in the face of ideological manipulation and censorship.

In the fourth article, Emily Lygo examines the fate of literature in translation in the Soviet Union during the Brezhnev years, in particular the translations published in the important journal *Novyi mir* from 1965 to 1981. In her analysis, Lygo shows that while there were changes in the translations published during that period, overall translation did not experience stagnation. As she indicates, different agents within the Soviet literary process – members of the Party, editors or translators – used translation in order to pursue their various agendas. In particular, Lygo demonstrates the various and specific strategies employed by the journal's editors and translators to get the texts past the censor, and sheds interesting light on the balance in *Novyi mir* in this period between translations from minority languages of the USSR and those from pro-Soviet or neutral Western writers.

The fifth essay, by Pilar Godayol, explores the translations of Jean-Paul Sartre's oeuvre into Catalan in the 1960s and early 1970s by researching the institutional censorship that these works underwent, starting from the time the publishers requested the permits from the Ministry of Information and Tourism until they received the final authorizations. Contextualizing the translations, Godayol concentrates on the analysis of the eight censors' reports, consulted in the General Archive of the Administration (AGA). Through her research she is able to see how the Franco dictatorship reacted to the possibility of translating works by Sartre into Catalan: who the censors were, what views they expressed and why. Remarkably, despite the fact that Sartre was a banned author, the Ministry finally authorized the translations. Once more, this contribution confirms that censorship is never a monolithic structure: at least one of the censors became a subtle protector of Sartre's works.

In the sixth contribution, Jeroen Vandaele demonstrates through his analyses of Michel Foucault's works that the translation of critical theory has received undeservedly scant attention. Addressing the general reader as well as Foucault specialists, he compares a chapter from *Surveiller et punir* (1975) ('Les moyens du bon dressement') with its English, Spanish and Norwegian translations. These translations, he argues, are by and large not 'the same text in a different language', but rather concepts that have been carved up in translation; shifts in analysis from a structural to a historical perspective; or syntactic adjustments that make Foucault sound like the writer of a book of instructions. In the end Vandaele suggests that Foucault studies themselves could benefit from a 'translational turn'.

The seventh article, by Patrick Zabalbeascoa, embarks on an analysis of Stanley Kubrick's 1962 big-screen version of Nabokov's 1955 novel, *Lolita*. Focusing on the humor and the subtleties of censorship, Zabalbeascoa provides a useful *tertium comparationis* with Adrian Lyne's 1997 film. Through convincing micro-textual analyses, the article offers fascinating insights into the nature of humor and the benefits of comical translations, and it shows how censorship, taboo and ideological misconceptions regarding an author's work can affect the audience's perception of it.

Lastly, in the eighth and final article of this special issue Stefan Baumgarten questions the role of the twenty-first century translator and Translation Studies themselves by looking at different translation phenomena from various viewpoints: theoretical, self-reflexive, ethical-ideological. This is an appropriately thought-provoking survey of where the discipline is currently at, and it offers some challenging ideas about how the world of translators and Translation Studies might change or be changed. Baumgarten explains that in contemporary society structures of domination and hegemony keep defining power relations, even though we are moving towards a post-neoliberal world order in which capitalist values are expected to become a more deeply engrained, and unquestioned standard. In his paper, Baumgarten attempts to inject the notion of 'hegemonic non-translation' into the discourse of translation theory, stressing the significance of enhanced 'self-reflexivity' and 'critical economics' for future research.

Collectively, in demonstrating the role ideology and censorship play in the act of translation, these eight articles help to establish a connection between the past and the present across different genres, cultural traditions and audiences. Focusing on issues that have thus far not been addressed in a sufficiently connected way and from a variety of disciplines, they analyze authentic translation work, procedures and strategies. The result of individual, original analyses, the papers presented here contribute new ideas that help to elucidate both the role of the translator throughout history as well as current practices. Thus, combining various chronological, geographical (Spain, Russia, France, Scandinavia and so forth) and textual perspectives on translation, this special issue makes its contribution to the discipline of Translation Studies by revisiting ideology and censorship as two important and often intertwined themes within translation theory, all the while attesting to their ubiquitousness.

Acknowledgements

We would like to thank Elisabetta Tarantino for her dedication and excellent research assistance, as well as her contribution to the success of the two conferences on Translation Studies organised by the European Humanities Research Centre (EHRC) of the University of Oxford. We are appreciative of the conference participants and the plenary speakers: Mona Baker, Theo Hermans, Judith Luna, Raquel Merino-Álvarez, Christina Schäffner, and Patrick Zabalbeascoa, for their suggestions, comments and ideas. We would also like to express our gratitude for the help and guidance of the *Perspectives* editorial office, most especially Jenny Tunstall and the Editor-in-Chief, Roberto A. Valdeón. Last but not least, we thank the reviewers who have generously devoted their time to the articles contained in this issue.

Disclosure statement

No potential conflict of interest was reported by the author.

Funding

Most of the articles forming part of this special issue were originally presented at two separate conferences on Translation Studies organized by Martin McLaughlin and Javier Muñoz-Basols at the European Humanities Research Centre (EHRC) of the University of Oxford: 'Translating European Languages: History, Ideology and Censorship,' 1–2 November 2013, and 'European Languages in Translation: Cultural Identity and Intercultural Communication,' 25–26 September 2014. Both events were generously supported by the John Fell Oxford University Press Research Fund (Grant ID: 113-270).

References

David, M., & Muñoz-Basols, J. (2011). Defining and re-defining diaspora: An unstable concept. In M. David & J. Muñoz-Basols (Eds.), *Defining and re-defining diaspora: From theory to reality* (pp. xii–xxiv). Oxford: Inter-Disciplinary Press.

Orwell, G. (1945/1989). *Animal farm*. London: Penguin.

Orwell, G. (1947). *Колгосп тварин*. (Ivan Chernyatyns'kyjj, Trans.). Munich: Prometej.

Pomerantsev, P. (2013, December 6). The Kremlin's attempt at soft power is back-to-front. *Financial Times*, p. 17.

Tymoczko, M. (2003). Ideology and the position of the translator: In what sense is a translator 'in between'? In M. Calzada Pérez (Ed.), *Apropos of ideology: Translation studies on ideology - ideologies in translation studies* (pp. 181–201). Manchester: St. Jerome.

Notes on Charles Darwin's thoughts on translation and the publishing history of the European versions of *[On] The Origin of Species*

Carmen Acuña-Partal

The history of the European translations of Charles Darwin's *[On] The Origin of Species* is discussed to demonstrate how ideological manipulation, censorship, and publishing strategies affected the reception of one of the most influential texts in the history of science. Darwin's involvement in the translation process is herein traced in his autobiographical writings and in the letters he exchanged with his continental translators and publishers. Aware of the decisive influence of translation on the correct understanding of his work abroad, and, in spite of his wishes to control the dissemination of his theories, Darwin had to cope with instances of overt ideological manipulation in some of the first versions he authorized, which forced him to seek out other translators to undertake new non-biased translations. The worldwide publishing success of the book came after his death, although manipulated, fragmented, or illegal editions in English and other languages also seem to have proliferated thereafter, in an increasingly complex book market not either exempt from the havocs wreaked by censorship or spurious commercial interests. The resulting overall picture sheds some light on central issues pertaining to the reception of classical texts in science barely examined in the field of Translation Studies to date.

1. Introduction

The history of the European translations of Charles Darwin's *[On] The Origin of Species* (*OS*) is outlined in this paper, with a focus on his involvement, as an author, in the translation process, and on his frustrated expectations with some of the versions he authorized, as well as the extent to which ideological manipulation, censorship, and publishing strategies affected the international reception of a book which, since its first edition in 1859, triggered an intellectual revolution that undermined the foundations of religion and morality on a worldwide scale. In order to respond to criticism by his fellow scientists, Darwin painstakingly combined the preparation of subsequent revised editions of *OS* in English in 1860, 1861, 1866, 1869, and 1872, which contain an endless number of textual changes, as summarized in Peckham (1959, p. 9), with his supervision of foreign versions, in close contact by mail with his continental translators and publishers.

The issue of the author's concerned presence and intervention in the translation process – well documented in the cases of Vladmir Nabokov or Umberto Eco – is dealt with by Groff and Ivančić, who, as Zanotti (2011, p. 85) points out, address 'the genetic aspects of translation, which have only recently started to attract scholarly attention'. While Groff (2011, p. 155) recounts his experience as a literary translator working closely together with Günter Grass as 'an interpretative attempt, the arbitrariness of which is minimized if not eliminated thanks to the work carried out with the author', Ivančić (2011, p. 163) describes Claudio Magris' involvement in the translation of his texts through an epistolary exchange with his translators, in which the writer's participation is regarded as dialogue rather than intervention or imposition. This fresh insight into an author's correspondence, also considered to be key reference material for historians of science within new methodological approaches to reception (White, 2008, p. 54), well deserves, in our view, to be further investigated in Translation Studies, and could add to Chesterman's (2009) idea of 'Translator Studies', as well as to Pym's (2009) aim to 'humanize' Translation History.

Our brief account of the history of the European versions of *OS* draws mainly on Darwin's own thoughts on authorship and translation in his correspondence and autobiographical writings, and on the work of a number of historians of science who allude to or value the role of translation when writing on the international reception of Darwinism.[1] In the first two sections of this paper we explore Darwin's interest in actively promoting his work abroad, his disappointed expectations with some of the early European versions of *OS* – which were widely disseminated and also the source of further indirect translations – and his perseverance throughout the years in authorizing and negotiating new editions with his translators and publishers, while, in a third section, we examine the resilience and enduring success of *OS* after Darwin's lifetime in a book market often affected by the havocs brought about by censorship and dubious commercial interests.

2. Darwin's early disappointed expectations: the German (1860), Dutch (1860), and French (1862) editions

Aware of the decisive influence of translation on the correct understanding of his theories abroad, prior to the publication of *OS* on 24 November 1859, Darwin confessed to London-based publisher John Murray his desire to see the book published in other languages: 'I am *extremely* anxious for the subject sake [sic] (& God knows not for mere fame) to have my Book translated; & indirectly its being known abroad will do good to English sale' (entry-2531).[2] In the hope that some naturalist would request authorization to translate the text – as, at that time, the initiative to publish a work in a foreign language was usually within the scope of the translator, who would aspire to gain permission directly from the author and negotiate a contract with a specific publishing house (Browne, 2002, p. 140) – Darwin readily negotiated the preparation of new editions and translations with his publisher.

On 4 February 1860, an eager Darwin sent a letter to eminent zoologist and palaeontologist Heinrich Georg Bronn, thanking him for his offer 'to superintend', to a certain extent, a translation which Schweizerbart was willing to publish in Stuttgart: 'I am most anxious that the great & intellectual German people should know something about my book' (entry-2687). On 14 February, he stressed the importance of choosing good German terms for 'Natural Selection', which Bronn, in a previous review of *OS*, had translated as 'choice of life-style', leaving on Darwin's mind the impression 'of the Lamarckian doctrine (which I reject) of habits of life being all important' (entry-2698).[3]

On 25 February, in the knowledge that it would be Bronn himself who would translate the work instead of merely supervizing it, Darwin wrote to clarify the meaning of several terms that the translator had queried and expressed his joy at the forthcoming publication of the first German version of *OS* (Darwin, 1860b), based on the second English edition (entry-2698). On 14 July, Darwin thanked Bronn for the third part of the translation he had received and, also, not without candour, for a final chapter of criticisms by the translator himself: 'I shall of course carefully read the whole chapter [...] I shall ever consider myself deeply indebted to you for the immense service & honour which you have conferred on me in making the excellent translation of my book' (entry-2867).

Darwin had scarcely expected a translator, however eminent, to adjust *OS*'s argument to suit himself. Armed with some heavy German dictionaries, he struggled through Bronn's pages to see what had been done, but it would be Miss Camilla Ludwig, the new German governess at Down House, who would finally translate the epilogue for him (Browne, 2002, p. 141). Darwin's initial satisfaction turned to bewilderment when he understood that the translator had therein voiced his disagreement with the main thesis of *OS*, in an unfavourable review 'sewn within its own binding', as Montgomery (1988, pp. 91–92) puts it. In a letter to Bronn dated 5 October, Darwin cautiously, and with a remarkable pinch of humour, mentioned the chapter of criticisms: 'The objections & difficulties, which may be urged against my view, are indeed heavy enough almost to break my back; but it is not yet broken!' (entry-2940).

Furthermore, Bronn's translation is, according to Rupp-Eisenreich (1996, pp. 834–835), somewhat cumbersome and unreliable. While the full English title was *On the Origin of Species by Means of Natural Selection, or the Preservation of Favoured Races in the Struggle for Life*, in Bronn's translation 'struggle for life' is rendered as 'battle, or war for one's being',[4] 'suggesting a war to the death for every creature', and 'favoured races' as 'perfected races',[5] thus introducing 'an element of racial hierarchy'. The implications fed into '"Social Darwinism" [...] never part of Darwin's own policy or vision' (Shaffer & Glick, 2014, p. 4). Moreover, Bronn left out a number of sentences of which he did not approve, such as the conspicuously cryptic 'Light will be thrown on the origin of man and his history' (Darwin, 1860a, p. 488).

On 28 July 1861, having received a parcel by post, Darwin expressed his surprise to British botanist J.D. Hooker: 'There is a Dutch (!) Translation of "Origin" come out' (entry-3221). The reception of the Dutch version (Darwin, 1860c), translated by renowned geologist and paleontologist T.C. Winkler, and published in Haarlem by A.C. Kruseman, was to be conditioned – like Bronn's German version – by the fact that Jan Van der Hoeven, professor at the University of Leiden, added to the work his own translation of a review criticizing the book, signed by mathematician and geologist William Hopkins (Bulhof, 1988, p. 279).

Bronn later suggested to Darwin the possibility of publishing a second German edition, and, in a letter dated 11 March 1862 (entry-3470), Darwin expressed his wish to include in the text the corrections which he had introduced in the third English edition of 1861, wherein he responded to Bronn's criticisms. Apologizing for the extra work heaped upon the translator, Darwin explained:

> I [...] have marked with a pencil line all the additions & corrections [...]. I very much hope you will add to the load of kindness already conferred on me by looking through the English Sheets & correcting the new German Edition by them. (entry-3519)

On 11 July, he forwarded him a footnote (entry-3652), not knowing that his translator had died of a heart attack on 5 July. The German edition of *OS*, which Bronn completed before passing away, finally appeared in 1863.

On 10 September 1861, Darwin asked Murray to send off 'a copy of last Edit. of Origin to Madelle. Clemence Auguste Royer', a self-taught free-thinker and proto-feminist exiled in Switzerland, 'as she has agreed with a Publisher for a French Translation' (entry-3250). Her contacts with the publishing house Guillaumin of Paris must have had a decisive influence on Darwin's acceptance of Royer's proposal to translate *OS*, as probably did her reading of a review by Swiss naturalist Edouard Claparède play a part on her resolution to undertake the translation. Guillaumin established an alliance with Parisian publisher Masson to print the first French edition authorized by Darwin, which Royer translated from the third English edition (Harvey, 1997, p. 64, 2008, pp. 356–357).

In June 1862, on receiving the book, Darwin recounted to American botanist Asa Gray some of his early thoughts about her, with a certain stupefaction:

> Royer [...] must be one of the cleverest & oddest women in Europe: is ardent Deist & hates Christianity, & declares that natural selection & the struggle for life will explain all morality, nature of man, politicks [sic] &c &c!!! (entry-3595)

Royer's 1862 translated text was yet another source of major disappointment for Darwin, since she wrote a controversial and long preface, wherein she presented the author's ideas as an alternative to the revealed religious truths, as an anticlerical diatribe against Catholics and Protestants (Browne, 2002, p. 143; Harvey, 1997, p. 64), and as a naturalistic justification of the economic laws by which, in her opinion, society must be governed. As Prum (2014, p. 395) rightly points out, these views irritated Darwin, 'whose work has hardly anything to do with what was later to be referred to as "Social Darwinism" [...]. His rejection of both racism and eugenics (to use modern terms) has been repeatedly and convincingly demonstrated by Patrick Tort'. In the title, *De l'origine des espèces ou des lois du progrès chez les êtres organisés*, the reference to 'the laws of progress' announces the Lamarckian bias noticeable throughout the text, as in her translation of 'natural selection' ('élection naturelle'), and of 'struggle for life' ('concurrance de vie'). For her, as for Lamarck, evolution is progressive, as it was, according to Hull (1988, p. 390), for the bulk of the European intellectual community, the concept of progress being by then 'pandemic', whereas 'Darwin's scheme of evolutionary adaptation was based entirely on contingency. Organisms shifted randomly' (Browne, 2002, p. 61).

On 11 July 1862, Darwin wrote to French naturalist J.L.A. Quatrefages de Breau: 'I wish the translator had known more of Natural History; she must be a clever, but singular Lady; but I never heard of her, till she proposed to translate my Book' (entry-3653). On 6 September, Darwin received a letter from Claparède, in which he bluntly called Royer's work into question: 'Her translation is heavy, indigestible, sometimes incorrect and the notes that accompany it will certainly not be to your taste' (entry-3715).[6] His words, as Harvey remarks (1997, p. 68), instilled in Darwin a certain fear that Royer's version might prejudice the acceptance of his ideas in France and other countries within the French cultural zone of influence. A few days later Darwin commented to Hooker (entry-3721):

> Claparède, who helped the French Translatress of the Origin [...], tells me he had difficulty in preventing her (who never looked at a bee-cell) from altering my whole

description, because she affirmed that an hexagonal prism must have an hexagonal base! Almost everywhere in Origin, when I express great doubt, she appends a note explaining the difficulty or saying that there is none whatever!! It is really curious to know what conceited people there are in the world.

In that same letter Claparède described Royer as 'a singular individual, whose attractions are not those of her sex' (entry-3715).[7] Other scholars, among them French philosopher Ernest Renan, allegedly concurred in seeing in her 'almost a man of genius'. As Browne (2002) observes:

> Women in those academic circles were expected mostly to facilitate the unimpeded flow of their menfolk's scientific ideas by translating, editing, proof-reading, and such like [...]. To rewrite and to politicise was unacceptable –unacceptable whatever the sex of the translator [...]. To be sure, Royer was inaccurate, misinformed, and following a cause. Yet Darwin and his friends may have found it a relatively simple matter to link these faults with her gender and dismiss her evolutionary outbursts as feminine curiosity. (2002, pp. 143–144)

Even if, in a letter to Edward Cresy early on in 1860, Darwin stated that it was 'an immense advantage to any scientific work and subject to be translated into French, as it can then be read in any country' (entry-2657), and he always showed great respect for French science, it would not be long before he became fully aware of the silence with which *OS* was to be received in France. This 'conspiracy of silence' was, in Molina's (1996, p. 913) opinion, due to a nationalistic prejudice derived from the predilection of the scientific community towards Lamarckian evolutionism, and, in Glick's (1992, p. 321) view, to its being rendered in a somewhat alien conceptual language, on the basis of its massive depiction of field observations. Conry (1974, pp. 222–223) further discusses the reception of *OS* within specific disciplinary traditions and identifies sources of resistance linked to a generational component. Nonetheless, Browne (2002, p. 144) suggests that the Lamarckian bias of Royer's translation may have ultimately benefited the dissemination of Darwin's theories in France.

Until the appearance of the first direct translations, in Tsarist Russia and other Slavic countries, like Poland, Darwin's work was disseminated through the controversial German (1860) and French (1862) versions. Botanist S.A. Rachinsky translated *OS* into Russian (Darwin, 1864), according to Babkov (1996, p. 1050) from the text of the second American edition and the first German edition by Bronn, 'under the explicit approval of censorship officials' (Levit, Levit, Hossfeld, & Olsson, 2014, p. 164). The first Russian translation was commercialized by Glazunov's publishing house in St. Petersburg, while the second edition came onto the market the following year, with corrections such as the editing of the reference to the animal and vegetable reigns in the title, reminiscent of Bronn's version.[8] Paul (1988, p. 407) comments on a temporary banning of *OS* in Russia in 1866, as a result of 'an immediate political-social scare and a general association of Darwinism with radicalism'.

3. Authorizing new European translations: the Italian (1864–1865), German (1867), French (1873, 1876), Spanish (1877), and Serbian (1878) editions

On 5 December 1863, Darwin joyfully recounted to Hooker the coming publication of an Italian translation of *OS*: 'There is an Italian Edit. of Origin preparing!!! This makes fifth foreign Edit, ie in five foreign countries' (entry-4353). As Darwin was ill, it was his wife Emma who asked John Murray to send a copy of the book to the translators, zoologist Giovanni Canestrini and Leonardo Salimbeni: 'As you have never hesitated to authorise a foreign translation he has taken upon himself to authorise a translation into Italian without consulting you' (entry-4352). For Paul (1988, p. 409), in Italy, the translation of *OS* published by Nicola Zanichelli e Soci in Modena between 1864 and 1865 was given 'an impeccable scientific presentation' by the translators, 'which avoided the type of situation that arose from the presentation of Darwinism in France by Clémence Royer as a new scientific basis for a secularistic *Weltanschauung*'. However, as Molina (1996, p. 918) points out, they both copied and criticized Royer's translation, as shown in the terms 'natural election'[9] and 'perfected races'[10] of the title.

After Bronn's unexpected demise, and, in order to correct the possible distorting effect of his translation in Germany and in countries such as Norway, the present Czech Republic, Estonia, or Lithuania (Engels & Glick, 2008, pp. 4–5), on 23 March 1866 Schweizerbart proposed to Darwin that a revised edition of Bronn's translation be published (entry-5038), which was entrusted to zoologist Julius Victor Carus and came out in 1867. On 7 November 1866, Carus consulted with Darwin about how to proceed with Bronn's notes and epilogue, which the new translator was reluctant to keep on the following basis: 'As the first two editions of his translation are existing, the history of the Sciences will take due notice of his position. But for my part I should not like to propagate his doubts' (entry-5269). Three days later, Darwin replied:

> I suspect that Bronn's translation is very defective, at least I have heard complaints on this head from quite a large number of persons [...], you will be fully justified in entirely omitting Bronn's appendix [...]. A new edition may be looked at as a new work. (entry-5273)

Finally, on 15 November, Carus remarked upon some 'quite ridiculous' mistakes that he had found, and adds: 'For myself I shall not append notes, as I do not think it proper to bring my individuality forward' (entry-5279).

On 11 February 1867, Carus sent Darwin a translation of the preface he had just prepared for the new edition, kindly asking him to give his opinion on the matter (entry-5397). Darwin was pleased to send a prompt laudatory reply to his new ally:

> It seems to me that you have treated Bronn with complete respect and great delicacy, and that you have alluded to your own labour with much modesty. [...] as you have omitted Bronn's objections, I believe that you have acted with excellent judgment and fairness in leaving the text without comment to the independent verdict of the reader [...], I have now the great satisfaction of knowing that the German public can judge fairly of its merits and demerits. (entry-5403)

At a later date, Francis Darwin (1887) commented that these letters marked the beginning of a close relationship which was to grow between his father and Carus, who would eventually become his most loyal and valued translator and endeavoured to faithfully reproduce in the translated texts, up until the sixth German edition of 1876, the amendments that Darwin introduced in the succeeding English editions of his work, in response to the criticisms and reactions that *OS* aroused.

> The conscientious care with which this work was done was of material service, and I well remember the admiration (mingled with a tinge of vexation at his own shortcomings) with which my father used to receive the lists of oversights, &c., which Professor Carus

discovered in the course of translation. The connection was not a mere business one, but was cemented by warm feelings of regard on both sides. (Darwin, 1887 III, pp. 48–49)

At the start of 1869, V.O. Kovalesky, who, on 2 April 1867, had informed Darwin that Rachinsky's Russian translation of 1864 was based on Bronn's German version (entry-6541), wrote to seek Darwin's permission to translate the additions to the fifth English edition and to incorporate them as a supplement into a new Russian version (entry-6950).

In October 1869, after receiving a letter from Swiss zoologist J.J. Moulinié expressing his desire to translate Darwin's next work on man, the British author saw in him an alternative to his difficult dealings with Royer and Masson (entry-6950). On 23 October, Darwin asked him whether it would be legally possible to publish a new French edition with a new publisher and without Royer's preface (entry-6955), and on 5 November Moulinié replied that Reinwald – 'with whom he continued to have pleasant relations as the publisher of many of his books into French' (Darwin, 1887 III, p. 110) – would be willing to release a new edition of *OS* provided prior agreement was reached with the former publisher (entry-6971). A few days later Darwin related the case to Hooker as follows:

> She has now just brought out a third edition without informing me, so that all the corrections, etc. in the fourth and fifth English editions are lost. Besides her enormously long preface to the first edition, she has added a second preface abusing me like a pickpocket of Pangenesis, which of course has no relation to the "Origin". So I wrote to Paris; and Reinwald agrees to bring out at once a new translation from the fifth English edition, in competition with her third edition […]. This fact shows that "evolution of species" must at last be spreading in France. (entry-6997)

Even though Darwin withdrew his authorization for Royer to henceforth translate *OS*, the French text (Darwin, 1870) continued to be reprinted for years to come.

On 15 November 1867, the British naturalist made the following recommendation to Moulinié: 'As your translation will have to compete with Mlle Royer's, who I am told writes very spirited French, you will [I] think have to keep this in view in regard to style'. He also kindly requested that he consult Royer's text with the aim of maintaining some important terms, and that Reinwald not add a translator's preface to the new French edition (entry-6989). On 4 March 1873, Reinwald detailed to Darwin the troubled completion of the long-underway French version of *OS*, hampered as it was by the Franco-Prussian War, by Moulinié's illness and subsequent demise, and by the additions from the sixth English edition that Darwin had asked the translator to include in the text (entry-8797). Moulinié's translation was finally published later that year (Darwin, 1873a), after being finished and corrected by Edmond Barbier, a French 'freethinker', of whom we hardly know anything (Prum, 2014, p. 296). It incorporated the content of a letter that Darwin sent to Moulinié in February 1872 (entry-8191), wherein the author declared that the reason for hiring a new translator was Royer's refusal to revise her translation.

At the beginning of the section entitled 'Additions and Corrections to the Sixth Edition' of the 1872 text of *OS*, Darwin commented on the complex overall picture already in sight as a result of the coexistence on the market of an increasing number of translated versions based on the different revised English editions he had produced:

> As copies of the present work will be sent abroad, it may be of use if I specify the state of foreign editions. The third French and second German editions were from the third

English, with some few of the additions given in the fourth edition. A new fourth French edition has been translated by Colonel Moulinié, of which the first half is from the fifth English, and the latter half from the present edition. A third German edition, under the superintendence of Professor Victor Carus, was from the fourth English edition; a fifth is now preparing by the same author from the present volume [...]. The Italian is from the third, the Dutch and three Russian editions from the second English edition, and the Swedish from the fifth English edition. (Darwin, 1872d, pp. xv–xvi)

In Janvier's opinion (1996, p. 1042), the strong influence of the Lutheran church may have played an important part in the somewhat delayed reception of Darwin's theory in Scandinavia. Both the above-mentioned Swedish version – translated by the young medical doctor A.M. Selling (Darwin, 1871) and published in Stockholm by L.J. Hiertas Förlagsexpedition – and the Danish edition (Darwin 1871a) – by botanist and author Jens Peter Jacobsen – are based on the fifth English edition. At that time, Danish was a shared written language in both Denmark and Norway and the two countries had, to a large extent, a common book market (Rem, 2014, p. 160). Heavily influenced by naturalist Ernst Haeckel, Jacobsen produced a rather Germanized and liberal version of *OS*, in which 'Natural Selection' was 'choice by quality',[11] and 'The Basic Laws of Nature: An Attempt to Declare the Unity of the Organic World'[12] was the title in the original nine instalments, later to be changed to a more literal translation for the full edition in book format released by Gyldendal of Copenhagen. Due to Jacobsen's fame in Danish culture, 'his translations have been tacitly celebrated as masterpieces and treasured as unique literary accomplishments', a myth in Danish literary studies that Clasen, Grumsen, Hjermitslev, and Kjærgaard (2014, pp. 107–108) believe worth reconsidering.

In June 1873, Hungarian naturalist Dapsy László informed Darwin that the Természettudományi Társulat, the Natural History Society, of Budapest was to print his translation of *OS* in August (Darwin, 1873-1874) (entry-8931). A partial Polish version of *OS*, translated by Waclaw Mayzel, was also published that year by Niwa in Warsaw (Darwin, 1873b). In October 1874, Milan M. Radovanović wrote to Darwin seeking his permission to translate *OS* into Serbian (entry-9643), but in August 1876 he explained that the text was yet to be published due to the Serbian–Ottoman War (entry-10580), in a letter to which Darwin replied thanking him for his concerns on the matter (entry-10582a). The Serbian translation was finally issued in Belgrade by the state printing house Državna štamparija two years later (Freeman, 1977, p. 109). In October 1875, Canestrini wrote to inform Darwin (entry-10220) that the second Italian edition of *OS* (Darwin, 1875), on which he worked on his own, had been published almost in full in Turin by Unione Tipografico-Editrice (Canadelli, Coccia, & Pievani, 2014, p. 511).

In May 1873, dissatisfied with Moulinié's performance as a translator of *OS* – in view of his use of the Swiss variety of French and of the text being stylistically poor – which could have a detrimental effect on the sales of the book (entry-8911), Reinwald suggested publishing a new version of *OS* based on the sixth English edition, which was finally translated by Barbier and came out in 1876.

Clémence Royer's translated text aroused much controversy in Spain, not only in its original version but also through the first incomplete Spanish translation of *OS*. The latter, based on the third French edition, was suspended after only a few instalments had come out in Madrid in 1872, as part of the Biblioteca Social, Histórica y Filosófica, printed by Jacobo María Luengo. It included Royer's prefaces, in which, in a footnote, the unknown Spanish translator explicitly warned the readers against her 'daring' assertiveness (Darwin, 1872b, p. x). In 1872, a summarized translation of *OS*, attributed by some historians to author Francisco María Tubino, was also published in Barcelona by Montaner y Simón, in *La Creación*, an eight-volume natural history encyclopedia edited by geologist and paleontologist Juan Vilanova y Piera (Darwin, 1872c). The first complete Spanish translation based on the sixth English edition of 1872 was finally published in Madrid in 1877. In April 1876, in response to a previous letter by Spanish journalist Enrique Godínez, Darwin had authorized him to carry out the translation (entry-10481). In March 1877 Darwin acknowledged receipt of the sheets of the Spanish version and apologized for not being able to read the text, as he was ill and overwhelmed with work. While he confessed that he had almost entirely forgotten the Spanish he had learnt for his *Beagle* voyage, he stated that what he had read seemed to him clearly expressed (entry-10908). At the beginning of this edition of *OS*, published in Madrid in 1877 by Biblioteca Perojo, a copy of the letters they exchanged is included, in both English and in Spanish, as proof of authorization and appraisal by Darwin (Acuña-Partal, 2013).

In his *Recollections of the Development of my Mind and Character*, written by Darwin in 1876, he speaks once more about the international reception of his theories and the translation of *OS* into foreign languages:

> Sixteen thousand copies have now been sold in England and considering how stiff a book it is, this is a large sale. It has been translated into almost every European tongue, even into such languages as Spanish, Bohemian,[13] Polish, and Russian [...]. I have Heard it said that the success of a work abroad is the best test of its enduring value. I doubt whether this is at all trustworthy; but judged by this standard my name ought to last for a few years. (Barlow, 1958, pp. 122–123, 129)

As Browne (2002, p. 256) points out: 'The wave of editions and translations taking evolutionism back and forth between Britain and continental Europe and America presented a social and intellectual phenomenon in its own right'. However, in spite of Darwin's eager wishes to promote and control the dissemination of his theories, the author was unable to predict or determine the fate of his ideas once having traversed transnational and linguistic borders:

> Taken together, these overseas publications necessarily fell into other cultural contexts and became associated with different issues. In retrospect it seems likely that Darwin was unprepared for the way his writings would be reinterpreted. German, French and American readers were coming to grips with an *Origin of Species* different from the one he thought he had written. Bit by bit, these foreign editions and translations may have forced him to acknowledge the independent life of his child. (Browne, 2002, p. 144)

4. The resilience and enduring success of *The Origin of Species* after Darwin's lifetime

The book's worldwide publishing success came after Darwin's death on 19 April 1882, although manipulated, fragmented, or illegal editions in English and other languages also seem to have proliferated thereafter. About the sales of *OS*, Peckham (1959) further remarks the following:

> The profits of the American pirates must have been enormous. It would be interesting to know the sales in foreign languages. But now that the book is no longer protected by

copyright, it would be as hopeless a task to search out all the reprints as it would be to discover those of its great [...] coeval, *The Rubáiyát of Omar Khayyám*. (1959, pp. 24–25)

Some significant instances of the constraints and hindrances yet to affect the reception of *OS* in translation are encountered in a number of European countries at the end of the nineteenth and over the course of the twentieth centuries. Engels and Glick (2008, pp. 4–5) comment on the particular importance of '*cross-cultural influences or inflections* induced by translations [...] determining directions not intended by the author', as in the persistence of inaccuracies derived from Bronn's biased German version in the first Norwegian edition of *OS*, translated by educator Ingebret Suleng in 1889–1890 (Lie, 2014, p. 188) from the sixth English edition.

According to Rayfield (2014, pp. 259–260), following a period of relatively strict censorship in the 1880s – imposed by Tsar Alexander III and Konstantin Pobedonostsev, Procuror of the Holy Synod – the 1890s and 1900s saw further Russian editions of Darwin's works, such as Timiriazev's (1896a) and Filippov's (1896b) translations of *OS* (Glick, 2014, p. xxxviii), the former to be republished after the revolution in the USSR, along with all the major works of Darwin, which came out from 1935 to 1941.

After three Spanish versions were released in the first decades of the twentieth century, translated by López White (1903), Zulueta (1921), and Barroso-Bonzón (1936), in the aftermath of the Spanish Civil War (1936–1939), *OS* was officially banned during the dictatorship of General Franco for more than a decade. In the 1950s, censorship authorized Ediciones Ibéricas to publish Barroso-Bonzon's translation (Darwin, 1950) –which Ediciones Bergua had printed before the war – as Darwin's text was no longer found to be contrary to Catholic morality, at a time of some openness of the Church and less ideological polarization of the recurring debates about science in Spain. Since 1976, once democracy was restored, the number of Spanish editions of *OS* rose significantly: previously authorized translations were reprinted, translations published in the nineteenth century or prior to the Civil War were reissued, and new translations of *OS*, of varying lengths, came out. The abundance and coexistence of reprints of such texts – as a result of publishing policies in Spain which stand in clear contrast to those found in other European countries like France, where Barbier's canonical translation was continuously reissued for over 100 years – have determined, to a large extent, the dissemination of Darwinism in Spain throughout the nineteenth and twentieth centuries.[14]

Hjermitslev (2014, pp. 131–133) refers to the case of Gyldendal issuing a 1909 revised second edition of Jacobsen's Danish original translation rendered by botanical student Frits Heide, who did not change the tone of Jacobsen's far from literal language (Darwin, 1909). Clasen et al. (2014, p. 106) further remark that Heide edited and revised an abridged edition (Darwin, 1913) still based on Jacobsen's original translation.

The first Greek translation of *OS*, by Nikos Kazantzakis, only came out in 1915, and was, as Zarimis (2014, pp. 649–650) points out, written 'in the "katharevousa", a puristic Greek, containing archaic forms' that only the well-educated could fully comprehend (Darwin, 1915). Moreover, for Darwin's last words in the *Origin*, 'are being evolved', Kazantzakis uses 'anaptyssontai', 'are being developed', implying a tendency to betterment or improvement, as seen in some of the aforementioned European translations.

In Nazi Germany, *Die Bücherei*, the official journal for lending libraries, published a set of 'Guidelines' (1935, p. 279) on which books to remove from libraries during the second round of 'purifications' (*Saüberung*), including: 'Writings of a philosophical and social nature whose content deals with the false scientific enlightenment of primitive Darwinism and Monism (Haeckel)'. In this regard, Bald and Pollack (2006, p. 246) remind us that *OS* was similarly prohibited in Yugoslavia in 1935, and banned in Greece in 1937, under the right-wing Metaxas regime (1936–1941).

Throughout the second half of the twentieth and the beginning of the twenty-first centuries, European publishers continued both to reprint old versions and to produce new translations of Darwin's masterpiece, with a significant rise in editions issued to coincide with Darwin commemorative anniversaries, some of which have helped bridge a number of gaps detected in the translation history of *OS*. While in Italy, until 1959 – when publisher Boringhieri of Turin released the first twentieth-century Italian version by Luciana Fratini (Darwin, 1959), based on the sixth English edition – the only translations of *OS* available were reprints of nineteenth-century editions (Canadelli et al., 2014, p. 519), in France, Barbier's 1876 translation became the standard French edition of *OS* during the twentieth century, though Royer's translation was also published as late as 1932. As Prum (2014, pp. 391, 396, 399) remarks, it was the part played by nineteenth-century French translators, their misreadings and mistranslations, together with the consequent potential influence of their biased versions on the French or French-speaking readership at large, which led to the preparation of a totally new retranslation of *OS* by Aurélien Berra, Patrick Tort, and Michel Prum himself, published in Paris by Honoré Champion (Darwin, 2009). With so many 'species' of *OS* coexisting in an already entangled market ruled, more often than not, by mere commercial interests, this is indeed a fine example of how the fruitful cooperation of translators, scholars, and publishers has been of invaluable service to the history of science in finally fulfilling the author's wishes on the dissemination of his theories through translation. It stands, in Tort's (2014, p. 415) own words, as 'the tribute that had been due to him for such a long time'.

Acknowledgement

This paper is a result of the Research Project 'La Traducción de Clásicos en su Marco Editorial: Una Visión Transatlántica' (FFI2013-41743-P, National Scientific Research, Development and Technological Innovation Plan), financed by the Ministry of Economy and Competitiveness of the Government of Spain.

Disclosure statement

No potential conflict of interest was reported by the author.

Notes

1. The texts of a number of Danish, Dutch, French, German, Polish, Portuguese, Russian, and Spanish translations of Darwin's *[On] The Origin of Species* are available at John van Wyhe, ed. (2002—), *The Complete Work of Charles Darwin Online* (http://darwin-online.org.uk/).
2. Entry numbers henceforth refer to transcripts and summaries of letters written by or to Charles Darwin, available at *Darwin Correspondence Database* (http://www.darwinproject.ac.uk/), from the printed series *The Correspondence of Charles Darwin* (Burkhardt et al., 1985—), and *A Calendar to the Correspondence of Charles Darwin: 1821-1882* (Burkhardt & Smith, 1994).
3. ('Wahl der Lebens-Weise').
4. ('Kampfe um's Daseyn').
5. ('vervollkommneten Rassen').

6. ('Sa traduction est lourde, indigeste, parfois incorrecte et les notes qui l'accompagnent ne seront certainement point de votre goût').
7. ('une personne singulière, dont les allures ne sont point celles de son sexe').
8. ('im Thier- und Pflanzen-Reich').
9. ('elezione naturale').
10. ('razze perfezionate').
11. ('kvalitetsvalg').
12. (*Naturlivets grundlove: Et forsøg på at hævde enheden i den organiske verden*).
13. In March 1878 Darwin authorized the publication of a Bohemian edition of *OS* to zoologist Anton Stecker (entry-11419).
14. A complete list up to 2001 is given in Gomis and Josa (2009) and discussed in detail in Acuña-Partal (2013).

References

Acuña-Partal, C. (2013). *Traductores, editores y traducciones españolas de* [On] The Origin of Species *y* The Descent of Man, *de Charles Darwin: Historia, autoría y plagio (1872–2001)*. [Translators, publishers and Spanish translations of Charles Darwin's [On] The Origin of Species and The Descent of Man: History, Authorship and Plagiarism (1872–2001)] (Unpublished doctoral dissertation). University of Málaga, Málaga.

Babkov, V. (1996). Darwinisme Russe. In P. Tort (Dir.), *Dictionnaire du Darwinisme et de l'évolution* [Dictionary of Darwinism and evolution] (pp. 1045–1108). Paris: PUF.

Bald, M., & Pollack, J. (2006). On the origin of species. In M. Bald (Ed.), *Literature suppressed on religious grounds* (pp. 240–246). New York, NY: Facts on File.

Barlow, N. (Ed.). (1958). *The autobiography of Charles Darwin 1809–1882. With the original omissions restored*. London: Collins.

Browne, J. (2002). *Charles Darwin*. London: Random House.

Bulhof, I. (1988). The Netherlands. In T. F. Glick (Ed.), *The comparative reception of Darwinism* (pp. 279–286). Chicago: The University of Chicago Press.

Burkhardt, F., & Smith, S. (Eds.). (1994). *A calendar to the correspondence of Charles Darwin 1821–1882*. Cambridge: Cambridge University Press.

Burkhardt, F., et al. (Eds.). (1985—). *The Correspondence of Charles Darwin*. Cambridge: Cambridge University Press.

Canadelli, E., Coccia, P., & Pievani, T. (2014). Commemorating Darwin in Italy: An overview (1882–2009). In T. F. Glick & E. Shaffer (Eds.), *The literary and cultural reception of Charles Darwin in Europe* (pp. 510–523). London: Bloomsbury.

Chesterman, A. (2009). The name and nature of translator studies. *Hermes. Journal of Language and Communication Studies, 42*, 13–22.

Clasen, M., Grumsen, S. S., Hjermitslev, H. H., & Kjærgaard, P. C. (2014). Translation and transition: The Danish literary response to Darwin. In T. F. Glick & E. Shaffer (Eds.), *The literary and cultural reception of Charles Darwin in Europe* (pp. 103–127). London: Bloomsbury.

Conry, Y. (1974). *L'Introduction du Darwinisme en France au XIX siècle* [The introduction of Darwinism in France in the nineteenth century]. Paris: J. Vrin.
Darwin Correspondence Project (http://www.darwinproject.ac.uk/).
Darwin, C. (1860a). *On the origin of species by means of natural selection, or the preservation of favoured races in the struggle for life* (2nd ed.). London: John Murray.
Darwin, C. (1860b). *Über die Entstehung der Arten im Thier- und Pflanzen-Reich durch natürliche Züchtung, oder, Erhaltung der vervollkommneten Rassen im Kampfe um's Daseyn* [On the origin of species in the animal and vegetable reigns by means of natural selection, or, preservation of the perfected races in the battle for one's being]. (H. G. Bronn, Trans.). Stuttgart: Schweizerbart.
Darwin, C. (1860c). *Het ontstaan der soorten van dieren en planten door middel van de natuurkeus* [The origin of species of animals and plants by means of natural selection]. (T. C. Winkler, Trans.). Haarlem: A. C. Kruseman.
Darwin, C. (1862). *De l'origine des espèces, ou des lois du progrès chez les êtres organisés* [On the origin of species, or the laws of progress among organized beings]. (C. Royer, Trans.). Paris: Guillaumin et Cie./V. Masson et fils.
Darwin, C. (1863). *Über die Entstehung der Arten im Thier- und Pflanzen-Reich durch natürliche Züchtung* [On the origin of species in the animal and vegetable reigns by means of natural selection] (2nd ed.). (H. G. Bronn, Trans.). Stuttgart: Schweizerbart.
Darwin, C. (1864). *O proiskhozdenii vidov v tsarstvakz zhivotnom i rastitel'nom putem estestvennogo podbora rodichei* [On the origin of species in the animal and vegetable reigns by means of natural selection]. (S. A. Rachinsky, Trans.). St. Petersburg: Glazunov.
Darwin, C. (1864–1865). *Sull'origine delle specie per elezione naturale, ovvero conservazione delle razze perfezionate nella lotta per l'esistenza* [On the origin of species by means of natural election, or the preservation of the perfected races in the struggle for existence]. (G. Canestrini & L. Salimbeni, Trans.). Modena: N. Zanichelli e Soci.
Darwin, C. (1867). *Über die Entstehung der Arten durch natürliche Zuchtwahl* [On the origin of species by means of natural selection] (3rd ed.). (H.G. Bronn & J. V. Carus, Trans.). Stuttgart: Schweizerbart.
Darwin, C. (1870). *De l'origine des espèces par sélection naturelle, ou des lois de transformation des êtres organisés* [On the origin of species by means of natural selection, or the laws of transformation of organized beings] (3rd ed.). (C. Royer, Trans.). Paris: Guillaumin et Cie./V. Masson et fils.
Darwin, C. (1871). *Om arternas uppkomst genom naturligt urval* [On the origin of species by means of natural selection]. (A. M. Selling, Trans.). Stockholm: L. J. Hiertas Förlagsexpedition.
Darwin, C. (1872a). *Om arternes oprindelse ved kvalitetsvalg* [On the origin of species by means of choice by quality]. (J. P. Jacobsen, Trans.). Copenhagen: Gyldendal.
Darwin, C. (1872b). *Del origen de las especies por selección natural; ó resumen de las leyes de transformación de los seres organizados* [On the origin of species by means of natural selection; or summary of the laws of transformation of organized beings]. Madrid: Jacobo María Luengo.
Darwin, C. (1872c). El origen de las especies [The origin of species]. In J. Vilanova y Piera (Ed.), *La creación* [The creation] (Vol. 1, pp. 1–38). Barcelona: Montaner y Simón.
Darwin, C. (1872d). *The origin of species by means of natural selection, or the preservation of favoured races in the struggle for life* (6th ed.). London: John Murray.
Darwin, C. (1873a). *L'origine des espèces au moyen de la sélection naturelle, ou la lutte pour l'existence dans la nature* [The origin of species by means of natural selection, or the struggle for existence in nature]. (J.-J. Moulinié, Trans.). Paris: C. Reinwald et Cie.
Darwin, C. (1873b). *O powstawaniu gatunków drogą naturalnego doboru* [The origin of species by means of natural selection]. (W. Mayzel, Trans.). Warsaw: Niwa.
Darwin, C. (1873–1874). *A fajok eredete a természeti kiválás útján* [The origin of species by means of natural selection]. (D. László, Trans.). Budapest: Természettudományi Társulat.
Darwin, C. (1875). *Sulla origine delle specie per elezione naturale* [On the origin of species by means of natural election]. (G. Canestrini, Trans.). Turin: Unione Tipografico-Editrice.
Darwin, C. (1876). *L'origine des espèces au moyen de la sélection naturelle, ou la lutte pour l'existence dans la nature* [The origin of species by means of natural selection, or the struggle for existence in nature]. (E. Barbier, Trans.). Paris: C. Reinwald et Cie.

Darwin, C. (1877). *Orígen de las especies por medio de la selección natural ó la conservación de las razas favorecidas en la lucha por la existencia* [Origin of species by means of natural selection or the preservation of favoured races in the struggle for existence]. (E. Godínez, Trans.). Madrid: Biblioteca Perojo.

Darwin, C. (1878). *Postanak vrsta pomoću prirodnog odabiranja* [The origin of species by means of natural selection]. (M. M. Radovanović, Trans.). Belgrade: Državna štamparija.

Darwin, C. (1889–1890). *Arternes oprindelse gjennem naturligt udvalg* [The origin of species by means of natural selection]. (I. Suleng, Trans.). Christiania: Bibliothek for de tusen hjem.

Darwin, C. (1896a). *Proiskhozdenie vidov putem estestvennogo otbora* [The origin of species by means of natural selection]. (K. A. Timiriazev, Trans.). St. Petersburg: O.N. Popov.

Darwin, C. (1896b). *Proiskhozdenie vidov putem estestvennogo podbora* [The origin of species by means of natural selection]. (M. Filippov, Trans.). St. Petersburg: A. Porokhovshikov.

Darwin, C. (1903). *Origen de las especies por medio de la selección natural ó conservación de las razas en su lucha por la existencia* [Origin of species by means of natural selection, or the preservation of races in the struggle for existence]. (A. López White, Trans.). Valencia: Sempere.

Darwin, C. (1909). *Om arternes oprindelse ved kvalitetsvalg* [On the origin of species by means of choice by quality] (2nd ed.). (J. P. Jacobsen, Trans.; F. Heide, Rev.). Copenhagen: Gyldendal.

Darwin, C. (1913). *Om arternes oprindelse ved kvalitetsvalg* [On the origin of species by means of choice by quality] (3rd ed.) (J. P. Jacobsen, Trans.; F. Heide, Rev.). Copenhagen: Gyldendal.

Darwin, C. (1915). *Peri tis geneseos ton eidon* [On the origin of species]. (N. Kazantzakis, Trans.). Athens: Fexis.

Darwin, C. (1921). *El origen de las especies por medio de la sélection natural* [The origin of species by means of natural selection]. (A. de Zulueta, Trans.). Madrid: Calpe.

Darwin, C. (1936). *El origen de las especies* [The origin of species]. (M. J. Barroso-Bonzón, Trans.). Madrid: Librería Bergua.

Darwin, C. (1950). *El origen de las especies por selección natural* [The origin of species by means of natural selection]. (M. J. Barroso-Bonzón, Trans.). Madrid: Ediciones Ibéricas.

Darwin, C. (1959). *L'origine delle specie* [The origin of species]. (L. Fratini, Trans.). Turin: Einaudi.

Darwin, C. (2009). *Origine des espèces par le moyen de la sélection naturelle, ou la préservation des races favorisées dans la lutte pour la vie* [Origin of species by means of natural selection, or the preservation of favoured races in the struggle for life]. (A. Berra, Trans.). Paris: Honoré Champion.

Darwin, F. (Ed.). (1887). *The life and letters of Charles Darwin, including an autobiographical chapter.* London: John Murray.

Engels, E. M., & Glick, T. F. (2008). Editor's introduction. In E. M. Engels & T. F. Glick (Eds.), *The reception of Charles Darwin in Europe* (pp. 1–22). London: Continuum.

Freeman, R. B. (1977). *The works of Charles Darwin: An annotated bibliographical handlist.* Folkestone: Dawson.

Glick, T. F. (1992). El impacto del darwinismo en la Europa mediterránea y Latinoamérica [The impact of Darwinism in Mediterranean Europe and Latin America]. In A. Lafuente & J. Sala Catalá (Eds.), *Ciencia colonial en América* [Colonial science in America] (pp. 319–350). Madrid: Alianza.

Glick, T. F. (2014). Timeline: Literary reception of Charles Darwin in Europe and Darwin commemorative celebrations. In T. F. Glick & E. Shaffer (Eds.), *The literary and cultural reception of Charles Darwin in Europe* (pp. 27–52). London: Bloomsbury.

Gomis Blanco, A., & Josa Llorca, J. (2009). *Bibliografía crítica ilustrada de las obras de Darwin en España (1857–2008)* [Illustrated critical bibliography of the works of Darwin in Spain (1857–2008)]. Madrid: CSIC.

Groff, C. (2011). Tradurre Grass con Grass [Translating Grass with Grass]. In C. Buffagni, B. Garzelli, & S. Zanotti (Eds.), *The Translator as author. Perspectives on literary translation* (pp. 151–156). Berlin: LIT.

Guidelines. (1935). In *Die Bücherei 2:6, 279* (R. Richter, Trans.). Retrieved from http://www.library.arizona.edu/exhibits/burnedbooks/documents.htm#guidelines

Harvey, J. (1997). *Almost a man of genius: Clémence Royer, feminism, and nineteenth-century science.* New Brunswick, NJ: Rutgers University Press.

Harvey, J. (2008). Darwin in a French dress: Translating, publishing and supporting Darwin in nineteenth-century France. In E. M. Engels & T. F. Glick (Eds.), *The reception of Charles Darwin in Europe* (pp. 354–374). London: Continuum.

Hjermitslev, H. H. (2014). The Danish commemoration of Darwin in 1909. In T. F. Glick & E. Shaffer (Eds.), *The literary and cultural reception of Charles Darwin in Europe* (pp. 128–159). London: Bloomsbury.

Hull, D. (1988). Darwinism and historiography. In T. F. Glick (Ed.), *The comparative reception of Darwinism* (pp. 388–404). Chicago: University of Chicago Press.

Ivančić, B. (2011). Dialogue between translators and authors. The example of Claudio Magris. In C. Buffagni, B. Garzelli, & S. Zanotti (Eds.), *The translator as author. Perspectives on literary translation* (pp. 157–172). Berlin: LIT.

Janvier, P. (1996). Darwinisme nordique [Nordic Darwinism]. In P. Tort (Dir.), *Dictionnaire du Darwinisme et de l'évolution* [Dictionary of Darwinism and evolution] (pp. 1042–1044). Paris: PUF.

Levit, I., Levit, G. S., Hossfeld, U., & Olsson, L. (2014). Russia and its neighbors. In S. Blancke, H. H. Hjermitslev, & P. C. Kjærgaard (Eds.), *Creationism in Europe* (pp. 162–179). Baltimore, MD: Johns Hopkins.

Lie, T. (2014). 'A matter of money … ': The first Darwin commemoration in Norway in 1882. In T. F. Glick & E. Shaffer (Eds.), *The literary and cultural reception of Charles Darwin in Europe* (pp. 181–189). London: Bloomsbury.

Molina, G. (1996). Darwinisme Français [French Darwinism]. In P. Tort (Dir.), *Dictionnaire du Darwinisme et de l'évolution* [Dictionary of Darwinism and evolution] (pp. 909–954). Paris: PUF.

Montgomery, W. M. (1988). Germany. In T. F. Glick (Ed.), *The comparative reception of Darwinism* (pp. 81–116). Chicago: University of Chicago Press.

Paul, H. W. (1988). Religion and Darwinism. In T. F. Glick (Ed.), *The comparative reception of Darwinism* (pp. 405–438). Chicago: University of Chicago Press.

Peckham, M. (Ed.). (1959). *The origin of species by Charles Darwin. A variorum text.* Philadelphia: University of Pennsylvania Press.

Prum, M. (2014). Charles Darwin's first French translations. In T. F. Glick & E. Shaffer (Eds.), *The literary and cultural reception of Charles Darwin in Europe* (pp. 391–399). London: Bloomsbury.

Pym, A. (2009). Humanizing translation history. *Hermes. Journal of Language and Communication Studies, 42,* 1–26.

Rayfield, D. (2014). Darwin, Chekhov and Mandelshtam. In T. F. Glick & E. Shaffer (Eds.), *The literary and cultural reception of Charles Darwin in Europe* (pp. 257–267). London: Bloomsbury.

Rem, T. (2014). Darwin and Norwegian literature. In T. F. Glick & E. Shaffer (Dir.), *The literary and cultural reception of Charles Darwin in Europe* (pp. 160–180). London: Bloomsbury.

Rupp-Eisenreich, B. (1996). Darwinisme Allemand [German Darwinism]. In P. Tort (Eds.), *Dictionnaire du Darwinisme et de l'évolution* [Dictionary of Darwinism and Evolution] (pp. 822–866). Paris: PUF.

Shaffer, E., & Glick, T. F. (2014). Introduction. In T. F. Glick & E. Shaffer (Eds.), *The literary and cultural reception of Charles Darwin in Europe* (pp. 1–14). London: Bloomsbury.

Tort, P. (2014). 1909: The great silence–remarks on the non-celebration of Darwin's centenary in France. (N. M. Huckle, Trans.). In T. F. Glick & E. Shaffer (Eds.), *The literary and cultural reception of Charles Darwin in Europe* (pp. 400–415). London: Bloomsbury.

Van Wyhe, J. (Ed.). (2002—). *The complete work of Charles Darwin online* (http://darwin-online.org.uk).

White, P. (2008). Correspondence as medium of reception and appropriation. In E. M. Engels & T. F. Glick (Eds.), *The reception of Charles Darwin in Europe* (pp. 54–65). London: Continuum.

Zanotti, S. (2011). The translator and the author: Two of a kind? In C. Buffagni, B. Garzelli, & S. Zanotti (Eds.), *The Translator as author. Perspectives on literary translation* (pp. 79–89). Berlin: LIT.

Zarimis, M. (2014). Darwinian reception and selected responses of two prominent Greek literary writers. In T. F. Glick & E. Shaffer (Eds.), *The literary and cultural reception of Charles Darwin in Europe* (pp. 649–666). London: Bloomsbury.

"¡No Pasarán!": Translators under siege and ideological control in the Spanish Civil War

Marcos Rodríguez-Espinosa

This paper traces the biographies of Paulina and Adelina Abramson, Irene Falcón, Maria Fortus, Ilse Kulcsar, Constancia de la Mora, Lise Ricol, and Lydia Kúper, a group of women who worked as translators during the Spanish Civil War. Before being appointed translators during this conflict, the professional training of some of them had been sponsored by the Red Army and the Comintern, the international communist organization created to spread, on a worldwide scale, the political changes of the Bolshevik Revolution. The Comintern recruited activists throughout the world, who eventually travelled to the USSR, where they received political indoctrination and sometimes linguistic training as translators. The Spanish Civil War was, for these translators, a unique opportunity to put translation at the service of 'the last great cause'. For most of them, the end of the Spanish conflict also meant the beginning of a long exile; not only due to the defeat of the Republic but also to their dissidence from Soviet orthodoxy. Some died far from their homelands, yet still had the chance to use translation as a weapon of resistance against General Franco; others were forced into a new exile after being exposed to the atrocities of Stalinism.

1. Introduction

Baker (2006), Salama-Carr (2007), and Inghilleri and Harding (2010) have, in recent years, published or edited collective works in which a number of contributors address the vital roles played by translators during the wars of the twentieth century in such key issues as military alliances, hierarchical power structures, territorial occupation, peace missions, or war narratives. Previous research on the presence of translators in the Spanish Civil War by Alcofar Nassaes (1971), Martínez de Pisón (2005), Rodríguez-Espinosa (2007), Aizpuru (2009), and Baigorri-Jalón (2012), based, in some cases, on war documents held in the Historical Archive of the Spanish Communist Party (Madrid), the Historical Memory Documentary Centre (Salamanca), and the Historic Archive of Basque Nationalism (Bilbao), personal interviews with translators, and the exploration of notebooks, manuscripts, and correspondence, has pointed out certain questions related to these translators, such as their military and ideological affiliation, their presence in the Francoist war zone, the enrolment of white Russians within the Soviet contingent, or Spanish exiles in the Soviet Union.

Drawing on a wide range of historical and literary scholarship, memoirs, biographies, and fictional texts, this paper discusses a series of questions connected to the personal narratives of seven women of different nationalities who worked as translators and interpreters in the Spanish Civil War. Thomas (2003), Beevor (2006), and Kowalsky (2004), among other leading historians of the Civil War, have underlined the international implications of the Spanish confrontation, the evidence of language and communication problems within the different nationalities on the front, and the presence of translators on the Loyalist battlefield. Following Inghilleri's (2010, p. 179) definition of military translators in their dual capacityas linguists and combat soldiers, we will first approach the linguistic training, operational effectiveness, and undercover intelligence activities of Maria Alexandrovna Fortus, Paulina Abramson, and Adelina Abramson; three military translators who, in late 1936, came with a Soviet expedition to help the besieged Spanish Republic.

The shortage of military translators in the Loyalist war zone will also lead us to examine the incompetence of the Soviet institutional framework in its failure to bring enough translators into service, as well as the motives behind the recruitment of polyglot civilian translators such as Lise Ricol, Lydia Kúper, and Irene Falcón. Moreover, we will analyze their close relationship with the Comintern, the international communist organization founded by Lenin, which emerged in the 1930s as a space for political activism in which foreign translators had been traditionally attached to its multilingual propaganda and translation sections.

Palmer's (2007, pp. 13–28) investigation into the US military occupation of Iraq in 2003 provides a unique insight into the diverse functions undertaken by translators and interpreters hired as 'fixers' by foreign press correspondents who lacked the essential knowledge of the country and thus had to rely on the interpreters in order to efficiently report on the complexities of the conflict. In this paper we will also explore the performance of translators Ilse Kulcsar and Constancia de la Mora in the Loyalist Foreign Press and Propaganda Office, with particular reference to their conflicting roles in the censorship apparatus, preventing foreign correspondents from sending dispatches that contradicted the inconsistent war narratives produced by the Republic.

The scarcity of scholarly literature available on the presence of translators and interpreters in world conflicts, in the opinion of Maier (2007, p. 9), has made personal memoirs, contemporary accounts, or fictional representations a relevant source of information pertaining to the translators' responses to work-related challenges and their lives as individuals. Spanish Civil War memoirs, in our case, will be analyzed as potential referencial material in order to disclose significant issues, such as the ethical implications of their tasks, their commitment to the cause they fought for, or the notion of translators as heroines or traitors, particularly relevant to the unpredictable political turmoil found in Loyalist Spain.

Finally, we will explore the role played by the female military and civilian translators studied in this paper in the new conflicts that shattered Europe at the end of the Spanish Civil War. The analysis will place particular focus on their engagement in new translation activities during their long exile in the Soviet Union as well as the role of literary translation as a space of political resistance in the course of General Franco's dictatorship, together with the public visibility and media recognition achieved by many of them in Spain and Latin America in recent years.

2. Soviet military translators in the Spanish Civil War: Maria Fortus, Paulina Abramson, and Adelina Abramson

The Spanish Civil War started with a distant military uprising in northern Morocco which soon developed into an international conflict, defined by Thomas (2003, p. 449) as a world war in miniature. The uncertainty of a major regional confrontation made France and Great Britain, together with other European nations, set up a Non-Intervention Committee in September 1936, which Preston (1986, p. 83) described as 'a sham that worked in the interest of the rebel forces in Spain, and hindered the efforts of the legitimate Republican government to stage an effective defense against the insurgents'. General Franco's insurrection had, in fact, been supported from the very beginning, as Beevor (2006, p. 157) notes, by a horde of Italian and German advisers, observers, technicians, combat personnel, and the most modern battlefield weaponry. The Soviet Union, for its part, had also proclaimed its neutrality through the Non-Intervention Agreement, hoping not to challenge the critical international balance of powers. Nevertheless, the double dealings of fascist and Nazi leaders during the summer of 1936 forced Stalin to change the nature of his collaboration with the Spanish Republic.

Later, in September, general Yan K. Berzin ('Grishin'), former head of Soviet foreign military intelligence (GRU), arrived in Madrid, a city littered with wall posters and leaflets bearing the slogan uttered by communist heroine Dolores Ibárruri during her epic radio speech, delivered just after the July military insurgence: 'The Fascists shall not Pass! They shall not Pass! / ¡Los Fascistas No Pasarán! ¡No Pasarán!' Berzin's main responsibility was to coordinate Operation X, the secret plan devised to deliver tanks, armored cars, airplanes, trucks, rifles, field artillery, and other weapons. This military equipment was accompanied by a contingent of combatant and non-combatant personnel, which, according to Beevor (2006, p. 183), never appeared to have been more than 2200, and included high-ranking military advisers, intelligence officers, pilots, tank drivers, flying instructors, and translators and interpreters. The performance of this last group, as we will see, proved to be crucial for proper collaboration between Soviet authorities and the Republican government.

The first of the 204 translators and interpreters sent to Spain were chosen mostly among female graduates from local universities and institutes, such as the Moscow Institute of New Languages. They were selected, as stated by Kowalsky (2004), by a special committee appointed by the Defence Commissariat, although the lack of expertise in Spanish of many candidates forced them to enroll in a three-month intensive course in Moscow. As most of their comrades in arms, Alcofar Nassaes (1971, pp. 141–142) emphasizes that Soviet military translators were highly politicized and intimidated by the presence of the political commissars of their units. Military linguists also kept their real identity hidden by assuming one of a Latin American citizen and using false names on their passports, which is probably why some Spaniards started calling them 'Mexicans'. Military translators were sent on different missions, such as official diplomatic meetings, military tactical advice, war machinery instruction, battlefield operations, undercover guerilla units, and message encoding and deciphering. They were expected to behave as combat soldiers and some of them, such as Sofia Bessmertnaia, who died in the battle of Brunete, met their demise in the war.

Volodarsky (2013, p. 174) refers to Maria Alexandrovna Fortus (1908–1980) as a legendary figure who combined her activities as an illegal resident agent and a military translator under the code name of 'Julia Jiménez Cárdenas'. She was fluent in Spanish and had a precise knowledge of the country's political affairs, as she had spent considerable time there in the company of her husband, Ramón Lluch Casanellas, a Catalan anarchist who arrived in the USSR as a political refugee after being associated with the assassination of Spanish Prime Minister Eduardo Dato in 1921. Soviet military adviser Meretskov (1968), alias 'Petrovich', praises her performance during the meetings of the Spanish Joint Chiefs of Staff and the inspection of trenches and fortifications shortly after her arrival in Madrid. Fortus also translated Meretskov's inspiring speech to an infantry brigade, which was nothing more than a unit of armed civilians from party and union militias, trembling in fear of nearby Francoist troops. In the presence of Enrique Líster, the Moscow-trained commander of the future Fifth Regiment, Meretskov, said emphatically that battle discipline was based on political consciousness, organizational capacity, and the support of the Spanish people. The translator's intimidating rendering of the Soviet adviser's words on the night of 7 November 1936 convinced Prime Minister Largo Caballero to urgently meet with his government in Valencia, because the rebel forces were already at the gates of Madrid. During the battle of Brunete in February 1937, as military adviser Malinovsky (1986, p. 56) recalls, Fortus shouted at a group of retreating soldiers: 'Who has castrated you? If you were not castrated, you would be men and you would not flee the battlefield!' The reckless intervention of the interpreter eventually stemmed their panic while under a large-scale Nationalist assault, but also made her the target of bitter complaints from Spanish Loyalist officers. Military translator Maria Fortus returned to the Soviet Union at the end of the Spanish war to join the infiltration intelligence units in eastern Europe during World War II and was officially awarded for her distinguished services on different occasions.

The scarce number of translators then available encouraged the recruitment of bilingual citizens born in Spanish-speaking American republics as well as from Latin American parents exiled in the Soviet Union. Miralles (2009, pp. 44–45) included among them the Uruguayans Dina and Fiodor Kravchenko and the Argentinians Aléxis Korobitshin, Pedro Loss, and sisters Paulina and Adelina Abramson; a select group of translators and GRU agents who were among the first to arrive in Spain. As a matter of fact, Commander Paulina Abramson (1915–2000) had managed to sneak into the country just a few months before the conflict broke out, apparently to work in Editorial Europa-América, a typical publishing enterprise financed by the Comintern. One of her first assignments was to translate for Soviet film-maker Roman Karmen while filming his war documentary *Ispaniia*. *Pravda* correspondent Mikhail Koltsov (1978, p. 134), who also required her linguistic support on his dangerous expedition to the northern front, narrates the hostile mutterings with which local men welcomed her military trousers in a Santander restaurant and her successful performance during his conversations with communist leaders in Asturias and with the president of the Basque government in Bilbao. In November 1936, Paulina joined the military intelligence of the International Brigades, translated for the Junta de Defensa de Madrid, and operated on the front line with the October Battalion. During this time she worked on a series of high risk assignments with her future husband, colonel Khadzi-Umar Mamsurov ('Ksanty'), a secret military agent who set up sabotage warfare units in the rebel rearguard. Paulina Abramson completed her military instruction at the Frunze Military Academy in Moscow and was subsequently promoted to Major of the Red Army. After World War II, she moved to Prague, where she became head of the Spanish section of the Military Institute of Foreign Languages (Abramson & Abramson, 1994).

Adelina Abramson (1917–2012), together with her father Veniamin Abramson, came into Spain by way of France under the false identity of 'Adelina Regis'. Soviet Air Force adviser General Yakov V. Smushkevich ('Duglas'), after excluding her from guerrilla missions on account of her youth, employed her linguistic expertise at the three Republican Air Force headquarters and at a new assembly plant in Reus (Barcelona), where Soviet aircrafts were being manufactured. The technical complexity of this task made Adelina Abramson compile a detailed bilingual glossary to be used by Russian and Spanish engineers and pilots. During World War II, Adelina Abramson was assigned as a military interpreter for the Italian contingent of prisoners captured during the Soviet advance towards the German front. She retired from her military duties in 1949 and was decorated with the Order of the Red Star (Abramson & Abramson, 1994).

3. Civilian translators in the Spanish Civil War: Lise Ricol, Lydia Kúper, Irene Falcón, Ilse Kulcsar, and Constancia de la Mora

During the first months of the Spanish Civil War, Section X imposed a rule that only Soviet personnel were to be permitted to work as translators. The shortage of qualified linguists and the chaotic communication between military advisers and the army of the Republic soon forced Moscow to open a language school in the Loyalist zone, but it only remained operational for a short time in 1937 (Kowalsky, 2004). The situation became so dire that they were forced to accept candidates among white Russians living in Spain, such as Constant Brusiloff (1895–1977), a czarist officer exiled since 1922. Arrested by the Loyalist police force in Santander during his honeymoon in the summer of 1936, Brusiloff was coerced into joining the official USSR consulate in Bilbao as one of the three translators involved with their operations in Asturias and the Basque Country (Aizpuru, 2009, p. 299).

The Soviet military establishment, however, did not completely trust these exiles and still preferred to call in foreign intelligence agents of the People's Commissariat for Internal Affairs (NKVD), or international communist cadres. Lise Ricol (1916–2012) was a translator in the French section of the Comintern who travelled to Spain as an interpreter of André Marty, Political Commissar of the International Brigades. At his side, Ricol carried out the task of organizing the logistics of the brigades, meetings with commanders of different nationalities, communications with the Spanish military and civilian authorities, as well as the ideological control of the units. Lise Ricol, whose family members were Spanish exiles in France, was later sent to the dangerous front line of Madrid, the 'heroic city'. There, still electrified by the psychological impact of the International Brigades on the morale of the population, she worked as the interpreter for Raymond Guyot, the General Secretary of the Executive Committee of the Young Communist International (KIM) (London, 1996, pp. 338–358).

The real purpose of this formal call was to meet the leaders of the Juventud Socialista Unificada (JSU), the new communist youth movement that unified socialist and communist organizations, which was to be the backbone of the new Republican army. The Spanish Communist Party (Partido Comunista de España), as Rees (1998, p. 143) demonstrates, had a leadership chosen by the Comintern and was imbued by its methods and doctrines. Due to its close relationship with Moscow, the party rapidly grew throughout the war from being a marginal force into a powerful political organization. Subsequently, it was to provide disciplined Russian-speaking militants who were later recruited as translators by Soviet military advisers.

One of the most notorious cases among them was translator Lydia Kúper (1914–2011), born in Lodz (Poland) to a Jewish family when the city still belonged to the Czarist Empire. After her father's death, she moved to Odessa, until the Russian Civil War forced her to seek refuge in Vigo (Spain), where her uncle was already a well-known dental practitioner. Kúper studied at the prestigious Faculty of Arts in Madrid and lived in the 'Residencia de Señoritas', the most exclusive and liberal female college in the country. Soviet authorities trusted Lydia Kúper to work as a translator, not only for her command of Russian and Spanish but also because she had married Gabriel León Trilla, a founding member of the Spanish Communist Party, with whom she had travelled to Moscow in the 1930s. International Brigade historian Castells Peig (1974, p. 657) identifies her under the name 'Lidia de Trilla' at the Loyalist Air Force base in Albacete, although later on she would also collaborate in translating material with the secret cipher bureau in Valencia. According to Martínez de Pisón (2007, p. 29), as a war-field interpreter for Soviet military advisers N. Ivanov, I. Maximov, and Rodion Y. Malinovsky ('Malino'), she witnessed the victory at the battle of Guadalajara and the beginning of the final defeat of the Republic, when Francoist troops cut all land links between Barcelona and Valencia in 1938.[1]

Irene Lewy Rodríguez (1908–1999), better known as Irene Falcón, was another early Spanish communist convert who became the interpreter of legendary communist leader Dolores Ibárruri, La Pasionaria, during the Spanish war and their exile in the USSR. Together with her husband César Falcón, a Peruvian journalist and communist activist, she launched the weekly magazine *Nosotros*, 'The Organ of the World Revolution', and the small publishing house Historia Nueva, where she was managing editor of a collection of feminist writings. After Irene Falcón joined the communist movement in 1932, she increased her feminist and revolutionary activities through organizations such as the Association of Antifascist Women (Asociación de Mujeres Antifascistas) (Falcón, 1996).

Spain paradoxically came to the attention of the Comintern after the Asturian miners' revolution of 1934, when most comrades were imprisoned and the party's newspapers and publications were also suspended. A new generation of Spanish communists, who would eventually rule the party for the next decades, was summoned to the Soviet Union to receive political or military instruction. Polyglot Irene Falcón arrived in Moscow, assigned to work as a proofreader and editor of classical Marxist and Leninist texts at the Publishing Co-operative of Foreign Workers in the Soviet Union.[2] The Bolsheviks, as Service (2012, p. 244) maintains, were people of the printed word, and communist subversive propaganda reached its foreign proselytes through translations printed both by small foreign publishers and Soviet state publishers. Military translator Paulina Abramson (1994, p. 40), whose father also collaborated with this publishing house, translating the works of Lenin and Stalin into Spanish, recalls the place as a 'small Babylon', populated with international activists hired to work as typists, proofreaders, or translators.

Irene Falcón and Lydia Kúper lived in the Hotel Lux, the residence in Moscow that lodged revolutionary exiles, international delegates, and high-ranking functionaries. More than half of the Executive Committee of the Communist International staff, according to Huber (1998, p. 43–44), were foreigners employed in the translation and press services of the Publishing Department. Bulgarian Comintern General Secretary Georgi Dimitrov had sent Irene Falcón, shortly after General Franco's *coup d'etat*, to a secret Moscow radio station to translate any kind of useful information about the Spanish confrontation into French or German. Back in Spain, Falcón continued this task by helping to set up the Antifascist World Press Agency/Agencia de Información Mundial Antifascista (AIMA), operated by the Spanish government and the Communist Party to disseminate their own version of the conflict, which, in the long run, turned out to be crucial for the formation of world-wide public opinion (Falcón, 1996).

An outstanding aspect of the international involvement in the Spanish Civil War was, as Thomas (2003, p. 305) points out, the fact that countless distinguished journalists converged south of the Pyrenees. Most Western newspapers justified, to a certain degree, Franco's uprising; in particular, as Beevor (2006, pp. 267–269) remarks, after the first reports of 'red massacres' had reached the world. Many other journalists, on the contrary, such as Jay Allen, George Steer, Ernest Hemingway, Martha Gellhorn, and Louis Fischer, wrote 'as resolute partisans, to the extent of activism' (Preston, 2009, p. 19), in favor of a Spanish Republic and, in so doing, struggled to convince Western public opinion that the Republic constituted the only legal democratic government of the nation.

The Loyalist Foreign Press, Propaganda and Censorship Department was run from the Telefónica skyscraper in Madrid, by International Telephone & Telegraph Company employees who were lost in what Preston (2009, p. 29) describes as 'a chaotic din of languages'. Dispatches were translated into Spanish, or, at best, French, but the erratic instructions received created dangerous breaches in military and political information. Julio Álvarez del Vayo, a Left-wing socialist with strong communist leanings and only recently named Minister of Foreign Affairs, appointed Luis Rubio Hidalgo to the position of Chief Censor at the Foreign Press and Propaganda Office in September 1936. Under Rubio Hidalgo, censorship was implemented much more efficiently. As a rule, censors were hired on the basis of their ability to read the dispatches in the language in which they were originally written. Moreover, as Vaill (2014, p. 54) notes, correspondents were given far more consistent standards as to what would and would not be authorized for publication, with a strict rule that no information could hint at anything other than victory for the Republic.

As novelist Arturo Barea (2001, p. 573) mentions in *The Forging of a Rebel*, he was appointed censor on the recommendation of a communist friend because he was fluent in French and he could translate 'the English of technical reviews'. Once the copy of the dispatch was returned, stamped, and initialed by the censors, the correspondents sent it by cable or telephone while switch censors made sure there were no deviations from the approved text. Barea and his colleagues searched dictionaries for double meanings and cut out phrases when the French argot or American slang remained obscure to them.

While the Telefónica building was the main target for rebel mortar fire and bombers flying over Madrid, the lack of translators compelled Rubio Hidalgo to hire reliable foreign activists who were in Spain at the time to fight fascism. Viennese polyglot Ilse Kulcsar (1902–1973), dubbed 'Ilsa de la Telefónica' by the correspondents, built a trustworthy relationship with foreign journalists and exerted an enormous influence on the news they reported due to her efforts in providing them with reliable information together with her ability to pull the right strings to ensure they obtained interpreters, hotel rooms, gasoline vouchers, safe-conducts, etc. Throughout 1937, when she was named Barea's deputy, Ilsa translated the hidden documents found in a flat by Doctor Norman Bethune, chief of the Canadian Blood Transfusion Unit, which contained classified information about the Nazi fifth column in Madrid (Eaude, 2009, pp. 178–181).

Constancia de la Mora (1906–1950), a communist hardliner whose grandfather had been Prime Minister of several governments of King Alphonse XIII, was named Chief of the Foreign Press and Propaganda Office in the summer of 1937. Fluent in English, French, and German, she was called to Albacete to act as interpreter when the organizational committee of the International Brigades transformed itself into a military council in late 1936 (Beevor 2006, p. 181). 'Connie', as she was called by the correspondents, performed similar duties at the side of foreign politicians and journalists and travelled extensively with members of the Loyalist cabinet to different European countries. British documentarian Thorold Dickinson also praised her cooperation with film crews who wanted to shoot in forbidden areas of the front line and interview relevant members of the Republican faction (Fox, 2007, p. 293).

The Loyalist Spanish government, as Beevor (2006, p. 274) recalls, concurrently provided two contradictory and incompatible versions of the war. An account for external consumption was designed to convince the French, British, and US governments that they were a liberal property-owning democracy, while home propagandists ruled by radical political organizations tried to accelerate mass mobilization and the revolutionary dimension of the conflict. Mora made sure the Foreign Press and Propaganda Office was not only a censoring filter of dispatches but also an influential weapon to give foreign journalists access to vehicles, letters of safe-conduct, interviews with military staff, reliable sources of information, translators, and interpreters, who would aid them in explaining the truth about the Spanish cause. More than 50 people, many of them foreign female activists, collaborated with the Press and Propaganda Office, which eventually moved from Valencia to Barcelona. Constancia de la Mora travelled to Moscow in December 1938 with her husband Ignacio Hidalgo de Cisneros, Senior Officer in the Loyalist Air Force, on a secret mission to buy weapons from Stalin. She was to be the official spokesperson of the Spanish Republic until its demise in 1939 (De la Fuente, 2006).

4. Translators as traitors, Trotskyists, and exiles

Translators operating in such an extremely polarized ideological battlefield as the Spanish Civil War, in which it was not always easy to distinguish between friend and enemy, often appeared as 'recurring objects of ambivalence, in-between figures, loathed and admired, privileged and despised' (Cronin, 2002, p. 55). The unpredictable evolution of the battlefront, together with the antagonistic political groups fighting inside the Republican war zone, created a conflicting situation in which their professional practice was constantly under scrutiny. 'Moving between factions, privy to sensitive information, and frequently called upon to pass on unwelcome news', as Mairs (2011, p. 65) notes, translators in this unstable context became more and more susceptible to being labelled traitors, a concept as old as the profession itself.

The strange disappearance of translator José Robles Pazos (1897–1937) is still today an unsolved mystery that has captivated historians, writers, and filmmakers in recent decades. Robles had left Spain during the dictatorship of general Primo de Rivera and, by the late 1920s, had become a lecturer at Johns Hopkins University and translated John Dos Passos' *Manhattan Transfer* (1929) and Sinclair Lewis' *Babbit* (1930) for the radical publishing house Cénit. Shortly after the arrival of the

Soviet delegation, his command of Russian apparently made him the ideal candidate to be appointed interpreter for General Vladimir E. Gorev ('Sancho'), Head of Military Intelligence. Robles was suddenly and inexplicably executed in early 1937, probably accused of having committed espionage or having carelessly revealed a piece of sensitive information (Preston, 2009, p. 76). Dos Passos unsuccessfully tried to find out the real reasons behind the death of Robles. His killing, together with other nasty events the American novelist witnessed in Spain, undermined his idealistic commitment to what Weintraub (1968) called 'the last great cause', and triggered his criticism of the escalating ideological and military control the Soviet Union and the Communist Party exerted over the Republic.

Some of the female war translators and interpreters noted herein were suspected of treason, as the contexts in which they worked often required them to carry out potentially conflicting duties. As Martínez de Pisón (2007, p. 30) points out, Lydia Kúper was held in NKVD custody after a fatal car accident claimed the life of Soviet Adviser Maximov, to whom she had been assigned, and was not released until it was confirmed that she had, in fact, been given permission to attend a theatrical performance in Madrid that day, put on by the communist poet Rafael Alberti.

Ilsa Kulcsar was expected to assume multiple roles within the Press and Propaganda Office in order to guarantee that its heavily censored reports on the war would, in some way, contribute to the victory of the Republic. Radical militiamen constantly blamed Ilsa Kulcsar for leaking sensitive information; and Koltsov, the journalist hailed as Stalin's 'eyes and ears' in Madrid, threatened to have her and Arturo Barea court-martialed (Vaill, 2014, p. 86). In a similar vein, Volodarsky (2013, p. 238) describes military commander General Gorev, when in the company of his translator Emma Lazarevna Wolf, as a popular figure at General Miaja's headquarters. In addition, Gorev also visited the Press and Propaganda Office nightly to flush out information on Ilsa Kulcsar's former activities in Austria as well as to peruse the censor-approved articles, which he believed to be an invaluable source of secret information.

After carrying out her mission to infiltrate and fill the Foreign Press Office with communists, Constancia de la Mora released Ilsa Kulcsar and Arturo Barea from their duties on the likely grounds that they had brought the evils of the censorship apparatus to light. Ilsa Kulcsar, who had been expelled from the KPO (Austrian Communist Party) in the 1920s, and later joined the SDAP (Social Democratic Workers' Party), was the perfect scapegoat in a political smear campaign which sought to brand her as a Trotskyist spy. Repeatedly interrogated by the Military Intelligence Service (SIM) in Barcelona, Kulcsar was later released thanks to the intervention of her husband Leopold Kulcsar, then under the orders of General Alexandr M. Orlov, NKVD station chief in Spain. Fortunately, friends from her days as a socialist speaker and journalist in London, such as translators and editors Gwenda David and Eric Mosbacher, as Vaill (2014, p. 348) remembers, helped Ilsa find a new home in England.

In 1939, translators Lydia Kúper and Irene Falcón left Spain for the USSR in the company of a select contingent of Senior Military and Government Officials. During their long exile there, they joined the team of translators and interpreters upon which the Communist Party of Spain had relied for their institutional communication with the Soviet authorities. Nevertheless, after World War II, Kúper, alongside other Spanish Civil War veterans, joined the prestigious team of translators at the state-owned Foreign Languages Publishing House, which translated literature, propaganda, and science. In the end, such a cunning decision on her part later saved her from Stalin's pogroms and the constant in-fighting, which, in the late 1940s, erupted within the exiled Communist Party of Spain. An agreement struck between the International Red Cross and the government of General Franco finally made it possible for her and other exiles to return to Spain in 1957.

This was not, however, the case for Irene Falcón, the closest aide to Secretary General Dolores Ibárruri in Moscow, or Lise Ricol-London, who, after the Spanish Civil War, joined the French *résistance*, was eventually captured by the Nazis, and shipped off to a concentration camp. In 1952, Czechoslovakian Stalinist zealots organized a spectacular purge of Trotskyist, Titoite, and Zionist conspirators known as the Slánský Trial, which ended with the execution of Irene Falcón's ex-lover, Comintern Executive Bedrich Geminder, as well as other former International Brigade volunteers. Lise Ricol's husband, Artur London, Deputy Minister of Foreign Affairs, was also sentenced to life imprisonment.

After the Slánský Trial, Irene Falcón was discharged from the State Radio Broadcasting Service and publishing houses and stripped of all political responsibilities and duties. Dolores Ibárruri, however, managed to get her enrolled as a student in the Department of Oriental Studies at Lomonosov Moscow State University. Three years later, Falcón was sent to China to work for Radio Beijing's broadcasting services in Spanish. She was eventually rehabilitated after the death of Stalin and granted permission to resume her political activities in the central committee of the Spanish Communist Party in 1960 (Falcón, 1996, pp. 290–302).

5. Translators and interpreters as war chroniclers

Memoirs and autobiographical narratives by Spanish Civil War translators and interpreters provide revealing insights into their performance in the war and of the history of the conflict itself. *In Place of Splendor* (1939) – the US bestseller written in collaboration by American ghostwriter Ruth McKenney and Constancia de la Mora – was, for instance, one of the first propagandistic accounts of the civil war which justified Soviet intervention and denounced the partiality of the International Non-Intervention Agreement towards the rebel uprising. Mora (1939, p. 287), who early on asserts the need for translators in the war zone, openly says that her boss, Hidalgo Rubio, was not the ideal candidate to run the Press and Propaganda Office because he did not understand the North American correspondents, 'with their Kansas rather than Oxford accents, and their journalese slang'. Later on, Mora (1939, p. 304) also recalls the decisive task performed by translators in the office, who rendered into different languages the military documents seized from the Italian units captured during the Battle of Guadalajara. This contributed to the preparation of *The White Book*, which the Republican government presented at the League of Nations as proof of Mussolini's intervention in the country. There is not a single reference, nevertheless, to communist infiltration in the Loyalist Army and government or to the execution of translator José Robles. Mora spent most of her later years in Mexico, where she became the translator of the Soviet ambassador Constantine Oumansky. Shortly before her death, she cut off all remaining ties with the Spanish Communist Party.

Through the Foreign Press and Propaganda Office, Ilsa Barea-Kulcsar and Constancia de la Mora participated in the battle with the hope of convincing international public opinion of the Republic's just cause. Ilsa's fierce independence and her resistance to the polarized ideological positions inside the Censorship Office finally made her a heretic and condemned her to ostracism. During her lengthy exile in England, Ilsa Barea turned translation once more into a source of income and political activism. Her English version of Arturo Barea's trilogy *The Forge* (1943), *The Track* (1944), and *The Clash* (1946), printed in one volume in the United States as *The Forging of a Rebel* (1946), and her struggle to have his other books published and translated into different languages were seen as acts of defiance and resistance against the regime of General Franco, who had banned Barea's masterpiece. The outlawed text, found in Spain only at clandestine bookshops, was, in effect, condemned to be read behind closed doors in editions printed in Argentina (1954) and Mexico (1959).[3] As a fictionalized autobiographical account of the civil war, the third volume of *The Forging of a Rebel* provides a unique source of inside information on Ilsa's performance as the official interpreter of Eleanor Rathbone, Duchess of Atholl, Ellen Wilkinson, and Katherine Stewart-Murray, members of a British parliamentary commission strongly opposed to the policy laid out by the Non-Intervention Agreement. Barea (2001, pp. 656–661) notes how his deputy, Ilsa Kulcsar, translated 'with a hidden flourish', which made him 'suspect that she had edited what both sides had said'. This intervention by the interpreter became particularly advisable when Ilsa found herself toning down questions and answers relating to the presence of Russian instructors in the Republican Air Force at a tea party organized by General José Miaja, idealized by communist propaganda as the 'Defender of Madrid'.

Translator Irene Falcón, a fervent convert to the communist movement, bravely condemned the Stalinist purges in her autobiography *Asalto a los Cielos* (1996), which included a detailed description of her activities as an independent publisher in the strained Spanish political atmosphere of the 1930s and a lengthy chronicle of her approach to translation in different Soviet publishing houses and broadcasting services.

Lise Ricol and her husband Artur London also faced Stalinist prosecution and hostility from their party comrades after the latter was released from prison in 1956. International Brigade translator Lise Ricol-London's memoirs, published in France in 1995 and 1996, however, retain an idealistic depiction of their fight against fascism in Spain, as well as a benevolent account of Constancia de la Mora's competent collaboration with world famous international reporters such as George Soria, Mikhail Koltsov, Ernest Hemingway, Martha Gelhorn, Robert Capa, Louis Fischer, and Jay Allen. Nevertheless, there are very few references to Ricol's association with the SIM in the less rewarding duties of interrogating foreign prisoners suspected of being clandestine fifth column activists.

Paulina and Adelina Abramson's war memoirs, *Mosaico Roto* (1994), a priceless source of biographical data of Soviet field translators, provides inside information about professional practices on the battlefield that deviated from the official military narratives by advisers Meretskov (1968) and Malinovsky (1986). Paulina Abramson (1994, pp. 56–61), for instance, portrays Roman Karmen as an egocentric film director who ordered injured militiamen to clench their fists to improve the scene he was shooting and never included her name in the film credits among the members of the production crew. Adelina Abramson (1994, pp. 118–119), for her part, discloses a heated argument she had with a Soviet officer after having witnessed him abuse and torture a group of Italian prisoners during an interrogation session in which she had acted as his translator.

Adelina Abramson and Lydia Kúper enjoyed a long period of high-profile public appearances in the media during the 2000s, which made their work as military interpreters visible to Spanish-reading audiences on both sides of the Atlantic. The degree of publicity that Kúper's translation of Tolstoy's *War and Peace* (2003) received also unearthed her long career as a literary translator, which started in Madrid in the late 1950s when she joined the leading publisher Manuel Aguilar to aid in translating a number of works of classic Russian literature by such authors as Alexander Pushkin, Fyodor Dostoyevsky, Ivan Goncharov, Anton Makarenko, Osip Mandelstam, Boris Pasternak, and Vladimir Makanin. In the company of other returned exiles from the Soviet Union, which Rodríguez-Espinosa (2007, pp. 243–258) has dubbed 'the Group of Moscow', Kúper further challenged Francoist censorship through the translation of a wide range of banned Soviet authors, later printed by communist Latin American publishers Grijalbo (Mexico) and Ediciones Pueblos Unidos (Uruguay).

Adelina Abramson was named president of the association Archive, War and Exile (Archivo, Guerra y Exilio, AGE), created to gather and preserve historical documentation on the Soviet contingent in Spain, postwar diaspora and the International Brigades. Adelina Abramson, together with other civil rights activists, became particularly popular with the public in general through conferences, interviews, and documentaries. Their popularity only grew after Spain, ruled by the Socialist Party, passed the Law of Historical Memory in 2007, which marked the official recognition of the nation's need to confront its horrendously painful and violent past. Loyalty to 'the last great cause', which led Adelina Abramson and her colleagues to translate in the Spanish Civil War, never ended, it only grew with time.

Disclosure statement

No potential conflict of interest was reported by the author.

Funding

This article was supported by the Research Project 'La Traducción de Clásicos en su Marco Editorial: una Visión Transatlántica' [FFI2013-41743-P] (National Scientific Research, Development and Technological Innovation Plan), financed by the Ministry of Economy and Competitiveness of the Government of Spain [I+D+I 2013].

Notes

1. Soledad Sancha was another Spanish communist who worked at the Soviet embassy in Madrid as interpreter of Alexander Orlov, NKVD station chief.
2. This state-owned publishing conglomerate corporation would change its name to Foreign Language Publishing House in 1939 and to Progress Publishers in 1963.
3. *The Forging of a Rebel* would be translated into 10 different languages. Spanish filmmaker Mario Camus finally turned Barea's masterpiece into a successful six-episode television series in 1990.

References

Abramson, P., & Abramson, A. (1994). *Mosaico roto* [Broken Mosaic]. Madrid: Compañía Literaria.

Aizpuru, M. (2009). *El informe Brusiloff: la Guerra Civil de 1936 en el Frente Norte vista por un traductor ruso* [The Brusiloff report: The Civil War of 1936 in the northern front seen by a Russian translator]. Irún: Alberdania.

Alcofar Nassaes, J. L. (1971). *Los asesores soviéticos en la guerra civil española (Los Mejicanos)* [Soviet advisers in the Spanish Civil War (The Mexicans)]. Barcelona: Dopesa.

Baigorri-Jalón, J. (2012). La lengua como arma: intérpretes en la guerra civil española o la enmarañada madeja de la geografía y la historia [Languages as weapons: Interpreters in the Spanish Civil War or the entangled skein of geography and history]. In G. Payas & J. M. Zavala (Eds.), *La mediación lingüístico-cultural en tiempos de guerra: cruce de miradas desde España y América* [Linguistic and cultural mediation in times of war: Exchange of glances from Spain and America] (pp. 85–108). Temuco: Ediciones de la Universidad Católica de Temuco.

Baker, M. (2006). *Translation and conflict: A narrative account*. London: Routledge.

Barea, A. (2001). *The forging of a rebel*. (I. Barea, Trans.). London: Granta Books.

Beevor, A. (2006). *The battle for Spain: The Spanish Civil War 1936–1939*. London: Phoenix.

Castells Peig, A. (1974). *Las Brigadas Internacionales en la Guerra de España* [The international brigades in the war of Spain]. Barcelona: Ariel.

Cronin, M. (2002). The empire talks back, heteronomy, and the cutural turn in interpretation studies. In M. Tymoczko & E. Gentzler (Eds.), *Translation and power* (pp. 45–62). Amherst, MA: University of Massachusetts.

De la Fuente, I. (2006). *La roja y la falangista. Dos hermanas en la España del 36* [The red and the falangist. Two sisters in the Spain of 1936]. Barcelona: Planeta.

Dos Passos, J. (1929). *Manhattan Transfer*. (J. Robles, Trans.). Madrid: Cénit.

Eaude, M. (2009). *Triumph at midnight of the Century: A critical biography of Arturo Barea*. Eastbourne: Sussex Academic Press.

Falcón, I. (1996). *Asalto a los cielos. Mi vida junto a Pasionaria* [Assaulting the skies. My life with Pasionaria]. Madrid: Temas de Hoy.

Fox, S. (2007). *Constancia de la Mora in war and exile: International voice for the Spanish Republic*. Brighton: Sussex Academic Press.

Huber, P. (1998). Structure of the Moscow apparatus of the Comintern and decision-making. In T. Rees &. A. Thorpe (Eds.), *International communism and the communist international 1919–43* (pp. 41–64). Manchester: Manchester University Press.

Inghilleri, M. (2010). 'You don't make war without knowing why': The decisions to interpret in Iraq. In M. Inghilleri & S. A. Harding (Eds.), *Translation and violent conflict, The Translator*. Special Issue, *16*(2), 175–196. doi:10.1080/13556509.2010.10799468

Inghilleri, M., & Harding, S. A. (Eds.). (2010). *Translation and violent conflict. The Translator*. Special Issue, *16*(2).

Koltsov, M. E. (1978). *Diario de la Guerra Española* [Diary of the Spanish War]. (J. Fernández, Trans.). Madrid: Akal.

Kowalsky, D. (2004). *Stalin and the Spanish Civil War*. New York, NY: Columbia University Press. Retrieved from http://www.gutenberg-e.org/kod01/index.html

Lewis, S. (1930) *Babbit*. (J. Robles, Trans.). Madrid: Cénit.

London, L. (1995). *L'écheveau du temps. La mégère de la Rue Daguerre. Souvenirs de résistance* [The skein of time. The shrew of the Rue Daguerre. Memoirs of resistance]. Paris: Éditions du Seuil.

London, L. (1996). *L'écheveau cheveau du Temps. Le printemps des camarades* [The skein of time. The spring of comrades]. Paris: Éditions du Seuil.
Maier, C. (2007). The translator as an intervenient being. In J. Munday (Ed.), *Translation as intervention* (pp. 1–27). London: Continuum.
Mairs, R. (2011). Translator, traditor: The interpreter as traitor in classical tradition. *Greece and Rome, 58*(1), 64–81. doi:10.1017/ S0017383510000537
Malinovsky, R. (1986). El gran entusiasmo revolucionario español [The great Spanish revolutionary enthusiasm]. In *Junto a los patriotas españoles en la guerra contra el fascismo. Memorias de los soviéticos participantes en la Guerra Civil de España* [With the Spanish patriots in the war against fascism. Memoirs of the Soviets who fought in the Spanish Civil War] (pp. 56–61). Moscow: Nóvosti.
Martínez de Pisón, I. (2005). *Enterrar a los muertos* [To bury the dead]. Barcelona: Seix Barral.
Martínez de Pisón, I. (2007). *Las palabras justas* [The precise words]. Zaragoza: Xordica.
Meretskov, K. A. (1968). *На службе народу* [In the service of the people]. Moscow: Политиздат. Retrieved from http://militera.lib.ru/memo/russian/meretskov/11.html
Miralles, R. (2009). Los soviéticos en España, 1936–1939 [The Soviets in Spain, 1936–1939]. In *Los rusos en la Guerra de España, 1936–1939 [The Russians in the War of Spain, 1936–1939]* (pp. 19–47). Madrid: Fundación Pablo Iglesias.
Mora, C. (1939). *In place of splendour: The autobiography of a Spanish woman*. New York, NY: Harcourt, Brace.
Palmer (2007). Interpreting and translations for western media in Iraq. In M. Salama-Carr (Ed.), *Translating and interpreting conflict* (pp. 13–28). Amsterdam: Rodopi.
Preston, P. (1986). *The Spanish Civil War 1936–39*. London: Weidenfeld and Nicolson.
Preston, P. (2009). *We saw Spain die. Foreign correspondents in the Spanish Civil War*. London: Constable & Robinson.
Rees, T. (1998). The highpoint of Comintern influence? The communist party and the civil war in Spain. In T. Rees & A. Thorpe (Eds.), *International communism and the communist international 1919–43* (pp. 143–167). Manchester: Manchester University Press.
Rodríguez-Espinosa, M. (2007). Acerca de los traductores del exilio español en la URSS: El grupo de Moscú y la difusión de la literatura rusa en España en la segunda mitad del siglo XX [Translators in the Spanish exile in the USSR: The group of Moscow and the dissemination of Russian literature in Spain during the second half of the twentieth century]. In J. J. Zaro & F. Ruiz Noguera (Eds.), *Retraducir. Una nueva mirada: La retraducción de textos literarios y audiovisuales* [Retranslation: A fresh look. The retranslation of literary and audiovisual texts] (pp. 243–258). Málaga: Miguel Gómez Ediciones.
Salama-Carr, M. (Ed.). (2007). *Translating and interpreting conflict*. Amsterdam: Rodopi.
Service, R. (2012). *Spies & commissars. Bolshevik Russia and the West*. Basingstoke: Pan MacMillan.
Thomas, H. (2003). *The Spanish Civil War* (4th ed.). London: Penguin Books.
Tolstoy, L. (2003) *Guerra y Paz [War and Peace]*. (L. Kúper, Trans.). Madrid: Taller de Mario Muchnik.
Vaill, A. (2014). *Hotel Florida: Truth, love, and death in the Spanish Civil War*. New York: Farrar, Straus and Giroux.
Volodarsky, B. (2013). *El caso Orlov. Los servicios secretos soviéticos en la guerra civil española* [The Orlov case. Soviet secret services during the Spanish Civil War]. (A. Guelbenzu, Trans.). Barcelona: Crítica.
Weintraub, S. (1968). *The last great cause. The intellectuals and the Spanish Civil War*. New York: Weybright and Talley.

The censorship of theatre translations under Franco: the 1960s

Raquel Merino-Álvarez ⓘ

Over the last decade, Spain's censorship records have been used by translation studies scholars as the main source to reconstruct the history of translated culture. Censorship archives are virtually the only source of information to research the history of theatre translations in Spain, since they provide access to materials that range from contextual information to actual manuscripts (from draft versions to final censored texts). This contribution will provide a glimpse into the history of theatre translations in the 1960s, a period of political openness from within the Ministry in charge of theatre censorship and of intense activity on Spanish stages. Using textual and contextual evidence gathered from Spanish censorship archives, the actual process that led to the 1966 stage production of Albee's *Who's afraid of Virginia Woolf?* will help illustrate how play scripts were evaluated when submitted to the censors' ideologically-biased scrutiny and to what extent ideological manipulation was forced into the production script. Such evidence shows that foreign plays were integrated in to Spanish theatre through translation and adaptation. It also reveals the role of censors, stage directors and professional translators in the censorship process that can be traced from the actual records.

Introduction

The Spanish censorship archives held in the General Administration Archive (Archivo General de la Administración [AGA], Alcalá de Henares, Madrid) are a rich source of documentation on virtually any aspect of Spanish history from the end of the Civil War (1939) until the decade after the death of Franco (1975–1985). From a cultural point of view, they provide information on publications and theatre or film productions. The enormous amount of data filed by a well-established bureaucratic tradition has helped researchers obtain greater knowledge of Spanish culture through the traces left in the censor's sieve. Censorship was obligatory and universal, and cultural products subject to the censors' scrutiny left an abundant register of information from over 40 years.

Researchers working on the history of Spanish theatre (London, 1997, 2012; Muñoz Cáliz, 2005, 2008; O'Leary, 2005) have been using the AGA archives to obtain information on Spanish playwrights and plays, making it possible to access richer textual as well as contextual information from this source. Access to censorship documents opens up new ways of dealing with old issues. With respect to translations, the records are at times the only source of reliable information, since historical accounts of theatre in Spanish (staged or published), focused as they are on the 'Spanish', have traditionally ignored the 'foreign' (translated into Spanish) and so an important part of Spanish theatre has habitually been overlooked.

The study of censored translations inevitably leads to a consideration of who the authors of the versions were and what role they played in importing foreign theatre to Spanish stages. From the evidence in the censorship archives, one is faced with a truly hidden story, and a new perspective of the history of Spanish theatre comes to light by focusing on names of Spanish playwrights, stage directors, producers, actors and translators.

Historical accounts of Spanish theatre dwell on authors, directors and actors, producers and theatre groups and venues, with little or no reference to foreign theatre or the work of translators who made productions of foreign plays possible. Even in the more recent and thorough volume edited by Delgado and Gies (2012) the role played by translations and translators is overlooked.

In this contribution we aim at filling that gap by focusing on foreign theatre translated and performed in the 1960s, presenting the polemical case of E. Albee's *Who's afraid of Virginia Woolf?(¿Quién teme a Virginia Woolf?)* (1962) translated by Méndez Herrera, a professional translator whose versions of foreign plays were usually at the center of controversy.

The censorship of theatre translations under Franco

Censorship was obligatory and universal under Franco's rule: it was applied to all types of cultural production, from printed books and periodicals to stage productions and films. In the case of theatre there was a specific Directorate within the Ministry for Information and Tourism in charge of assessing plays and films (*Dirección General de Cinematografía y Teatro*) (Gutiérrez Lanza, 2011) and the documents derived from the censorship process are now available at the AGA.

The TRACE (TRAnslations CEnsored, www.ehu.es/trace) project was designed to look specifically at translation in the censorship process (Rabadán, 2000). Researchers who had been investigating the history of (film, prose, poetry, theatre) translations in Spain using traditional sources of information found in the Spanish censorship archives a means of extending their knowledge of Spanish 'translated culture' (Santoyo, 1983). More importantly, the archives offered the chance to shed light on obscure and totally unknown areas of that Spanish translated culture. The lists of authors, national and foreign alike, and titles of plays, original and translated, which were duly filed when submitted to the censor by producers, editors or exhibitors, have become a sort of archaeological site that may be excavated and studied. The sheer number of records and files makes sampling the archives a hard task but the results of preliminary studies helped establish, in a fairly accurate manner, which authors or plays were imported through translation at the time. The history of theatre translations in Spain, as seen from censorship archives, has been charted by building catalogues of translations and analyzing the information in order to select target corpora (Gutiérrez Lanza, 2011; Merino-Álvarez, 2007).

Following a series of TRACE theatre studies (Bandín, 2007, 2011; Merino-Álvarez, 2007; Pérez López de Heredia, 2004, 2005), specific corpora have been identified and studied using selection criteria derived from the analysis of catalogues of translations compiled from censorship archives. Quantitative methods have been combined with qualitative studies 'on selected sets of cases' derived from the analysis of the information held in the catalogues (Merino-Álvarez, 2012, p. 126). At first the focus was on the most representative authors for a specific source country (US, Britain and Ireland), language (English) or period; but subsequently also on the topics deemed 'dangerous' by censors. For example, the polemical issue of adultery has been studied through the compilation and analysis of a corpus of translations and adaptations of Graham Greene's *The Complaisant Lover* (Merino-Álvarez 2012, pp. 133–134). The play's stance on sexual morality challenged the 'open' censorship policy[1] of the 1960s: a six-year long censorship process, fraught with difficulties, resulted in a successful 1968 premiere which proved that Greene's theatrical trajectory in Spain was not 'effete' (London, 1997, p. 63).

A study on how the topic of homosexuality entered Spanish stages through translations has traced the issue back to 1950, when Tennessee Williams' *Streetcar named Desire* was first filed as a censorship record. William's play, translated into Spanish by José Méndez Herrera, seems to be the first of a trend of translations of plays by foreign playwrights (E. Albee, M. Anderson, M. Crowley and P. Shaffer) that helped introduce topics barred for native playwrights (Merino-Álvarez, 2010, p. 154).

The findings of research done on censorship archives show that even under the so-called official open policy of the 1960s, elaborate negotiations between censors and producers or directors were needed, especially over sensitive topics. Moral sexuality or the equally pernicious issue of foul language was very often at the center of such negotiations. The case of Edward Albee's *Who's afraid of Virginia Woolf?*, translated by José Méndez Herrera, is paradigmatic in this respect.

The role of professional translators in Spanish theatre censorship

In the world of theatre, translation is usually an invisible process that is taken for granted or overlooked. When asked about this aspect of their activity, writers, directors or actors, even those who put their name to adaptations, seem to consider the process of translation as the first necessary step, albeit not as important as the actual writing or rewriting and adaptation (Merino-Álvarez, 1994). Translation, as the process of rendering a text from one language to another, when mentioned, if at all, seems to define the first draft ('literal translation') that would lead to a fully-fledged final version. What is more, the foreign text rendered into Spanish – labeled 'translation', 'version' or 'adaptation' – was not necessarily presented for censorship or even published under the name of the person who undertook the transfer from one language to another.

Professional translators like Méndez Herrera usually lacked the means, the power, or even the will to exercise their rights, and were forgotten once the translation commission was over. The fact is that most of the actual names of the professionals who rendered foreign plays into the target language are usually unknown to us today and the few that may be identified with the actual process of translation can only be traced using sources such as censorship archives since 'translator' and 'adaptor' were required fields on application forms. When compiling catalogues of translations from archives such as the AGA, 'translator' or 'adaptor' (or assumed translator or adaptor) then stands for the name identified along with that of the original writer as author of the Spanish version, and as such is filed in censorship reports and manuscripts,[2] or in published versions of translated plays.

In the role of 'assumed translators' we find actors, directors, playwrights and professional translators. Any of them taken individually or as a group could be the subject of a study on the history of theatre translations in Spain. However, in addition to the directing or acting for which they were better known, their roles as translator-adaptors when considered in the light of their 'original' text production may contribute to a deeper knowledge of the history of Spanish theatre (original and translated) in general (Merino-Álvarez, 2012, pp. 135–136).

Méndez Herrera's translations

Méndez Herrera was a professional translator who produced versions of plays by Shakespeare (for which he was awarded the Spanish National Prize for Translation in 1962) and works by various playwrights (Albee, Miller, Williams). His name can be traced in the censorship files from the early 1940s until the end of the 1970s and the study of his career as a theatre translator could illustrate the whole period of the Franco dictatorship and would no doubt merit an entire book.

Very much in tune with the invisible nature of the translation process, Méndez Herrera's work as a translator has not been studied, and virtually no reference to him can be found other than for his role as translator of authors like Dickens, Shakespeare, Stevenson or Priestley. Only recently has his name been quoted in newspaper articles in relation to his son, Alberto Méndez, author of *Los girasoles ciegos,* a successful novel adapted for the screen. We know from these brief references that he worked for the FAO (UN Food and Agricultural Organization), and led an exile's life in Rome (Valls, 2005) working as a translator for various Spanish publishing houses.

Méndez Herrera's career as theatre translator was long and fruitful, starting before the Civil War and continuing afterwards from his Roman exile. His command of foreign languages led him to make a living out of translation and to have close links with Spanish culture. He was well respected as a professional translator and this unusual position in Spanish theatre culture meant that his name was systematically acknowledged in reports, manuscripts and published translations. As a theatre translator his name can be found in 18 entries in the AGA theatre database from 1941 until 1977, and over 20 translations by Méndez Herrera have been recorded in TRACE-theatre catalogues, compiled from direct consultation of censorship documents, of both published plays and scripts for theatrical productions (see Appendix).

During the censorship under the Franco regime, Méndez Herrera translated many controversial plays. His version of *A Streetcar named Desire* was first banned in 1950 but the successive rewritings submitted to the censor (the first approval was granted in 1951) were instrumental in introducing Williams' plays and contentious topics, particularly homosexuality, to Spanish stages (Pérez López de Heredia, 2004, pp. 162–169). In the 1960s Méndez Herrera's translations of Shaw's *Pygmalion* and Miller's *After the Fall* and *The Price* reached Spanish stages, as did his translations of plays by Fabbri and Pirandello and other commercial hits.[3]

Who's afraid of Virginia Woolf?

Although the entire corpus of Méndez Herrera's translations would merit a detailed study, we will focus on his translation of Edward Albee's play. The actual title, *Who's afraid of Virginia Woolf? (¿Quién teme a Virginia Woolf?),* is not recorded in the AGA theatre database, and could only be identified and documented through direct sampling in the censorship archives. This polemical play reached the stage (16 February 1966, Teatro Goya, Madrid) after a complex process of censorship in the heyday of the 1960s Spanish 'apertura' or policy of openness (Muñoz Cáliz, 2006).

The first petition for a stage production of Albee's *Who's afraid of Virginia Woolf?* (censorship AGA number 215/65) was signed by José Osuna (8 November 1965), director of the production scheduled for the Teatro Marquina. The name of the translator is specified along with the representative of the author in Spain, Andrés Kramer. The play was evaluated by the usual selection of three censors, in this case Fr. Artola, Mr. Baquero and Mr. Mostaza. They all deemed that the play could be authorized and classified 2, for audiences over 18, but a series of cuts were proposed, mostly isolated words and expressions considered to contain excessively strong language.[4]

The religious censor, Fr. Artola, proposed around 26 cuts in over 20 pages of the manuscript on expressions deemed 'indecent', 'extreme' and 'harsh', such as 'mierda' (shit, 'screw you' in the original), 'testículo derecho' (right testicle, 'right ball' in the original) or 'montar a la anfitriona' (mount the hostess).

One of the censors, Mr. Mostaza, clearly states in his report that the script could easily be approved for Teatros de Cámara y Ensayo (Club Theatres) with no modifications, but that a commercial stage would require the text to be trimmed (he actually suggests 13 deletions of words and short expressions in the manuscript). Approval for Club Theatres usually implied no cuts, since the restriction of smaller audiences and one-night productions was deemed enough. Monléon (1971, p. 70) points out that club theatre performances were the back door that enabled the introduction of new topics to Spanish commercial stages and favored the creation of a 'leftish theatre'.

Censor (and theatre critic) Mr. Baquero did not propose specific cuts, but rather referred to 'limitations', being inclined to find a way to authorize the play with restrictions. The nature of these limitations could be geographical (approval for Madrid only), or a matter of age (over 18). Adaptations and modifications to tone down the language of the play and make it 'less crude' were recommended. Another measure proposed to accommodate the text was the addition of a note about the 'corrosive tone' of the original play in the theatre program for the production. Success abroad and the prize awarded to the American production in the 1962–1963 season were used as counter-arguments that would favor authorization. Baquero backs up his report quoting the official theatre censorship norms (published in the Official Gazette-BOE, 1964) that could be used to strike a balance in the final decision. He claims that while norms eight and 18 recommend banning plays that justify divorce, adultery, unlawful sexual relations or prostitution, or present a 'lascivious climate', norm six might be quoted to justify 'degradation' on stage, and even risk the spectators' adverse reaction to evil behavior if a proper moral conclusion is reached (Informe, 1964, p. 18).

The case for authorizing Albee's play required additional reports from the rest of the members of the theatre censorship Board, who were summoned to a general meeting or *Pleno*. Among the seven reports issued is Father Fierro's, which defined the play as 'harsh, disagreeable, but not immoral'. Another censor, Mr. de la Torre, representative of the Spanish Society of Authors (SGAE), saw no serious objections, but pointed out a few words that could be modified while praising the overall quality of the play and the 'exemplary' ending. In his report, he mentions polemical plays that had previously been approved (Miller's *A View from the Bridge,* or Williams' *A Streetcar named Desire*) adding that the language in those was no less dangerous or daring. Mr. Barceló, theatre critic in the Catholic newspaper *El Alcázar*, thought that adapting the language would not temper the atmosphere of the play. He seemed to be concerned about the 'receptivity of our audiences', and for him it was a question of either 'full approval' or an 'outright ban'. The reports were discussed in the plenary meeting of the theatre censorship Board (16 November 1965) and the play was classified 'authorized for over 18' with cuts and adaptations. The quality of the text and the fact that it had reached the main international stages were taken as strong arguments in favor. The cuts agreed by the Board were a small selection of those proposed individually by censors.[5]

Along with censors' reports and the minutes of the Board's meeting, we find other documents filed in censorship record 215/65 once rehearsals were under way. A letter sent by director José Osuna (registered 1 February 1966) states that 'the suggested changes' had been followed in the rehearsals and that 'all expressions that could have harmed the feelings of the average spectator' (violar/rape, testículo/testicle, hijo de puta/son of a bitch, escroto/scrotum) had been replaced by equivalent words with 'the same intention but weaker effect'. He says that words and expressions which are not 'intrinsically bad, just bad taste' (mierda/shit or vete a hacer puñetas/go to hell) were being retained in the stage production rehearsals, since they were the linguistic means of establishing the psychology of the characters. On the stage, the director argues, they are matter-of-fact, habitual ways for the characters to express themselves. The Board did not approve these changes and ratified the original restrictions.[6] Osuna sent a second lengthy letter, addressed to the Director General, in an attempt to have the banned expressions restored, but this petition was also rejected. The Director General mentions the letter in his *Memoirs* (a day to day account of his activity as Head of the Theatre and Film Censorship Directorate): 'Osuna requests permission for a few more "shits" to adorn Albee's *Who's afraid of Virginia Woolf?*' (García Escudero, 1978, p. 194, our translation). García Escudero compares Albee's play to the polemical *The purple dress of Valentine* by F. Sagan: 'It is surprising that our society – and not just the pious sector – still has that puritan attitude, they find scandal in what is said and not in what is done. Of course *Virginia Woolf* is moral but *Valentine* is not' (1978, p. 199, our translation). Appearances, double morality and references to strong language or value judgments on plays (immoral vs. strong) are frequent topics in García Escudero's *Memoirs* (1978).

Director José Osuna was officially informed (8 February 1966) that his second petition was not accepted and the restrictions of the authorization were maintained. The first *Guía de Censura* (blue cardboard certificate used as proof of authorization for production), specifying the modifications agreed by the Board was issued on 12 February 1966.[7] The dress rehearsal was reviewed by the censorship inspectors, who filed positive reports ('no incidents', 14 February 1966). The play's premiere took place on 16 February 1966 at Teatro Goya, Madrid, where it became a box-office success.[8]

The premiere (Llovet, 1966) brought about strong reactions in the press, most notably the editorial published in the Catholic newspaper *El Diario Regional* entitled 'inexplicable show', which triggered the reaction of the Director General García Escudero who wrote a letter to be published in the newspaper and dated 21 March 1966, addressed to the director of *El Diario Regional* (Pérez López, 1992, p. 848) and filed in the record along with a copy of the note sent to the representative of the *Ministry for Information and Tourism* in Valladolid, asking him to make sure the matter was managed with diligence. The letter is a detailed account of the reaction to the premiere of *Who's afraid of Virginia Woolf?*, with quotes from press reviews by the leading Madrid theatre critics. García-Escudero argues that the editorial in *El Diario Regional* is biased, since only negative reactions are quoted. He cites whole sentences from the reviews, aiming to show that the overall impression of theatre critics was balanced. He goes further and informs the reader that the play was passed with the votes of the majority of the censorship Board.

This was not the first time the Director General had to explain the decisions of the censorship Board. In 1964 he wrote a 50-page report (Informe, 1964) in answer to a series of ecclesiastical documents that harshly attacked the *apertura* or open policy of the Ministry for Information and Tourism team, working under Fraga as Minister (1962–1969) and García Escudero as Director General for Film and Theatre (1962–1967).

Both his *Memoirs* (1978) and the unpublished Report (Informe, 1964*)* are sources that add a new dimension to the information filed in the AGA archives in relation to Theatre Censorship in the 1960s. García Escudero is conscious of his role as censor, but he is also aware of his difficult position as 'censored censor'. When writing about the frictions between ministerial authorities and prominent playwrights like Buero Vallejo, who often criticized the limitations imposed by censorship, Garcia Escudero reflects:

> I could have told him [Buero Vallejo][9] the story of the censored censor and that of the three types of censorship: the one he speaks about and which I represent; another, the social censorship which I suffer; and a third type, which nobody speaks about: that of the businessmen and the industry, the worst type, and he and I have to face it equally (1978, p. 223).

The negotiations on cuts and modifications that led to the Spanish stage production of Albee's play had their counterparts elsewhere. In the 1962 Broadway premiere, the play's running time was reduced by 15 minutes (Bottoms, 2000, p. 34). Other productions across the US accommodated modifications suggested by the local authorities. The London 1963 production had to face the warnings and more than 60 cuts proposed by the Lord Chamberlain's office (Bottoms, 2000, pp. 44–45). But it was the US film adaptation that brought about the strongest clamor against the Production Code of the Motion Picture Association of America. Written and run by Catholics, the Code had been instrumental in eliminating homosexuality from the film version of *Cat on a hot tin roof*, but allowed the film adaptation of Albee's drama. The United States regulatory committee did not manage to censor its 'gritty language' which 'brazenly violated the rigid guidelines that had dictated the content of American movies since 1934' (Lord, 2011). When the National Catholic Office for Motion Pictures saw the play's 'redeeming value' the film was classified and exhibited for adults over 18 (Bottoms, 2000; Leff, 1981; Quicke 2010) in 1966.

The American censors' battle and the arguments used to propose cuts in the film version of Albee's play were in essence no different from those of their Spanish or British counterparts,[10] and foul language was once more gauged against the play's redeeming ending. Against all odds and all censoring bodies, whether American or Spanish, Albee's play was a world success in the 1960s which helped overcome restrictive barriers (Lavery & McGuire Roche, 2013; Semonche, 2007), because the times seemed to be changing on both sides of the Atlantic.

Conclusion

Albeit working under a totalitarian regime, Spanish theatre censorship was, in the way it functioned and under the strong influence of religious morality, as restrictive in sensitive cases as its counterparts in countries that enjoyed elected governments and a long democratic tradition. Censoring bodies in the 1960s were strongly influenced by religious organizations, and sexual morality was often at stake when playwrights and filmmakers tried to oppose established norms. The censorship case of *Who's afraid of Virginia Woolf?* helped change attitudes: it did introduce foul language and a shocking view of marital relations on the stage (with cuts in Spain and the UK), and adapted to the big screen, it opened the way for a new classification system based on age restrictions in the US. The very fact that the play was at the center of public controversies gained its author worldwide fame, and the directors and producers in various countries benefited from the publicity as well.

The success of *Who's afraid of Virginia Woolf?*, boosted by the echoes of the censoring process, made Albee an extremely popular author in Spain. The 1966 production of his play was a clear sign of change; confirming that a relaxation within the governmental structure in charge of censorship was at work. Caught in a flux of resistance and reaction, García Escudero and his team managed to restructure the Board for film and theatre censorship and to publish the norms and select censors who were more professional and less political. Constant attacks came from left and right, but the basis for a transition to a renewed governmental structure was laid down. The old moral code that reactionary forces still tried to maintain was overcome by the reality of everyday life in the 1960s. Spanish theatre producers imported foreign plays through translation to spearhead change on stage, knowing that censorship was more lenient on the 'foreign', but once landmark productions like *Who's afraid of Virginia Woolf?* broke the ice, native products could follow suit.

Disclosure statement

No potential conflict of interest was reported by the author.

Notes

1. Between 1962 and 1969 decisions taken by the new team at the Directorate General for Cinema and Theatre (Ministry for Information and Tourism) under Minister Fraga Iribarne were 'more permissive and tolerant than under his predecessors' (Gutiérrez-Lanza, 2011, p. 305). Muñoz-Cáliz (2005) refers to the 1960s policy of 'opening up' from within the Ministry that contrasted with previous stricter positions under minister Arias Salgado (1950–1962) and the subsequent return to ultra-Catholic positions with Sánchez Bella (1969–1973).
2. It is not unusual to find in a given censorship record different names filed under 'translator' for the same 'translation'. For example, the Spanish text of Albee's *The Zoo Story* was first filed as translated by García-Rey but all the subsequent manuscripts filed in the AGA and even the 1991 publication of the play were under the name of William Layton (Merino-Álvarez, 2005). Other cases gave rise to confrontation between the actual translator and the person named as author of the 'version' for the stage. *Canta gallo acorralado* (*Cock-a-Doodle Dandy*) by O'Casey was filed by the censorship office as a version by playwright Antonio Gala. The translator, Ana Antón-Pacheco, complained to the authorities and the theatre company about the use of her text without prior permission.
3. The Spanish translation of Lawrence Roman's *Under the Yum Yum tree* was first filed as record number 267–61, and attributed to Méndez Herrera. In later exchanges of documents with censorship authorities it was presented as 'adapted' by actress Catalina Montes, who along with Roman's representative in Spain, Andrés Kramer, fought a long and bitter censorship case in which the name of the translator, a much less powerful figure in the theatre system, was no longer mentioned. The main issue at stake was pre-marital relations and the play was considered 'too strong'. After several attempts to have the script approved and

endless negotiations with the censors (many a letter started 'with every wish to cooperate with the censor'), the final authorization was granted with restrictions (audiences over 18 with cuts, 25 April 1962).
4. Quotes in this section, either censors' comments or expressions from the manuscript have been taken from AGA record 215/65, which consists of 60 pages of brief non-paginated documents. All quotations from the records consulted are in our translation.
5. The certificate granting permission for the stage production of *Who's afraid of Virginia Woolf?* (*¿Quién teme a Virginia Woolf?*) states the following cuts and modifications. Cuts (act I, pages 1, 7, 8, 46, 47, 55, 61; act II pages 30, 43, 49 and 50): me cago en, mierda, acostarse, mala leche, saliva, escroto, te violaré, hacer puñetas, hacérselo encima, hija de su madre, testículo derecho, marica, el trasero, recuperé mi virginidad, hijo de puta, montar a la anfitriona. Adaptations (act I, pages 7, 8, 11, 14, 32, 38, 54, 59 and 61; act II pages 3, 16, 25, 44 and 50): mala leche > mala uva, vete a la mierda > vete a tomar viento fresco, vete a hacer puñetas > vete a hacer gárgaras, su testículo derecho > su riñón derecho. The manuscript, marked with these cuts and modifications, was used by the censors in charge of reviewing dress rehearsals, and is most probably the text found in the AGA record consulted for this contribution.
6. The manuscript, filed in the record, shows that the banned expressions and modifications Osuna was trying to restore were retained. Among others we find: 'vete a hacer puñetas' (go to hell), crossed out and substituted by the lighter 'vete a hacer gárgaras' (go jump in the lake); 'testículo derecho' (right testicle) changed to 'riñón derecho' (right kidney); or 'hijo de puta' substituted by 'hijo de Satanás' (Satan's son).
7. The second *Guía* was filed on 13 January 1968, and two performances by Carátula Theatre Group (Canary Islands) were permitted.
8. A petition to have the play on a tour of the provinces was sent on 26 July 1966 and a limited route was approved with the same restrictions (audiences over 18 with cuts). The play was approved for the following towns: Valladolid (3 days), León (2 days), Palencia (1 day), Burgos (1 day), Logroño (2 days), La Coruña (4 days), Oviedo (2 days), Gijón (3 days), Santander (4 days) and Salamanca (2 days). Usually the criteria for allowing a play in one town rather than in another, as well as the number of performances or days was justified with arguments to do with the 'maturity' or 'experience' of theatregoers in those towns.
9. Arcadio Baquero, theatre-critic and member of the *Board* from 1963 to 1967, in an interview published shortly before he died, said:

> when I was asked to become a member of the Censorship Board, before giving an answer I asked my good friends in the theatre profession and they all advised me to accept. They said that censorship could help them enormously. I do think that was the case (Muñoz Cáliz, 2004, p. 19, our translation).
> Among these friends was Buero Vallejo, who had turned down proposals to become a member of the Board since he thought any official relation with the authorities could undermine his position as a critical playwright. When asked about the 1960s open policy, Baquero states that García Escudero's period was indeed open, adding that among the members of the Board were many liberals and well-known theatre professionals (Muñoz Cáliz, 2004, p. 19, our translation).

10. Expressions like 'goddam', 'screw you', 'bugger', 'plowing pertinent wives', 'hump the hostess' or 'mount her like a goddam dog' that offended censors' ears in America were basically the same that had been marked by Spanish and British censors for deletion or modification.

ORCID

Raquel Merino-Álvarez ⓘ http://orcid.org/0000-0002-3772-0461

Funding acknowledgements

This work was supported by the University of the Basque Country, UPV/EHU, the Consolidated Research Group TRALIMA [grant number GIC12/197], the Basque Government [grant number IT728/13]; and the Spanish Ministry for Economy and Competitiveness, MINECO [grant number FFI2012-39012-C04-01T].

References

Bandín Fuertes, E. (2007). *Traducción, recepción y censura de teatro clásico inglés en la España de Franco. Estudio descriptivo-comparativo del Corpus TRACEtci (1939–1985)* [Translation, reception and censorship of English classical theatre in Franco's Spain. A descriptive-comparative study of TRACEtci (1939–1985) corpus] (Unpublished doctoral dissertation). University of León, León.

Bandín Fuertes, E. (2011). *Las páginas olvidadas del teatro español: traducciones y adaptaciones del teatro clásico inglés durante el franquismo* [The forgotten pages in Spanish theatre: Translations and adaptations of classical English theatre under Franco's rule]. *Represura. Revista de Historia Contemporánea española en torno a la represión y la censura aplicadas al libro 7*. Retrieved from http://www.represura.es/

Bottoms, S. J. (2000). *Albee: Who's afraid of Virginia Woolf?* Cambridge: Cambridge University Press.

Delgado, M., & Gies, D. T. (Eds.). (2012). *A history of theatre in Spain*. Cambridge: Cambridge University Press.

García Escudero, J. M. (1978). *La primera apertura. Diario de un director general. La larga batalla de la censura en cine y teatro* [The first opening. Memoirs of a director general. The long battle for cinema and theatre censorship]. Barcelona: Planeta.

Gutiérrez Lanza, C. (2011). Censors and censorship boards in Franco's Spain (1950s–1960s): An overview based on the TRACE cinema catalogue. In D. Asimakoulas & M. Rogers (Eds.), *Translation and opposition* (pp. 305–320). Bristol: Multilingual Matters.

Informe sobre la Censura Cinematografica y Teatral [Report on cinema and theatre censorship]. (1964). *Ministerio de Información y Turismo. Dirección General de Cinematografía y Teatro* [Ministry for information and tourism. General directorate for cinema and theatre]. Unpublished manuscript.

Lavery, D., & McGuire Roche, N. (2013). Hollywood's *Who's afraid of Virginia Woolf?*: Breaking the code. In W. R. Bray & R. Barton Palmer (Eds.), *Modern American Drama on Screen* (pp. 187–202). Cambridge: Cambridge University Press.

Leff, L. J. (1981). Play into film: Warner brothers' *Who's afraid of Virginia Woolf? Theatre Journal*, 33, 453–466. doi:10.2307/3206770

Llovet, E. (1966, February 17). Estreno de ¿Quién teme a Virginia Woolf? en el Goya [Premiere at Goya of Who's afraid of Virginia Woolf?]. *ABC*, p. 93. Retrieved from http://hemeroteca.abc.es.

London, J. (1997). *Reception and renewal in modern Spanish theatre: 1939–1963*. Leeds: W. S. Maney & Son Ltd, Modern Humanities Research Association.

London, J. (2012). Theatre under Franco (1939–1975): Censorship, playwriting and performance. In M. Delgado & D. T. Gies (Eds.), *A history of theatre in Spain* (pp. 341–371). Cambridge: Cambridge University Press.

Lord, M. G. (2011, March 30). How Elizabeth Taylor's 'sexual intensity' helped tear down the production code. *The Hollywood Reporter*. Retrieved from http://www.hollywoodreporter.com/

Merino-Álvarez, R. (1994). *Traducción, tradición y manipulación. Teatro inglés en España 1950–90* [Translation, tradition and manipulation. English theatre in Spain 1950–90]. León: University of León / University of the Basque Country.

Merino-Álvarez, R. (2005). La investigación sobre teatro inglés traducido inglés-español, 1994–2004 [Research on theatre translation English-Spanish]. *Cadernos de Literatura Comparada*, 12/13, 99–119.
Merino-Álvarez, R. (2007). La homosexualidad censurada: estudio sobre corpus de teatro TRACEti (desde 1960) [Censored homosexuality: Studies on TRACEti corpus since 1960]. In R. Merino-Álvarez (Ed.), *Traducción y censura en España (1939–1985). Estudios sobre corpus TRACE: cine, narrativa, teatro* [Translation and censorship in Spain (1939–1985). Studies on TRACE corpus: cinema, narrative, theatre] (pp. 243–286). Bilbao: Universidad del País Vasco/Universidad de León. Retrieved from http://hdl.handle.net/10810/10169.
Merino-Álvarez, R. (2010). Building TRACE (translations censored) theatre corpus: Some methodological questions on text selection. In M. Muñoz & C. Buesa (Eds.), *Translation and cultural identity: Selected essays on translation and cross-cultural communication* (pp. 116–138). Newcastle: Cambridge Scholars.
Merino-Álvarez, R. (2012). A historical approach to Spanish theatre translations from censorship archives. In I. García-Izquierdo & E. Monzó (Eds.), *Iberian studies on translation and interpreting* (pp. 123–140). Oxford: Peter Lang.
Monleón, J. (1971). *Treinta años de teatro de la derecha* [Thirty years of right-wing theatre]. Barcelona: Tusquets.
Muñoz Cáliz, B. (2004). Entrevista a Arcadio Baquero Goyanes, Miembro de la Junta de Censura Teatral entre 1963 y 1967 [Interview. Arcadio Baquero Goyanes, member of the Theatre Censorship Board between 1963 and 1967]. *Las puertas del drama. Revista de la Asociación de Autores de Teatro, AAT, Libertad de Expresión I*, 18, 17–21.
Muñoz Cáliz, B. (2005). *El teatro crítico español durante el franquismo visto por sus censores* [Spanish critical theatre under Franco as seen by censors]. Madrid: Fundación Universitaria Española.
Muñoz Cáliz, B. (2006). *Expedientes de la censura teatral franquista* [Records of Francoist theatre censorship]. Madrid: Fundación Universitaria Española.
Muñoz Cáliz, B. (2008). Los expedientes de la censura teatral como fuente para la investigación del teatro español contemporáneo. [Theatre censorship records as a source for investigations into Spanish contemporary theatre]. *Teatro (Revista de Estudios Escénicos)*, 22, 27–40.
O'Leary, C. (2005). *The theatre of Antonio Buero Vallejo: Ideology, politics and censorship*. Woodbridge: Tamesis.
Pérez López, P. (1992). *Católicos, políticos e información: Diario Regional de Valladolid, 1931–1980*. [Catholics, politicians and information: Diario Regional de Valladolid, 1931–1980]. Valladolid: Universidad de Valladolid.
Pérez López de Heredia, M. (2004). *Traducciones censuradas de teatro norteamericano en la España de Franco (1939–1963)* [Censored translations of US theatre in Franco's Spain (1939–1963)]. Bilbao: University of the Basque Country.
Pérez López de Heredia, M. (2005). Inventario de las traducciones censuradas de teatro norteamericano en la España de Franco (1939–1963) [Catalogue of censored US theatre translations in Franco's Spain (1939–1963)]. In R. Merino-Álvarez, J. M. Santamaría, & E. Pajares (Eds.), *Trasvases culturales: literatura, cine y traducción, 4* Cultural transfers: literature, cinema and translation, 4] (pp. 97–112). Bilbao: University of the Basque Country. http://hdl.handle.net/10810/10537
Quicke, A. (2010). The era of censorship (1930–1967). In J. Lyden (Ed.), *The Routledge companion to religion and film* (pp. 32–51). Abingdon: Routledge.
Rabadán, R. (Ed.). (2000). *Traducción y censura inglés-español, 1939–1985. Estudio Preliminar* [Translation and censorship English-Spanish, 1939–1985, preliminary study]. León: University of León.
Santoyo, J. C. (1983). *La cultura traducida. Lección inaugural del curso 1983–84* [Translated culture. Inaugural lecture, academic year 1983–84]. León: University of León.
Semonche, J. E. (2007) *Censoring sex: A historical journey through American media*. Plymouth: Rowman & Littlefield.
Valls, F. (2005, October 15). Alberto Méndez, o la dignidad de los vencidos [Alberto Méndez or the dignity of the defeated]. *El País*. Retrieved from http://www.elpais.com.

Appendix 1. Translations by José Méndez Herrera

Title of play	Author	Record number /year submitted	Approved
Una visita en la noche	Casas Bricio, Antonio	2575/41	1941
El angelus	Martín Alonso, M.	3815/43	1944
En la hora del diablo	Martín Alonso, M.	0734/45	1947
Un tranvía llamado Deseo	Williams, Tennessee	0217/50	1951
La heredera	Goetz, Augustus y Ruth	129/51	1952
Cocktail Party	Eliot, T. S.	28.02.52	1952
El cero y el infinito	Kingsley, Sidney	164/52	1952
Cuento de invierno	Shakespeare, William	056/53	1953
Un tranvía llamado Deseo	Williams, Tennessee	217/57	1957
El árbol del amor (provisional)	Roman, Lawrence	267/61	
Mi querido embustero	Kilty, Jerome	313/61	1962
La sonata a Kreutzer	Watt, Hannah	0002/63	1964
Pigmalión	Shaw, George Bernard	166/63	1963
La noche de la iguana	Williams, Tennessee	7/64	1965
Robo en el Vaticano	Fabbri, Diego	0030/64	1964
El gorro de cascabeles	Pirandello, Luigi	0123/64	1964
Después de la caída	Miller, Arthur	0237/64	1966
¿Quién teme a Virginia Woolf?	Albee, Edward	215/65	1966
La piedad en noviembre	Brusati, Franco	0206/66	1966
Las troyanas	Eurípides	0196/69	1974
El precio	Miller, Arthur	0011/70	1970
Un enemigo del pueblo	Ibsen, Henrik	403/71	
Los lúnaticos	Middleton, Thomas	0370/72	1973
Hamlet	Shakespeare, William	0313/73	1973
Viernes día de libertad	Claus, Hugo	0417/77	1977

Sources: AGA & TRACE-theatre

Between ideology and literature: Translation in the USSR during the Brezhnev period

Emily Lygo

The USSR's de-Stalinization and liberalization under Khrushchev opened up the country to the West and led to a boom in the translation of foreign and especially Western literature. After the Thaw, however, Soviet society is generally seen to have moved into a period of stagnation, characterized by a cooling in its enthusiasm for America and the West more generally. This article will examine the fate of translated literature in the less congenial environment of the Brezhnev years, looking in particular at translations in the journal *Novyi mir* in 1965–1981. It will show that, although there were changes in the profile of the translations published during the period, overall, translation cannot be said to have undergone stagnation. It asks how translation was used by different agents: the Party, editors, and translators. It will argue that translation continued to be seen by the Party as symbolic of the 'friendship of the peoples', but was used by editors and translators to publish artistically diverse and challenging works. It will show how various strategies were employed by the journal's editors and translators to present texts in such a way as to get them past the censor.

The term 'stagnation' is widely applied to the Brezhnev era (1965–1981) and especially to its second half, and is seen to have set in in political, economic, and cultural spheres. It describes not only a lack of growth, interest, and vigour but also a slow reversion, after the Khrushchev Thaw, to neo-Stalinist conservatism. In particular, it is associated with increasingly anti-Western rhetoric. In spite of détente and improvement in Cold War tensions, the USSR was no longer prepared to nurture interest in and sympathy towards America and the capitalist West more generally. Rhetoric about bourgeois society failing, injustice, double standards, hypocrisy, and crisis constituted a powerful message about capitalism's inherent contradictions and inevitable degeneration. In the time of Khrushchev, the USSR had opened up to the West, but, in the time of Brezhnev, it is widely considered to have closed the door again.

The more famous controversies and illiberal moments of the literary history of the stagnation have often led to a sense that all the positive gains of the Thaw were lost. Even during the Thaw, the campaign against Pasternak in 1960 was a reminder that not all remnants of the Stalin period had been expunged; there was a marked return to these after the fall of Khrushchev. The trials of Brodskii in 1964, Siniavskii and Daniel in 1965,

Ginzburg and Galanskov in 1967, and the expulsions of Brodskii in 1972 and Solzhenitsyn in 1974, as well as the furore over the publication of *Metropol'* in 1975, all point to a significant change in political climate. What is more, the leakage of writers to the West via exile and emigration throughout the 1970s, known as the third wave of Russian emigration, was no doubt a product of the stagnation.

The Soviet literary scene of the Brezhnev period was certainly not, however, comparable to the wasteland created by Stalinism in the 1940s. Indeed, the gradual recovery of writers anathematized during the Stalin period, which was such a significant part of the cultural Thaw under Khrushchev, continued into the Brezhnev period as well. Works by and about writers such as Osip Mandel'shtam, Marina Tsvetaeva, and Mikhail Bulgakov appeared in the thick journals through the 1970s. And although the refusal to publish *Metropol'* in 1975 clearly indicated the limits of what was permissible in print, the 1970s saw a striking range of contemporary prose writers published in the USSR, even if later some emigrated (these included Vasilii Aksenov, Andrei Bitov, Viktor Erofeev, Fazil' Iskander, Iurii Trifonov, and Vladimir Voinovich).

Recent work on the Brezhnev and, more generally, the late Soviet period has started to challenge this notion of stagnation. In part, this research has focused on the dissident and underground movement: work by Savitskii (2002), Lygo (2010), and Sabbatini (2008) among others has shown that unofficial literary activity was an important sphere for cultural development during this period. However, scholars have also unpicked the idea that mainstream Soviet politics and culture were afflicted with stagnation. Bacon and Sandle's *Brezhnev reconsidered* (2002) examines Brezhnev as a leader and political culture under Brezhnev, seeing the roots of the dramatic changes of *perestroika* in the Brezhnev era. An international workshop in Amsterdam in 2012, 'Reconsidering stagnation' covered a wide range of cultural areas: the Aesopian language of cultural products, socialist humour and jokes, the cult of the Great Patriotic War, cinema, literature, arts and theatre, Soviet science fiction, bard music, tourism, fashion, fascination with the West and foreign consumer goods, and the emergence of Soviet rock 'n' roll.

This article sets out to examine whether or not the publication of literary translation in the USSR, which was, after all, a notable way that a window could be held open to the West, diminished in quantity or variety or was otherwise subject to stagnation in the Brezhnev period.

Scholarship on the publication of literary translation in the post-Stalin period has tended to concentrate on the Thaw, the so-called 'decade of euphoria' that brought the USSR back into contact with the rest of the world, and especially the West, after the xenophobia of the late Stalin period (Friedberg, 1977). There has been little attention paid to the publication of translations in the Brezhnev period, but Sergei Zav'ialov's work on the publication of translations of poetry that was experimental and modernist in its affinities asserts that the window on the West that is associated so strongly with the Thaw did not close in the mid-1960s, and that from 1955 there was an epoch of translation that lasted largely uninterrupted for 30 years (Zav'ialov, 2008, para. 1). While Zav'ialov does not comment on the reason why literary translation was relatively immune to the increasing ideological conformity in the 1970s and early 1980s, Friedberg suggests that the practice of translating Western literature continued into the post-Khrushchev period in part because readers were keen to read it (Friedberg, 1977, p. 337). Editors had to balance ideology and censorship with pragmatic considerations of how to appeal to Soviet readers, and, since Western literature was in high demand among readers, they found various ways to accommodate it and at the same time protect themselves from possible recriminations from the ideological authorities.

The strategies that both translators and editors could employ to facilitate the publication of foreign and especially Western literature were largely determined by the system of Soviet censorship during the period. While censorship existed throughout the Soviet period, its organization and institutions evolved over time, and in the post-Stalin period responsibility shifted somewhat from the central organs to literary professionals. Historians of censorship in the USSR note generally that censorship increased after the period of the Khrushchev Thaw, from about 1968; this apparently accelerated in the wake of the Soviet invasion of Czechoslovakia and the crushing of the Prague Spring, which had seen censorship removed as part of its programme of 'socialism with a human face'. T.M. Goriaeva shows that there are documents produced by the Party and censorship authorities in the 1970s that refer to certain literary works of the 1960s as anti-Soviet, even though those works were passed by the censors and published at the time (Goriaeva, 2002, pp. 349–350). This neatly encapsulates how the definition of what was acceptable for publication changed over time. Arlen Blium argues that the letters of protest against censorship written by Aleksandr Solzhenitsyn and Lidiia Chukovskaia in the late 1960s, together with an appeal to the Supreme Soviet by a group of writers asking for a new law on the free dissemination of and access to information and for the removal of Glavlit's (the main censorship organ of the USSR) control over literature, led the authorities to increase censorship to combat such dangerous tendencies (Blium, 2005, pp. 17–18).

The position of Glavlit in relation to Party institutions and hierarchy changed several times during the Thaw, a period that saw frequent reshuffling of institutions and their organization under Khrushchev's energetic but sometimes chaotic leadership. In 1966, however, it was restored to its former position as formally answerable to the Council of Ministers of the USSR, but in practice usually to the ideological departments of the Central Committee of the Communist Party of the USSR (Blium, 2005, pp. 15–17). Even though this restoration would seem to point to continuity in its role and influence, in fact by the late 1960s and in the 1970s, Glavlit's authority was significantly diminished. In as early as 1965, Blium describes a degree of loosening of control over the thick literary journals and books that were issued by the major, trustworthy publishing houses; a new protocol was introduced that required manuscripts to be submitted for publication only at the final draft stage (Blium, 2005, p. 24). Herman Ermolaev gives concrete examples of Glavlit's diminished authority in the 1970s and 1980s. The writer Vadim Kozhevnikov, chief editor of the Moscow 'thick' journal *Znamia* for 19 years in the late Soviet period, claimed that at no point during his tenure as editor did Glavlit hold up the publication of a manuscript. If there was a delay, it was because his editorial board had deemed it necessary. He also gives evidence that Glavlit's opinion of a text was not seen as binding or even authoritative by some journals: in 1983 the organ passed the second volume of Boris Mozhaev's novel *Peasant men and peasant women* for publication, but it was subsequently turned down by the editors of *Novyi mir*, *Nash sovremennik*, and *Druzhba narodov* (Ermolaev, 1997, p. 183).

As the above examples indicate, with the decrease in Glavlit's prestige and power was a corresponding increase in the authority of editors and editorial boards. Goriaeva quotes the writer Anatolii Kuznetsov as explaining that writers never met censors, never came into contact with them, and that this was in part because editors had, by this time, come to understand the system so well that they did not need the input of Glavlit employees to know what could and could not be permitted in print (Goriaeva, 2002, p. 345). Ermolaev and Blium concur that power moved to editorial boards, and Blium recalls Dirk Kretzschmar's observation that, in effect, all published works of literature became collaborative works under this system (Blium, 2005, p. 18).

The system of censorship was applied to literature in translation as well, so translations which necessarily involved the work of both author and translator became even more 'collaborative' when editors and censors had input into a text before it was published. Historians of censorship in the USSR have generally given little attention to the publication of translations, although Goriaeva gives examples of how the erotic scenes of John Updike's novels were censored, and the final chapters of Arthur C. Clarke's *2001: A Space Odyssey* were omitted. Similarly, she records, translations of literary criticism on foreign literature were censored, so from a history of English literature a paragraph about Arthur Koestler's and George Orwell's anti-communist writings was excised (Goriaeva, 2002, pp. 354–356). Ermolaev's study of censorship, which compares translated texts with their originals and analyses word choice, omissions, and changes, shows that references to the West, and in particular the economic and technological superiority of the West, were censored during the late Soviet period (Ermolaev, 1997, p. 214).

Samantha Sherry has examined specifically the censorship of translations in the USSR during the Thaw period (Sherry, 2013). She shows that in the post-Stalin period translators and editors bore far more responsibility for the censorship of translated literature than they had during the Stalin period. Like original literature, translated texts were not passed to the censorship organs until the last stage of the publishing process; it was expected that the literary professionals involved in the processes of translation and publishing would have taken most of the necessary decisions to produce a translation suitable for publication. She argues that translators and editors were thus involved in a complex balancing act, involving, on the one hand, adherence to the norms of Soviet publishing and, on the other, faithfulness to the literary text being translated. While editors and translators understood 'the rules of the game' and were able to produce texts that were ideologically acceptable, they were not necessarily content with conforming to established norms. The removal of the Party from the process until its final stage led to a situation, Sherry shows, in which there was more space to negotiate the publication of interesting works that were not too distorted by censorship.

Both Zav'ialov and Sherry base their analyses on publications by *Inostrannaia literatura*. This is not surprising: this journal was dedicated to the publication of foreign literature in the USSR, and was therefore the specialist journal for the area. Its history, indeed, reflects the history of the fortunes of translated literature in the USSR: its precursor publication, *Internatsional'naia literatura*, existed until 1943 but was closed during the xenophobic late Stalin years when contact with the West and Western culture was minimal. The launch of *Inostrannaia literatura* in 1955 was one of the key indications that the Thaw after the death of Stalin was truly underway. Even under the relatively liberal conditions of the Thaw, however, this journal was less accessible to the public than others: it was not possible just to go and read it in a library or to subscribe to it. So, while it does tell us what was translated for a specialist audience, it does not tell us much about what was read by a broader section of the Soviet public. It is important to remember, too, that it did not have a monopoly over the publication of translated literature. Most of the 'thick' journals published translations alongside original Russian-language works. Because translated literature constituted only a part of these journals' publications, it is possible to trace over time whether the space allotted to this category of texts increased or diminished.

This study examines the publication of translated literature in the journal *Novyi mir* to test the hypothesis that the publication of translated literature, like other areas of cultural activity, did not in fact undergo a period of stagnation during the late Soviet period. There are several reasons for choosing this journal: it regularly published translated works and it also had a higher print run and was more available (though by no means fully) to the general readership than *Inostrannaia literatura*. What is more, this journal had made a series of landmark publications during the Khrushchev Thaw under Simonov and especially Tvardovskii, and had gained a reputation as the most liberal journal. This liberalism was particularly focused on de-Stalinization, but also included a more sympathetic, conciliatory attitude towards the West. *Novyi mir* published a significant number of American writers during the Thaw, perhaps most notably J.D. Salinger (Friedberg, 1977, p. 199). Tvardovskii, who was responsible for most of these landmark publications, including, in 1962, Solzhenitsyn's *One day in the life of Ivan Denisovich*, remained chief editor of the journal until 1970, when a Party-initiated but Writers' Union-led shake-up of the editorial board forced his hand and he retired from his position. He was replaced by Valerii Kosolapov, whose appointment was intended to return ideological conformity to the journal (Kozlov, 2013, pp. 230–231).

This position of *Novyi mir* as a liberal journal, but one not entirely devoted to translated literature, makes it an appropriate publication to use to examine how, if at all, the stagnation affected the publication of translated literature in the USSR. This article will consider whether the balance of political and geographical representation in translated literature changed over time, and in particular look at the balance between translations from the minority languages of the USSR, and from both pro-Soviet and more neutral writers from the West, to see whether there was a significant change in the representation of these groups. It will then consider what the publications of translated literature in *Novyi mir* during the period can tell us about the strategies that translators and editors used to negotiate the demands of ideology and censorship.

My survey of the journal *Novyi mir* from 1965 to 1981 recorded the number of separate publications of translated literature there were for each journal issue. The figures in the survey reflect the tables of contents, therefore, and not the number of pages that translation occupies: a 100-page prose work is counted as one publication and so is a single poem. This means the survey does not show how much space in the journal, measured in number of pages, was dedicated to translations; it does, however, indicate the range of works published and whether these works were presented as the work of an individual author or as representative of a group of authors. When a long work was serialized over several issues, each separate publication was counted. While there are undoubtedly limitations to what these statistics can show, they nonetheless give a sense of the variety of the translations published. The works were categorized according to the geographical and political position of their authors; the categories used were adapted from those used by Sergei Zav'ialov in his survey of modernist style poetry in *Inostrannaia literatura* (Zav'ialov, 2008). From his work I have borrowed the following descriptions: 'historical figures', 'Western communists', 'Left-leaning Western writers', 'writers from socialist countries', and 'writers from capitalist countries who are apolitical'; to these I have added the category 'writers from the Soviet republics'. Beyond the statistics I collected, I noted trends that emerged from the survey, and these are also brought to bear on my discussion. The survey's results are recorded in Table 1.

Overall the number of translations published fell across the period, but this was mainly because the number of translations of writers from the republics fell. The number of writers from socialist countries also decreased somewhat; the anomalously high number in 1979 was due to the publication of works from a conference of writers from socialist countries. The numbers of Western writers – either Left-leaning or otherwise – do not show any clear pattern of change, but it is notable that *Novyi mir* published more Western writers who could not be said to be political than Left-leaning writers. The reason

Table 1. Writers published in translation in *Novyi mir*, 1965–1981.

	Historical figures	Writers from Soviet republics	Writers from socialist countries	Western communists	Western Left-leaning writers	Apolitical writers from Western capitalist countries	Total
1965	2	12	3		4	5	26
1966	1	13	2		4	7	27
1967	3	20	2		1	3	29
1968		19	1			7	28
1969		16	2	1	1	3	22
1970		13	3	1	1	4	22
1971		12	2	1	1	4	20
1972	1	19	1			2	23
1973	2	11	1		4	9	26
1974	2	14	1	1	1	4	23
1975		9	4	1		1	15
1976		8	1			2	11
1977	3	4				4	11
1978	3	4				3	10
1979		9	7	1		3	20
1980	1	5		1		4	11
1981		8				4	12

for this editorial decision was probably motivated by a combination of pragmatic and political reasons: such Western writers were popular and attracted readers, so it was pragmatic to include them to help boost the journal's popularity. However, they were also politically more liberal and progressive than pro-communist writers, and thus were a way that the journal could continue with its politically progressive position of the Thaw: Western writers had more leeway in their works than their Soviet counterpart writers, who were suffering from difficult conditions of publication in the post-Thaw period due to both harsh censorship and ideological control and also the gerontocratic and bureaucratic literary system dogged by inertia and the paper shortage.

Of course, the appearance of a text in translation did not necessarily mean that it was a faithful reproduction of the original, including all its aspects, that would appear to challenge Soviet literary norms. As Friedberg showed in his study of translated literature published during the Thaw era, instances of obscene language, sexual references, and political comments that were not favourable towards the USSR were often expunged or at least softened. Sherry has shown that this was not always at the hand of a Glavlit censor but often the work of translators and editors. These literary professionals knew the rules of the game and were prepared to make some adjustments to the text if it would result in it being passed for publication (Sherry, 2013). This strategy for achieving publication will be discussed below in the context of the publications during the Brezhnev period.

Neither political nor pragmatic reasons for editorial decisions would appear to explain the reduction in representation of writers from the republics of the USSR. The number of writers from the republics published in translation appears to drop quite dramatically from 1975. In fact this is not quite the case, and to examine the change that occurs at this time, the particularities of the representation of writers from the republics need to be explained. Throughout the period, most writers from the republics are represented overwhelmingly by poetry, in contrast with Western writers, whose works are mostly prose. Exceptions include Byelorussian writers, and in particular Vasil' Bykov, and to some extent writers from Ukraine and the Baltic States. However, writers from the Caucasus and central Asia tend to be poets. There are probably various reasons for this. The predominance of poetry among writers from the republics may be in part due to the strong oral tradition that these new literatures, which underwent significant encouragement to develop into part of Soviet literature, were based upon.

A more cynical explanation for the decrease in attention paid to the national writers, however, might be that, while it was necessary politically to include a good variety of such writers, by representing them through poetry less space had to be devoted to them. Going back to the 1930s, there is evidence of translators' scorn for the quality of much of the work they had to translate from the minority languages, and it is highly possible that this attitude prevailed in the post-war period (Zemskova, in Burnett & Lygo, 2013, p. 197). The Brezhnev period saw a return to policies of Russification and the rise of Russian chauvinism once more in the USSR; this tendency to minimize attention to the national minorities and to see them in terms of their nationality rather than their individual talent would appear to be part of a more general reluctance to see these nationalities as equal partners in the Soviet project.

From about 1975, when the figures show a decrease in the number of publications of writers from the republics, the journal stopped publishing these writers individually and shifted towards featuring groups of writers from a republic that appear as just one item in the contents. Earlier in the decade, poets such as Kaisyn Kuliev, a Balkar poet, and Mustai Karim, a Bashkir poet, had selections of their poetry published in the journal quite frequently, but from about the middle of the decade, the minority writers appear typically under headings such as 'Poetry from Uzbekistan' or 'New poetry from Ukraine'. There had always been such selections of poems, but these came to dominate the representation of the nationalities, with individuals, and especially individual poets, almost disappearing from the journal's pages. The feature uniting the poems in these selections was their ethnic and cultural background, and this led to a reductive view of the work of the national writers as representative of a national spirit or a national literary tradition. This use of selections of poets published together is in stark contrast to the way that Western writers were almost always represented as individuals. There were occasional exceptions to this rule, such as contemporary or historical collections of French or Italian poets, and collections of American poems or songs united by a theme, for example their opposition to the Vietnam War.

Another difference between the representations of Western writers and those from the republics is that the latter rarely had any commentary accompanying them, whereas Western writers tended to be furnished with paratext in the form of introductions or afterwords, the emphasis of which tended to focus on the writer's individual circumstances and the evolution of his or her literary work. The contrast in this representation might suggest the assumption that literature translated from the minority languages of the USSR was, after all, Soviet, and therefore needed no introduction to a Soviet reader, but could also indicate again a hierarchical view, which sees these writers as unworthy of the individual attention that Western writers routinely receive.

Even if it was easier for editorial boards to publish progressive work from the West than from the USSR, it is possible to see in the works of Western writers published in the journal features that made them ideologically acceptable for publication in the USSR; these tended to be features of their content, rather than their form. Given the history of Soviet emphasis on content and censure of preoccupation with form, this is understandable. In general, writers whose works involved criticism of Western society, and in particular issues such as inequality, were promising candidates. The most common nationalities translated are West German and American: there are 12 American authors published in the period, and although only four West German, Heinrich Böll's work appears very frequently. There are issues specific to each of these that commonly seem to have qualified works for publication in translation in the USSR. West German works frequently deal with the recent Nazi past; this reminder of the Second World War fits comfortably with the Soviet commemoration of the conflict that was so prominent in the late Soviet period, providing a reassertion of the guilt of the Nazi enemy. American works quite often involved the criticism of race relations, which chimed with Soviet rhetoric about the United States' hypocrisy in claiming to be the home of freedom and equality. There were writers, especially among the Americans, whose works were generally critical of the direction their Western societies were developing in, such as short stories by John Cheever, which Maurice Friedberg describes as 'about the demise of a simpler America, coupled with satirical barbs at the synthetic commercialized civilization replacing it' (Friedberg, 1977, p. 198). Stories such as Cheever's are far more than just social criticism, as will be explored below, but they gave a portrayal of American life with enough drawbacks and problems to be seen as suitable for Soviet readers. The problems of civil rights and racism associated with the southern settings of Truman Capote's and Flannery O'Connor's works seem likely to have been helpful in securing these works' publication.

Many works of literature in translation that appeared in *Novyi mir* during the Brezhnev period touched upon themes that coincided with the Soviet line, since there were many Western writers during this period engaged in the criticism of their own systems. Thus there was no shortage of works potentially qualifying for translation. These works of literature had a great deal more to interest readers than simply an echo of Soviet anti-Americanism or anti-fascism. What is particularly noticeable is that the formal qualities of the works are at the more experimental end of the spectrum when compared with Soviet prose of the time. It is not that there were not works published in the 1970s USSR that introduced less standardized, normative diction and style, but the very colloquial and informal narration, the non-standard language including obscenities (usually not printed in full in Russian), and the more experimental plot construction in a good number of works were certainly innovative in comparison with most published Soviet literature.

What is surprising is that there were also publications of works by Western writers whose main feature was their formal experimentation. Nathalie Sarraute's *Les Fruits d'or* published in Russian translation in April 1968, for example, was apparently critical enough towards the West to pass for publication, but its most distinctive feature was its experimental form. The work was published with an afterword by one of the editorial committee, Vladimir Lakshin, which guided the reader in how to approach Sarraute's 'anti-novel', which consisted entirely of interior monologues. At one point, Lakshin pointed to how Sarraute navigated a path between the Scylla and Charybdis of two literary sins in Soviet terms: hermeticism on the one hand and dry, academic imitation of art on the other.

> Nathalie Sarraute's mocking of "hermetic" literature and "hermetic" criticism demonstrates how keenly she feels the redundancy and meaninglessness of literature that has been formalized through and through. But at the same time it is not characteristic of her to produce lifeless, academic art that imitates classical discipline and clarity. (Sarraute, 1968, p. 172)

Sarraute was a progressive writer, and had Russian roots as well, but even so, the publication of her novel is an example of how strikingly progressive and experimental works could and did appear in the Soviet press during the Brezhnev period.

Lakshin's afterword to *Les Fruits d'or* is an example of the kind of paratext that Soviet editors used to present texts in translation to the Soviet readers; in *Novyi mir* they occured under Tvardovskii's editorship in particular. The paratext could take the form of an introduction or an afterword, and ranged between a few lines of text to several pages; its length appeared to offer a key to understanding how difficult a text was felt to be, both for the Soviet reader and to get past the censor. Its function was to offer an interpretation for the reader. Some examples include an essay on the background to modern American folksongs (Iz pesen sovremennoi Ameriki, 1966, p. 99); a few paragraphs on the life and thought of Rilke, carefully balancing his mysticism with his 'deeply humanitarian ideas' (Bazhan, 1967, pp. 22–23); the afterword on Nathalie Sarraute's experimental novel and its approach to the question of what art is (Sarraute, 1968, pp. 169–73); an introduction to Camus' position in literature, asserting that his theoretical works are not as important as his literary ones, that he struggled with the problem of balancing individual morality with social responsibility, and acknowledging that he did disassociate himself from the French Communist Party (Camus, 1969, pp. 155–156); and an introduction to Lao She as a writer who criticized Chinese nationalism but fell victim to the Cultural Revolution, and thus avoided association with either of these enemies of Soviet communism (Lao She, 1969, p. 83). An introduction to François Mauriac dwelled on the balance between his Catholicism and his friendship with socialists, and even goes as far as to say that the religiousness of Mauriac's characters should be seen as 'deeply unreligious' (Mauriac, 1970, pp. 105–6). Similar texts can be found about writers such as Kurt Vonnegut and Heinrich Böll. In each case, they pointed the Soviet reader towards the 'correct' understanding of the writer and the work, and often dealt with delicate issues associated with the author.

To some extent this practice of using paratext would appear to be a strategy for dealing with censorship: by informing the reader of the correct ideological approach to a text, the editors hoped to facilitate its publication. However, it is interesting to note that the practice became progressively less common in *Novyi mir* under the editorship of Kosolapov, in spite of the fact that the journal continued to publish interesting and sometimes challenging literature in translation. Although in the earlier years after Tvardovskii's removal the practice continued for some works, there was a tendency for the paratext to become shorter, and to foreground not so much the artistic merits of the work as the fact that the author had already appeared in other publications in the USSR, which is to say had already been passed by a censor. Later in the 1970s, works more frequently appeared with little or no paratext, for example a novella by Gabriel García Márquez in 1974 was prefaced by no more than a few lines of biography and bibliography (García Márquez, 1974, p. 106); a story by Muriel Spark appeared in 1977 with a sparse three-paragraph introduction; (Spark, 1977, p. 139) and in 1979 a novel by John Steinbeck had no introduction or afterword whatsoever (Steinbeck, 1979).

It would appear that, in fact, Tvardovskii's editorial team saw the paratext not only as a way to help a text pass for publication but also to introduce to the reader the notable, interesting features of a writer and a text; it suggests the editorial board saw readers as engaged in literary questions, as the kinds of 'critical' or 'creative' readers Nailya Safiullina identifies as emerging during the late 1930s in her study of readers' letters to the journal *International'naia literatura*. These were readers who 'were able to assess translated literary works primarily for their aesthetic, rather than ideological, merits'

(Safiullina, 2009, p. 130). Under Kosolapov's editorship, such issues are not flagged for the reader; this suggests that the journal did not encourage or particularly recognize an analytical approach to the literature it was publishing.

The difference between Tvardovskii's and Kosolapov's editorships in the approach to paratext accompanying translations suggests that its use was largely determined by editorial decisions; editors and their editorial boards were, after all, the bodies largely responsible for second-guessing and negotiating ideology and censorship in Soviet publishing in the Brezhnev period. Paratext was one way of shaping the journal's contents into a form acceptable for publication; another was the choice of texts themselves to be translated and the degree of censorship of its contents and language, an area dealt with in some detail by existing scholarship. As Samantha Sherry (2013) has discussed, Russian scholars' views of the censorship process tended to be totalizing and left little room for the agency of translators and editors, but her own work highlights these levels of censorship as areas of negotiation:

> [T]he increasing importance of editorial and self-censorship in the post-Stalin period could introduce potentially heterodox discourses and, to a limited degree, led to the destabilization of censorial and ideological norms. (Sherry, 2013, p. 739)

In her study based on *Inostrannaia literatura*, Sherry describes stages in the process of censorship: first, translators made certain censorial changes to texts they wished to see in print; afterwards, editors often cut and reworded further to ensure a text complied with the required norms. The initial process of choosing texts to be translated also seems to have been negotiated to some extent. For Western literary works, it appears that translators had to have professional standing in order to access special holdings of foreign books (Sherry, 2013, p. 737), but certain works were more accessible, for example poetry in the languages of Warsaw pact countries that was published in journals imported and sold in the USSR. This is the likely source of Polish poems that Vladimir Britanishskii (2012) describes translating for his own pleasure and not necessarily for publication. His translations sometimes did not appear in print for decades:

> Polish translations were for me, for both [Natal'ia] Astaf'eva and me, a work of art, we did not translate to order, and translated only works that we identified with, and consequently some of our translations were not published immediately at all, but ten, twenty, even thirty years later. (Britanishskii, 2012, n. p.)

Britanishskii's attitude towards translation reminds us that for many it was a labour of love, motivated by a literary sensibility that worked hard to preserve as much of the integrity of a work as possible under the conditions of Soviet publishing.

The translations published in *Novyi mir* during the Brezhnev period examined here demonstrate that the publication of literature in translation was not subject to stagnation in any straightforward or obvious way, at least in this journal. It is striking that translations of Soviet writers writing in languages other than Russian receive less attention and space in the journal than Western writers; apparently ideological principles such as the friendship of nations, the variety of Soviet literature, and equality among the peoples of the USSR were not particularly imperative in this era of Russification. It appears that the pragmatic considerations of selling journals and the strategies of editors and translators were instrumental in making a good variety of published literature in translation available to the Soviet reading public. Literature in translation published in the late Soviet period was certainly not confined to echoes of Soviet rhetoric produced by sympathetic foreign communists. Even if authors' criticisms of their own systems were welcome in the Soviet Union, in some cases these works from the West brought a level of formal innovation and experimentation to the Soviet press unparalleled in published Soviet literature of the time.

References

Bacon, E., & Sandle, M. (2002). *Brezhnev reconsidered*. Basingstoke: Palgrave Macmillan.
Bazhan, M. (1967). Povest' o nadezhde. (variatsii na temu R. M. Rilke) *Novyi mir*, *12*, 22–30.
Blium, A. (2005). *Kak eto delalos' v Leningrade: tsenzura v gody ottepeli, zastoia i perestroiki, 1953–1991*. St. Petersburg: Akademicheskiĭ proekt.
Britanishskii, V. (2012). *Vladimir Britanishkskii. Avtobiografiia. Okhripshie pesni*. Retrieved from http://www.stihi.ru/2012/12/30/9930
Burnett, L., & Lygo, E.(Eds.). (2013). *The art of accommodation: Literary translation in Russia*. Oxford & Bern: Peter Lang.
Camus, A. (1969). Padenie. *Novyi mir*, *5*, 112–156.
Ermolaev, H. (1997). *Censorship in Soviet literature, 1917–1991*. Lanham, MD: Rowman & Littlefield.
Friedberg, M. (1977). *A decade of euphoria. Western literature in post-Stalin Russia 1954–64*. Bloomington: Indiana University Press.
García Márquez, G. (1974). Nedobryi chas. *Novyi mir*, *11*, 106–191.
Goriaeva, T.M. (2002). *Politicheskaia tsenzura v SSSR: 1917–1991*. Moscow: ROSSPEN.
Iz pesen sovremennoi, Ameriki. (1966). *Novyi mir*, *12*, 99–103.
Kozlov, D. (2013). *The readers of Novyi Mir. Coming to terms with the Stalinist past*. Cambridge, MA: Harvard University Press.
Lao, She. (1969). Zapiski o Koshach'em gorode. *Novyi mir*, 83–103.
Lygo, E. (2010). *Leningrad Poetry 1953–75. The Thaw generation*. Oxford & Bern: Peter Lang.
Mauriac, F. (1970). Podrostok bylykh vremen. *Novyi mir*, *1*, 105–96.
Sabbatini, M. (2008). *Quel che si metteva in rima: Cultura e poesia underground a Leningrado*. Salerno: Europa Orientalis.
Safiullina, N. (2009). Window to the West: From the collection of readers' letters to the journal *International'naia literatura*. *Slavonica*, *15*, 128–161.
Sarraute, N. (1968). Zolotye plody. *Novyi mir*, *4*, 169–73.
Savitskii, S. (2002). *Andegraund: istoriia i mify Leningradskoi neofitsial'noi literatury*. Moscow: Helsinki Slavic Faculty.
Sherry, S. (2013). Better something than nothing: The editors and translators of *Inostrannaia literatura* as censorial agents. *Slavonic and East European Review*, *91*, 731–758.
Spark, M. (1977). Abbatisa kruskaya. *Novyi mir*, *9*, 139–79.
Steinbeck, J. (1979). Zabludivshiisia avtobus. *Novyi mir*, *3*, 121–80.
Zav'ialov, S. (2008). 'Poeziia – vsegda ne to, vsegda drugoe': Perevody modernistskoi poeziiv SSSR v 1950–1980-e gody. *Novoe literaturnoe obozrenie*, *92*. Retrieved from http://magazines.russ.ru/nlo/2008/92/za10.html

Censorship and the Catalan translations of Jean-Paul Sartre

Pilar Godayol

After more than 20 years during which no translations of foreign texts were permitted in Spain if they were not in tune with the Francoist regime, the work of Jean-Paul Sartre arrived in the 1960s in the form of translations into Catalan, despite the fact that his books had been on the list of Books Prohibited by the Catholic Church since 1948. The last years of the dictatorship, between 1965 and 1973, saw the publication of seven translations into Catalan of Sartre's work. The aim of this study is to investigate the institutional censorship that these works underwent from the time the publishers requested the permits from the Ministry of Information and Tourism (MIT) up until the final authorizations were given. After a brief contextualization of the translations, this article concentrates on the analysis of the eight censors' reports consulted in the General Archive of the Administration (AGA) situated near Madrid, in Alcalá de Henares. Seven permits were authorized and one rejected. The investigation enables us to see how the Francoist dictatorship reacted to the possibility of translating into Catalan works by Sartre, who were the censors who wrote the reports, what views they expressed and why, in spite of his being a banned author, the MIT finally authorized the translations.

1. Preliminary considerations

The year 2015 marks the 50th anniversary of the first translation into Catalan of a work by Jean-Paul Sartre. It was *Les Mots*, published by Gallimard in 1964, the year in which the author was awarded the Nobel Prize for Literature, which he rejected. Towards the end of the Francoist dictatorship, Sartre touched down in Spain with this significant title translated into Catalan. This was followed by six more translations. Between 1965 and 1973, seven of Sartre's works were published in Barcelona and, like all translations at that time, had to be submitted previously to the administrative censorship that operated from Madrid.

Five decades later, our aim is to study and contextualize the course of institutional censorship that *Les Mots* and the other six translations were obliged to follow before publication, taking into account that Jean-Paul Sartre was an existentialist and pro-Marxist writer vetoed by the Catholic Church. Our methodology will be based on the concept of 'microhistory' that Jeremy Munday presents in 'Using primary sources to produce a microhistory of translation and translators: theoretical and methodological concerns' (2014). Munday suggests applying the concept of 'microhistory', of the Italian historian Giovanni Levi, to the context of translation 'in order to better understand how detailed analysis of the everyday experience of individuals can shed light on the bigger picture of the history of translation in specific socio-historical and cultural contexts' (2014, p. 65). Munday underlines the importance of 'primary sources', often 'under-utilised in translation studies research' (2014, p. 64), and these he divides into 'Post-hoc accounts and interviews' (2014, p. 68) and 'Archives, manuscripts and personal papers' (2014, p. 71). This investigation focuses on part of Munday's 'more formal extra-textual primary resources' (2014, p. 71), the archives. Nevertheless, it also uses other primary sources such as memoirs or interviews and also articles and extracts from the press of the period.

This article investigates the eight censors' reports on titles by Jean-Paul Sartre proposed for translation into Catalan in the 1960s and beginning of the 1970s. Seven of these titles were approved and one prohibited. The study of the reports, consulted in the General Archive of the Administration (AGA) in Alcalá de Henares, enables us to answer the following questions: (1) What attitude was adopted by the Francoist regime with regard to the requests for permits to translate into Catalan works by Sartre, an author whose books had been on the list of Books Prohibited by the Catholic Church since 1948? (2) Who were the censors responsible for producing the reports? (3) What arguments did they put forward to defend or oppose his ideas? (4) Why, in spite of his being a banned author, did the Ministerio de Información y Turismo (MIT) finally authorize the translations? (5) And finally, why were the first translations of Sartre authorized by the MIT during the Francoist dictatorship those published in Catalan?

2. Censorship and Catalan translation during the Francoist dictatorship (1939–1975)

After the Civil War, Franco's regime strangled the activity of publishing companies in Spain for many years. From 1938 onwards, any text had to undergo the process of censorship prior to publication. Backed by laws and regulations, the administration's censors exercised a complete control over the social media. Books, newspapers, magazines and leaflets were inspected each with a distinct and specific procedure. During the first two decades of the dictatorship, translations into Catalan, Galician and Basque were banned. Today there are a good number of publications dealing with censorship and translation during the Francoist dictatorship. Some of these are panoramic and others study specific cases (see, amongst others, Abellán, 1980; Cisquella, Erviti, & Sorolia, 1977; Gutierrez-Lanza, 1997; Hurtley, 1986; Laprade, 2005; Larraz, 2014; Merino, 2008; Merino & Rabadán, 2002; Moret, 2002; Pérez, 1989; Rabadán, 2000; and Vandaele, 2010). More recently numerous works on censorship and Catalan translation have appeared (see, amongst others, Bacardí, 2012; Cornellà-Detrell, 2010, 2013; Gallofré, 1991; Llanas, 2006; Sopena, 2009, 2013; and Vallverdú, 2004, 2013).

The writer and chief editor of the publishing house Edicions 62 between 1965 and 2003, Francesc Vallverdú, establishes five phases (1939–1978) in the action of the censors with regard to Catalan books, which can be summarized as follows (2013, p. 10–12): (1) Between 1939 and 1945, the aim was to destroy not only all books in Catalan but also the readership. (2) Between 1946 and 1951, after the victory of the Allies in World War II, the prohibition on publishing in Catalan was met with increasing resistance which led to an initial but arbitrary tolerance of minority titles in Catalan such as religious texts, local monographs or poetry. (3) Between 1952 and 1962, the Minister of Information and Tourism, Gabriel Arias Salgado, brought out some 'New norms relating to regional languages', which perpetuated the criteria of the previous period. In this phase as in the previous ones, translations continued to be banned. (4) Between 1962 and 1966, the new minister of the MIT, Manuel Fraga Iribarne, modified the criteria for the publication of books in Spain and began to allow translations into Catalan: it was not a complete opening up, but it did mean a certain 'liberalization' of the censorship. Translations into Catalan boomed, with the growth of the industry and of specific publishers such as Edicions 62, created precisely during this period. (5) Between 1966 and 1976, the Press and Printing Law of 1966 was in force, the so-called Ley Fraga, which invalidated the Press Law of 1938. That is to say, the change was from 'compulsory previous censorship' of the originals to 'voluntary consultation', a disguised censorship that continued until 1976 and in some cases until 1978.

Between 1962 and 1968, translation played a leading role in book production in Catalonia. Vallverdú provides data: of a total production of 2831 titles in Catalan, more than a thousand were translations, 'a historical record' (2013, p. 13). Over these seven years, translation represented 38% of the total production, an extremely high percentage in comparison with other countries. The highest point was in 1965, when 55% of the total were translations, 'an excessive proportion unheard of in any other country' (2013, p. 13). During this same period, translations into Spanish represented between 20% and 30% of production, those into Danish represented 20% and into other languages 10% (Vallverdú, 2013, p. 13). It was in this context of exceptional prosperity in the history of Catalan translation that the first seven translations into Catalan of the work of Jean-Paul Sartre made their appearance (amongst other studies of the reception of Sartre in Spain, see Behiels, 2006; Díaz, 1983; and Roviró, García-Duran, & Sarrate, 2005). It should be mentioned that after a short period of time, in 1973, the bubble burst and with the economic crisis, 'translations into Catalan dropped to 8.3%; (Vallverdú, 2013, p. 13).

2. The Catalan translations of Jean-Paul Sartre (1965–1973): brief notes

We can distinguish two periods in the Catalan translations of Jean-Paul Sartre: a) the arrival in profusion during the last years of the Francoist dictatorship, and b) timid reappearances during the last two decades of the twentieth century and the beginning of the twenty-first, motivated by the death of the author (1980), the tenth anniversary of his death (1990) and the celebration of the centenary of his birth (2005). Of 15 translations in all, seven are from the first period and were the result of a historical and social context that fomented an interest in his political and existentialist works. The future publication of the article 'Las traducciones catalanas de Jean-Paul Sartre' (The Catalan translations of Jean-Paul Sartre) (Godayol, in press) will provide further information on the complete list of translations.

Table 1 presents essential data relating to the translations of the first period.

Jordi Llovet explains the two main reasons why the publishers in Proa, having previously obtained authorization from the MIT for *La nausée,* decided to put the publication of *Les mots* before that of *La nausée*: 'the fact that Jean-Paul Sartre was awarded the Nobel Prize for Literature in 1964, that is to say, in the same year that the translation of *Les mots* went to press, and the fact that he rejected it' (2005, p. 5). Josep M. Corredor, the translator of *Les mots* and writer of the prologue (Bacardí & Godayol, 2011, p. 154), was an essayist and university lecturer, living in exile in Perpignan. His translation created heated controversy as can be seen in the documents reproduced by

Table 1. Jean-Paul Sartre translations into Catalan between 1965 and 1973.

ORIGINAL TITLE	YEAR OF THE ORIGINAL	TITLE OF THE CATALAN TRANSLATION	YEAR OF THE TRANSLATION	TRANSLATOR	PARATEXT	PUBLISHER
Les mots	1964	*Els mots*	1965	Josep M. Corredor	Prologue (Josep M. Corredor)	Aymà (Barcelona)
La nausea	1938	*La nàusea*	1966	Ramon Xuriguera	Prologue (Ramon Xuriguera)	Aymà (Barcelona)
Réflexions sur la question juive	1946	*Reflexions sobre la qüestió jueva*	1967	Ramon Folch i Camarasa	No	Nova Terra (Barcelona)
Les mouches, *Huis-clos* (1944), *La putain respectueuse*, *Morts sans sépulture* (1946), *Les mains sales* (1948) and *Les Troyennes* (1965)	*Les mouches* (1943), *Huis-clos* (1944), *La putain respectueuse* (1946) *Morts sans sépulture* (1946), *Les mains sales* (1948) and *Les Troyennes* (1965)	*Teatre (A porta tancada. Les mosques. Les mans brutes. Morts sense sepultura. Les troianes)*	1968	Manuel de Pedrolo	Introduction (Xavier Fàbregas)	Aymà (Barcelona)
Esquisse d'une théorie des emotions	1939	*Esbós d'una teoria de les emocions*	1969	Miquel Adrover	No	Edicions 62 (Barcelona)
Baudelaire	1947	*Baudelaire*	1969	Bonaventura Espinosa	Introduction (Ricard Torrents)	Anagrama (Barcelona)
Questions de method	1957	*Qüestions de mètode*	1973	Carme Vilaginés	No	Edicions 62 (Barcelona)

Montserrat Bacardí in *La traducció catalana sota el franquisme* (Catalan translation under Franco's regime) (2012, pp. 226–230). Shortly after the publication of the translation, Corredor wrote to the editor of the magazine *Serra d'Or* complaining that he had not been able to check the proofs of the translation and accusing the publisher's corrector of bad practice. The publisher, Aymà, replied, in the same magazine, lamenting Corredor's reaction and defending the practice of correcting, to a greater or lesser degree, translations by prestigious writers. Catalan lecturers from various French universities later signed a statement in favor of Corredor and in defense of the translation. In 2005, when Proa brought out a new edition of *Els mots*, in the same translation (not revised) by Corredor, Llovet praised his version (2005, p.5).

In a letter of 25 November, 1965, Joan Baptista Cendrós[1] informed Josep Queralt, the former owner of Proa who died in Perpignan that same year, that 'after taking many steps we have managed to get permission to publish *La nausée*' (Vall, 1990, p. 56). In 1966, Sartre's first novel was published by Aymà as *La nàusea*, in a translation by the narrator, essayist and left-wing politician Ramon Xuriguera, who also wrote the prologue (Bacardí & Godayol, 2011, p. 600). In the midst of the controversy over Corredor's translation '*La nàusea* became all the rage' (Bacardí, 2008, p. 71). It should be mentioned that Xuriguera was also the first translator into Catalan of Simone de Beauvoir, with his version of *Une mort trés douce*, published in the same year as the first translation of Sartre, 1965, and just before Xuriguera's death (Godayol, 2013b).

After the publication of *Reflexions sobre la questió jueva* (1967), *Teatre* (1968), *Esbós d'una teoria de les emocions* (1969), and *Baudelaire* (1969), the prolific first period of translations of Sartre into Catalan was rounded off in 1973 with *Qüestions de mètode,* published by Edicions 62 in a translation by the psychologist and writer Carme Vilaginés (Bacardí & Godayol, 2011, p. 585). Her husband, Francesc Vallverdú, was chief editor of Edicions 62 at that time. Vilaginés had already translated the second volume of Simone de Beauvoir's *Le deuxième sexe* (1968) when she was commissioned to translate the work by Sartre (Godayol, 2013a, 2013b).

The literary critic Joan Triadú wrote an article in the magazine *Serra d'Or* in which he explained the translating boom of the 1960s in terms of the imperative need to retrieve as quickly as possible 'a generation lacking translated novels' (1968, p. 39). Although he insisted that this was still insufficient, he praised the fact that in five or six years more than a hundred titles had appeared 'thanks, often, to competent writers, or to good translators' (1968, p. 39). Josep M. Corredor, Ramon Xuriguera, Ramon Folch i Camarasa, Manuel de Pedrolo, Miquel Adrover, Bonaventura Vallespinosa and Carme Vilaginés (Bacardí & Godayol, 2011), those responsible for the first translations into Catalan of Sartre's works, fit Triadu's description. Most of them were well-known writers of Catalan literature, a profile that was to be found frequently in those years when the majority of intellectuals combined the two activities, usually for financial reasons. It is important to point out that there have been new editions of some of these translations, but none of these works have been re-translated.

3. The censorship dossiers of Jean-Paul Sartre

The eight censors' reports referred to here are held in the General Archive of the Administration in Alcalá de Henares. Seven of these were favorable and the translations published between 1965 and 1973 by Aymà, Nova Terra, Edicions 62 and Anagrama. Ordered by the date of opening of each dossier, and taking into account that *Le mur* was rejected, the reports are shown in Table 2.

Table 2. Censorship dossiers of Jean-Paul Sartre.

DATE OF OPENING	DOSSIER	BOOK	PUBLISHER	AUTHORIZATION/ REJECTION
6 August, 1964	AGA 21-15326, dossier 03882 (1964)	La nausée	Aymà	Authorized
25 June, 1964	AGA21-15408, dossier 04588 (1964)	Le mur	Aymà	Rejected
9 December, 1964	AGA 21-15724, dossier 07297 (1964)	Les mots	Aymà	Authorized
27 January, 1966	AGA 21-17023, dossier 00776 (1966)	Réflexions sur la question juive	Nova Terra	Authorized
6 May, 1968	AGA 21-18900, dossier 03386 (1968)	Teatre	Aymà	Authorized
29 November, 1968	AGA 21-19396, dossier 09889 (1968)	Questions de méthode	Edicions 62	Authorized
23 December, 1968	AGA 21-19509, dossier 11300 (1968)	Esquisse d'une théorie des émotions	Edicions 62	Authorized
21 February, 1969	AGA 66-02746, dossier 02550 (1969)	Baudelaire	Anagrama	Authorized

The order of the dates of opening of each administrative procedure for obtaining authorization does not correspond to the order of the final dates of publication. Since on occasion, the permits were held back or one rejected, we will refer to the eight cases in the order in which the permits were requested from the MIT, which will enable us to show their varying circumstances and the bureaucratic ups and downs they experienced before the texts could be published.

The first three permits were requested by Aymà: *La nausée* on 26 June, 1964, *Le mur,* on 6 August, 1964, and *Les mots*, on 9 December, 1964. This publishing company, which was founded in the 1940s and initially published in Spanish, was bought in 1962 by the patron Joan Baptista Cendrós, who merged it with other publishing entities and collections till it became known under the general name of Proa. Cendrós engaged the poet, narrator, playwright and translator Joan Oliver as Literary Editor to reactivate the company with the publication of a combination of original works and translations of well-known foreign writers. Aymà was also the publishing house that brought out, in 1966, the first translation into Catalan of Simone de Beauvoir, with *Une mort très douce* (Godayol, 2013b).

These three permits requested by Aymà in 1964 and a fourth requested by Nova Terra in 1966 for the translation of *Réflexions sur la question juive,* were subject to the Law of 1938 and the protocol of censorship differed from that applied to the later requests which came under the Law of 1966. These first four translations were therefore subject to obligatory previous censorship as opposed to the voluntary consultation applied to the other four. The change from the Law of 1938 to the new Law of 1966, the so-called 'Ley Fraga', meant 'the replacement of highly restrictive measures, the product of wartime, by those of a dictatorship that [...] considered that in this field it was in its interests to clean up its image' (Llanas, 2006, p. 24–25). The first impression was that the new law was more liberal, but this was only superficial. The margin for interpretation of the law was unclear and confusing, as it 'established a deliberately blurred border-line between tolerated freedom and what was called, in the phraseology of the time, "punishable libertinism"' (Llanas, 2006, p. 25). Added to this ambiguity was the 'arbitrariness of criteria of the readers of the administrative censorship' (Llanas, 2006, p. 25). Publishers found themselves condemned to absolute arbitrariness and 'absolute defencelessness' (Llanas, 2006, p. 25), a situation that resulted in 'an increase in self-censorship by authors and publishers' (Behiels, 2006, p. 1). Various autobiographical writings of publishers such as Carlos Barral (2001) or Josep Maria Castellet (1987, 2009) corroborate the complexities, risks and incoherencies of this law.

With the Law of 1966, consultation to the MIT could be carried out in two ways, either before or after the production of the book. The deposit of six copies prior to publication was mandatory whether or not the book was being submitted to previous voluntary consultation. Books that were presented for voluntary consultation might be authorized, suppressed or be subject to administrative silence, but in all cases, they were delayed. Books that were only deposited, but not subjected to censorship at that moment, could be published much more quickly but risked being withdrawn as the result of a later report. In reference to this option, Douglas Laprade comments: 'the freedom to publish without the censors' approval was illusory and publishers regarded this new possibility as a sword of Damocles' (2005, p. 70).

Apart from the total of four permits requested by Aymà, two were requested by Edicions 62, one by Nova Terra and one by Anagrama. Edicions 62 and Nova Terra, under suspicion from the regime for publishing mainly in Catalan (Llanas, 2006, p. 26, 30) were not allowed to choose between the two options permitted by the Law of 1966. The reason was that the Law of 1966 required publishers to be included in the register of Publishing Companies of the MIT. Edicions 62 and Nova Terra were refused the mandatory registration number, though after many interviews and meetings, they obtained it, the former in 1973 and the latter in 1974. As a consequence, this obliged these publishers to continue to apply for approval (voluntary consultation) from the MIT before commissioning a translation. Edicions 62 and Nova Terra also suffered from the bibliophobia of the extreme right at that time, who 'with the tolerance and/or complicity of the police attacked anti-Francoist publishing houses and bookshops' (Llanas, 2006, p. 31–32).

In spite of the offensives and the complexities of the system, the publishers did not desist. With regard to the importing of foreign literature, the aim was clear: to retrieve international classics of all time and spread the specifically ideological ideas of contemporary writers. Josep Maria Castellet, literary editor of Edicions 62 from 1964 to 1996, recalled that each original or translated title 'was politically and ideologically loaded' (Miralles, 2012, p. 8). He also referred to the censors: 'They put pressure on us right to the end. You never knew what you could publish and what you couldn't; the censorship was very arbitrary' (Miralles, 2012, p. 8).

3.1 The censorship and La nausée *(25 June, 1964)*

Aymà presented the MIT with the first request to translate Sartre into Catalan on the 25 June, 1964. The text chosen was *La nausée*, which had appeared in Paris in 1938. An edition of 3000 copies was requested and it was calculated that the book would have approximately 250 pages. The machinery of censorship then got under way. As was usual, the first step was to request readers' reports from two censors. In general, there were two types of censor: on the one hand, academics and intellectuals, who included members of the Church and of the Armed Forces, either active or in the reserve, and on the other, the employees of the MIT, whose work consisted of reading originals. In this particular case, given the international fame of the author, two eminent academics and irrefutable authorities of the Francoist Church were chosen: Father Saturnino Álvarez Turienzo and Father Santos Beguiristain.

The day after the request for authorization reached the MIT, Saturnino Álvarez Turienzo (La Mata de Monteagudo, León, 1920) was asked to report on the text. Álvarez Turienzo was an eminent member of the order of St. Augustine.[2] He was a specialist in philosophical works and had, according to Mireia Sopena, 'a social viewpoint that was wider than that of the stunted Francoist world' (2013, p.149). It should be mentioned that Álvarez Turienzo was also the censor responsible for four of the six reports that were requested for the translations of works by Simone de Beauvoir in this period. Some months after reporting on *La nausée*, he was asked to assess two feminist texts, *The Feminine Mystique* by Betty Friedan and *Le deuxième sexe* by Simone de Beauvoir. Friedan's work was approved and published immediately, in August, 1965, but de Beauvoir's was not published until June, 1968 (Godayol, 2013a, 2014).

Sartre's text enjoyed a better fate than de Beauvoir's feminist essay as Álvarez Turienzo authorized it immediately and without erasures. His review, clever as it is, reveals his admiration for Sartre's work. Even though it points out controversial aspects, ('certain passages are crude in language and in contents'), it finally recommends publication for two reasons: on the one hand because 'by now, the work is well-known because of the many accounts that speak of its plot and difficulties', and on the other because 'it is a narrative whose content is dense, to the extent that it is unlikely to have an effect on the general public'. Álvarez Turienzo insists that the specialized subject-matter of the novel and the limited erudite readership for whom it is intended rule out any risk of the work's reaching an uneducated public.

After Álvarez Turienzo's positive verdict of the 20 July, Father Santos Beguiristain (Bell Ville, Argentina, 1908 – Obanos, Navarra, 1994), a member of the Falange and a doctor in Theology and Canon Law,[3] was asked for a second report. On the 22 September, 1964, he emitted a favorable assessment, though with an erasure. In general, Santos' report is perspicacious and direct. From the start he makes it clear that the work had been listed in the Books Prohibited by the Church since 1948, that is to say, in the list of books censored by the Franco-friendly Roman Catholic Church. He describes the book as 'difficult to read, difficult to understand'. From an orthodox Francoist ecclesiastical standpoint, he admits publication since 'it will not reach the general public because of its obscure, philosophical character'. He demands only one erasure: 'On page 54, there is a passage which mocks pious customs in Spain, and this must be removed.'

Aymà received the positive verdict for the publication of the book on the 24 September, 1964. It was accompanied by a typed report from the Director General of Information in which the publisher was informed that, as it was a book that was prohibited by the Church, the MIT 'limits itself to permitting the circulation of the book, leaving to the publisher the responsibilities that are incumbent on him'. The publishers had to take on themselves all possible misfortunes. Their implication at this time was decisive: the arbitrariness led them to take many publishing risks, amongst others, financial loss when books were withdrawn, or accusations from individuals or institutions such as the Church, which could end up in the Courts of Justice. Six months later, on 12 March, 1965, Aymà presented a request to include in the edition a prologue by the translator, Ramon Xuriguera.[4] This was accepted and *La nausée* reached the bookshops a year later, in 1966, after *Les mots* for which the permit for translation had been requested six months after that of *La nausée*.

3.2 The censorship and Le mur *(6 August, 1964)*

On 6 August, 1964, Aymà requested authorization to publish the translation of Sartre's first narratives, *Le mur*. An edition of 3000 copies was requested. Two days later, Álvarez Turienzo was asked for an assessment. He gave his disapproval six days later in a short and conclusive typed report.[5] He states that none of the narratives 'is undeserving of reproof, some of them seriously so'. He criticizes the 'revolutionary atmosphere' of one, 'the reading of which could foment the type of terrorism that at times is hinted at', and the 'unacceptable moral crudeness' of others, while the last he judges as 'a case of disagreeable homosexuality, in addition loaded with political intention'. Álvarez Turienzo did not hesitate to declare that 'It should not be authorized'. The publishing house did not bother to appeal. The work was too subversive and so it is to be supposed that censors and publishers knew that they could go no further.

During the period of transition to democracy, after the death of Franco, Proa commemorated the death of Sartre in 1980 with the publication of the narratives that had brought the author to the fore in 1937, *Le mur* (1937), in a translation by poet and translator Agustí Bartra.

3.3 The censorship and Les mots *(9 December, 1964)*

On 9 December, Aymà requested authorization to publish *Les mots*, which had appeared during that same year, published by Gallimard. The very next day, the MIT asked for a reader's report from the censor J.V.S., who, to judge by the speed with which he gave his verdict – four days later – we assume to be a member of the permanent staff of the MIT.[6] This report is brief and discreet. It concludes that, although the author deals with sacred matters 'with impudence', 'he does not go as far as to be blasphemous or disrespectful'. Although 'he maintains his atheism', Sartre 'does not explain the process of his religious thinking nor does he defend his position'. For these reasons, J.V.S. authorizes publication without reservations.

The following day, the 15 December, Álvarez Turienzo was asked to submit a report.[7] The text is sober, clear and tends to subtly dedramatize the danger of the author's ideas: 'He explains all his scepticisms, including that regarding religion, without insisting on any particular stand'. It concludes: 'It is Sartre as usual in his corrosive, cold and lucid manner of expressing himself, leaving nothing untouched. The book has no other trend.' Álvarez Turienzo submitted the favorable report without erasures on 16 January, 1965. 10 days later, Aymà received the authorization, accompanied by a typed report from the Director General of Information, in which the publishing house was reminded that, as the book was prohibited by the Church, the MIT did not assume any responsibilities, as with *La nausée*, transferring these to the publisher.

3.4 The censorship and Réflexions sur la question juive *(27 January, 1966)*

On 27 January, 1966, Nova Terra requested authorization to translate *Réflexions sur la question juive*, published in Paris in 1949. Though it was not registered in the MIT until 1974, Nova Terra had been founded in 1958 by a group of lay people and members of the Church with 'the collective spirit of solidarity of the progressive social Christianity of the time' (Llanas, 2006, p.116) and modeled itself on the Éditions Ouvrières of Paris. Two days after the request was received, the first and only report was entrusted to Álvarez Turienzo, who gave his authorization on the 2 February.[8] In the briefest and least argumentative of styles, the censor describes the text as 'notes on the historical situation of the Jews' and concludes 'It can be authorized'. On the 4 February, 1966, Nova Terra received the positive report from the MIT with the condition that the six copies required should be deposited after publication of the book, a condition that was complied with a year later, on 12 May, 1967.

In the course of his activity as censor of the first four texts by Sartre (later reports were entrusted to other colleagues of the MIT), Álvarez Turienzo became a subtle protector of this French philosopher. Though he did not authorize *Le mur* because of its clearly subversive content, in the following three reports he always minimized the possible causes for mistrust by the body of censors and pointed out the instructive interest of the author's works. Knowing as he did that Sartre was considered a bête noire by the Francoist regime, he always referred to the author's international fame, the specialized subject-matter of his works and the limited edition proposed by the publishers, key arguments that favored the authorization of the translations. His statements were similar to those of publishers in their appeals after a translation had been prohibited. For example, in his appeal against the prohibition of Simone de Beauvoir's *Le deuxième sexe*, Ramon Bastardas of Edicions 62 resorted to very similar arguments (Godayol, 2013a, p. 81).

3.5 The censorship and Teatre *(19 April, 1968)*

On 19 April, 1968, Aymà presented a third successful request, this time for the publication of translations of plays by Sartre. Of a total of six, three had been refused authorization in 1958: *Les mouches*, *Morts sans sépulture* and *La putain respectueuse* (included in the reader's report by Pedro Borges Morán). Provision was made for 1000 copies of 300 pages. On the following day, a report was requested from Borges Morán (Nuez de Aliste, Zamora, 1929).[9] The holder of an Arts Doctorate from the Complutensian University of Madrid and a specialist in the History of America, Borges Morán was more intransigent than Álvarez Turienzo and never particularly magnanimous with dissident authors (Sopena, 2013, p. 157). His report is very brief: in five or six lines he summarizes the plot of each work and finally authorizes all of them. With reference to *La putain respectueuse*, he observes that 'in spite of its title, it is far from being scandalous or morbid'. He also adds that 'the prostitute is presented as having certain humane values, independently of her professional activity'. Contrary to his reputation as implacable, in this report, submitted on 3 May, 1968, Borges is fairly permissive with the author and the works.

Three days later, Manuel Pui, a censor on the staff of the MIT, was asked for a second report, which he submitted three days later with his approval.[10] Pui points out that two of these plays were being performed at that time in Madrid and that the critics, especially the newspaper ABC, had been favorable, 'receiving them with applause that was even enthusiastic'. It must be mentioned that, at this time, commercial theatre was strictly controlled, but that performances aimed at a limited public in small city theatres 'had more possibilities' (Behiels, 2006, p. 2). It was for this limited public that Sartre's work was performed.

Though Pui refers to the fact that 'it is well-known that Sartre's philosophy lies outside Christianity and that he sympathizes (though apparently less now) with communist theories', he finally seconds Borges' approval. The formal approval was received on the 10 May. Given that the Law of 1966 determined that voluntary consultations should be dealt with in no more than 30 working days, this was respected in this case since only 21 passed between the request and the receipt of the approval.

3.6 The censorship and Questions de méthode *(16 November, 1968)*

On 16 November, 1968, Edicions 62 requested authorization to translate the historical-philosophical essay *Questions de méthode,* published in Paris in 1957. M. Zapico, a censor on the staff of the MIT, was asked for a first report, which he submitted 10 days later.[11] With no beating about the bush, he authorizes the work because 'it is philosophical and serious, and not directly a political harangue' and because Sartre 'should be read by scholars'. The next day, a second report was entrusted to another staff censor, who gave his approval on the 2 December.[12] Less reserved than the first, this report analyses the differences between Marxism and existentialism and points out that the author finally 'criticises Marxism because it is incapable of guaranteeing freedom'. With the approval of both censors, the authorization was sent to Edicions 62 on the 3 December. The whole process had taken 18 days. However, questions of context and the publisher's programming led to the translation's being postponed for four years.

On 28 June, 1973, in the midst of the economic crisis of the 1970s, when the publishing boom had come to an end, Edicions 62, in accordance with the authorization, presented the six copies to be deposited. However, a further report was requested and this time signed by Mampel, an indecisive and arrogant staff censor of the MIT, who tended to be acrimonious and take a restrictive stand (Sopena, 2013, p. 157-158).[13] This was the case here. On the 17 July, 1973, Mampel submitted his assessment, in which, while authorizing the work, he demanded many mutilations ('pages 18, 28, 29, 82, 83, 157, 158 and 162'), which resulted in whole passages being eliminated.

When faced with this intellectual insult and financial loss, Josep Maria Castellet presented an appeal on the 30 July, requesting a revision of the proposed cuts 'both because of their number and their content'.[14] As most publishers of Sartre would have done, Castellet underlined the importance of the author and the historical and philosophical interest of the work. He pointed out that the work made Marxist theorists uncomfortable since 'it questions, from a contemporary standpoint, all the theoretical construction of those thinkers'. He also insisted on the specialized scientific subject-matter of the essay and the limited erudite readership to whom it was addressed. Finally he mentioned the financial question: 'If the decision to eliminate these fragments were to be maintained [...], it would cause us serious financial loss, since the book is in an advanced phase of production'. In fact, the book had already been printed.

The MIT did not rectify its decision, but decided to settle the matter by means of what is known as administrative silence, or tacit consent, which meant waiting for six months before distributing the book. This was a procedure used by the regime when foreign policy was considered to have priority over the circulation of a banned book. On the 4 March, 1974, Edicions 62 (which by this point, after six different requests to be included in the MIT Register, had been assigned number 1063) again sent six copies to the MIT, which finally gave authorization on the 7 March, 1974. Although according to the date of the procedure this was the sixth request for a permit, this title was the seventh and last of Sartre's works to reach the bookshops before the death of General Franco.

3.7 The censorship and Esquisse d'une théorie des émotions *(23 December, 1968)*

On the 23 December, 1968, Edicions 62 requested authorization to translate *Esquisse d'une théorie des émotions*, published in Paris in 1939. Provision was made for 1500 copies of 80 pages. Two days later, on Christmas Day, an unidentified reader was asked for a report, which was submitted with a positive verdict on the 22 January, 1969.[15] Concise and permissive, it stated that 'it is a brief psychological study of "emotion" beginning with James and Janet and going beyond them following a strictly phenomenological method in the style of Husserl and Heidegger'. The matter was clinched with a 'Nothing in particular'. After two days, the authorization was sent to the publishers of Edicions 62 who, six months later, on the 7 June, complied with the MIT's requirement of the deposit of six copies prior to distribution.

3.8 The censorship and Baudelaire *(21 February, 1969)*

On the 21 February, 1969, the publishing house Anagrama presented a request for a permit to translate Sartre's biography of Baudelaire, published in Paris in 1947. Anagrama (number 564 in the Register) was an irritating publishing house for the regime. It was founded in the second half of the 1960s by Jorge de Herralde Grau and, publishing mainly in Spanish, it began by establishing three collections simultaneously, two of more or less political essays 'Argumentos' and 'Documentos', and one of Catalan literary essays 'Textos', though this existed only briefly. *Baudelaire* came out in 'Textos' after the MIT's authorization had been requested on the 21 February and was granted on the 14 March. Approval had been given in a brief report by an unidentified censor.[16] It concluded with 'Nothing in particular. It can be published'. Eight days later, on the 22 March, 1969, six copies were handed in to the MIT, which wound up the procedure the same day.

4. Conclusions

Jeremy Munday's insistence on the application of 'microhistorical research' to translation studies is an invitation to study 'archives, manuscripts and translator working papers' because 'such sources [...] can give crucial insights into both historical circumstance and translation' (2014, p. 66). We have accepted that invitation with our investigation into the censorship reports on Jean-Paul Sartre's works. Although it was 'with inevitable disorder and delay' (Torrents, 1969, p. 7), Jean-Paul Sartre touched down in Catalonia during the 1960s, at a crucial and unrepeatable moment in the history of Catalan translation. Why Jean-Paul Sartre? Why authors such as Simone de Beauvoir, Antonio Gramsci, Karl Marx or Herbert Marcuse? Why, despite the MIT, did so many contemporary authors, internationally famous for their ideologies, appear in Catalan in the late sixties? It was thanks to the convergence of various circumstances that Sartre and other dissident intellectuals were able to make their entrance into Spain in Catalan during the apparent opening up of the last years of Franco's dictatorship. Our final considerations refer to this situation:

(1) Francesc Vallverdú explains an anecdote involving an un-named journalist of the newspaper *Le Figaro* (1965). This French correspondent claimed that 'the censorship treated translations into Spanish more harshly than those into Catalan' and that 'in Catalan one could find translations of Marx, Sartre, Gramsci that did not exist in Spanish' (2004, p. 186). This was irrefutable: at

that time, various authors were translated into Catalan before being translated into Spanish. What the French journalist does not say is that these authors, who had been banned for many years by the Francoist regime in Spain, had been translated in Latin America where publishers had no competitors and had bought the rights for reproduction in Spanish. Moreover, for long periods all Catalan texts were prohibited, which never happened in the case of Spanish. Like that of de Beauvoir (Godayol, in press),[17] the case of Jean-Paul Sartre is paradigmatic of this apparently paradoxical situation. In spite of the interventions of the MIT, the seven translations of Sartre's work into Catalan during those years were the first to obtain a positive verdict and the first to reach Spain. However, they had all been translated into Argentinian Spanish. Three publishers in Buenos Aires bought the rights and began to publish some works in the 1940s.[18]

(2) Apart from the expansionist policy of publishers in some countries in Latin America, while dictatorships flourished in the Iberian Peninsula, we have to bear in mind the fact that some writers, Sartre amongst them, had taken a stand against Franco's authoritarian regime and had refused to sell the rights to Spanish publishing companies. In an article in the newspaper *Avui* on the 27 April 1980 (p. 3), on the occasion of Sartre's recent death, Josep Maria Corredor, the translator of *Les mots* (1965), recalled the writer's intellectual commitment against dictatorial impositions and his support of national singularities such as the Basque or the Catalan. Proof of this is also to be seen in the preface that Sartre wrote for the book published in 1971 by Giselle Halimi, *Le procès de Burgos* (The Burgos trial).[19] With Sartre's consent, this preface was published in 1973 in a Catalan translation by Lluís Creixell as an offprint by Edicions Esquerra Catalana dels Traballadors (E.C.T.) in Perpignan, safe from the Francoist censors' supervision.

(3) This study of the eight censorship dossiers on the translations of Sartre provides representative cases of the type of actions carried out by the Francoist censorship under the Law of 1938 (1938–1966) and that of 1966 (1966–1976). All Sartre's works were authorized in a first resolution, except for one that was prohibited in 1964. In the censors' reports an evolution can be seen towards more permissiveness. Regarding this, Mireia Sopena has made a panoramic study of the censorship of the translations in the collection 'Llibres a l'Abast' of Edicions 62, which includes Sartre's last title and some by other contemporary ideologists, and has found, with regard to the censors' reports, that between 1963 and 1977 'the emphatic language and the space dedicated to the political valuation of the book were gradually reduced over the years' (Sopena, 2013, p. 424). Since Sartre was a controversial foreign writer, the readers' reports were mainly delegated to reputed academics who supported the regime. The most important of these was Father Saturnino Álvarez Turienzo, responsible for reports on the first four titles. In spite of his complicity, obviously limited, Sartre was considered, in general, to be a *bête noire*, but, as time went on, restrictions were relaxed because his international reputation gave him some level of protection against ideological persecution. It was not in the interests of the regime to hear accusations from the opposition within the country or from the foreign press or to be seen to persecute recognized contemporary writers. At the same time, the specialized subject matter and the limited edition were arguments in favor of the approval of the translations.

(4) Finally, there was one last factor that helped in the introduction of Sartre through Catalan at that time: for years he had been admired and followed by publishers, authors and an anti-Francoist reading public. If behind every title, there are some patrons, it is only right to wind up this article with reference to one of those principally responsible, along with Maria Aurèlia Capmany, Josep Maria Corredor, Joan Oliver, Francesc Vallverdú and Ramon Xurriguera, amongst others, for the fact that Sartre, in spite of being an author banned by the Francoist regime, became one of the most popular writers of the time: the publisher Josep Maria Castellet (1926–2014). Inspired by Sartre's thinking at an early age, Castellet became one of the disciples of existentialist ideology in Spain during the post-war years. On the 15 April, 1980, on the occasion of Sartre's death, he recalled his first contact with the master as an illumination, something which might well have been shared by all his generation:

> I was twenty-four years old. No book of literary theory had ever caused me such commotion. I became, from one day to the next, a convinced Sartrean. What Sartre was saying in this book was exactly the right thing for me to read in the Francoist Spain of those years; it gave me what I needed, without knowing it precisely. It was what I was missing in order to build my little trench of personal resistance. (1980, p. 68)

Acknowledgement

This article is the result of work by the consolidated research group 'Gender Studies Research Group: Translation, Literature, History and Communication' (GETLIHC) (2014 SGR 62) of the University of Vic–Central University of Catalonia (UVic-UCC), and the Research Project I+D "Traducción y censura: género e ideología (1939-2000)" (Ministerio de Economía y Competitividad, FFI2014-52989-C2-2-P). Translation of the article by Sheila Waldeck.

Notes

1. Joan Baptista Cendrós was an industrialist and activist who bought the Editorial Aymà in 1962 and Proa a year later, and finally merged them. For several years the names alternated until the new company became known as Proa.
2. Typed reader's report by Saturnino Álvarez Turienzo, dated in Madrid, 20 July, 1964 (AGA 21–15326, dossier 03882)
3. Typed reader's report by Santos Beguiristain, dated in Madrid, 22 September, 1964 (AGA 21–15326, dossier 03882).

4. Typed letter from Aymà to the Director General of Information, dated the 12 March, 1965 (AGA 21–15326, dossier 03882).
5. Typed reader's report by Saturnino Álvarez Turienzo, dated in Madrid, 14 August, 1964 (AGA 21–15408, dossier 04588).
6. Typed reader's report by J.V.S, dated in Madrid, 14 December, 1964. (AGA 21–15724, dossier 07297).
7. Typed reader's report by Saturnino Álvarez Turienzo, dated in Madrid, 16 January, 1965 (AGA 21–15724, dossier 07297).
8. Typed reader's report by Saturnino Álvarez Turienzo, dated in Madrid, 4 February, 1966 (AGA 21-17023, dossier 00776)
9. Typed reader's report by Pedro Borges Morán, dated in Madrid, 3 May, 1968 (AGA 21–18900, dossier 03386).
10. Typed reader's report by Manuel Pui, dated in Madrid, 9 May, 1968 (AGA 21–18900, dossier 03386)
11. Typed reader's report by M. Zapico, dated in Madrid, 28 November, 1968 (AGA 21–19396, dossier 09889).
12. Typed reader's report by an unidentified author, dated in Madrid, 2 December, 1968 (AGA 21–19396, dossier 09889). Most readers were unidentified and/or referred to by a number. Miguel Abellán (1980) attempted to compile a list of all censors and Mireia Sopena (2013) gave a list of those that censored three different series of translated essays at Edicions 62.
13. Typed reader's report by Mampel, dated in Madrid, 17 July, 1973 (AGA 21–19396, dossier 09889).
14. Typed administrative appeal by Josep Maria Castellet, dated in Barcelona, 30 July, 1973 (AGA 21–19396, dossier 09889).
15. Typed reader's report by an unidentified author, dated in Madrid, 22 January, 1969 (AGA 21–19509, dossier 11300 [1968]).
16. Typed reader's report by an unidentified author, dated in Madrid, 13 March, 1969 (AGA 66–02746, dossier 02550).
17. The author of this article is in the process of analyzing the censors' reports on works by Antonio Gramsci, Karl Marx and Herbert Marcuse in order to ascertain if the same criteria were applied as in the cases of de Beauvoir and Sartre.
18. Losada brought out *La náusea* in 1947, *Baudelaire* in 1949, and *Teatro* in 1950, in translations by Aurora Bernárdez, and *Crítica de la razón dialéctica* in 1963 and *Las palabras* in 1964 translated by Manuel Lamana; the National University of Córdoba published *Esbozo de una teoría de las emociones* in 1959 in a translation by Irma B. Bocchino de González, and Sur published *Reflexiones sobre la cuestión judía* in 1960, translated by José Bianco.
19. In this text, Sartre defends the 16 Basques judged by the military tribunal of Burgos and recognizes the validity of the Basque people's struggle for independence and socialism.

ORCID

Pilar Godayol http://orcid.org/0000-0003-2513-5334

References

Abellán, M.L. (1980). *Censura y creación literaria en España (1939–1976)*. Barcelona: Ediciones Península.
Bacardí, M. (2008). Ramon Xuriguera i la traducció. *URC. Revista literària, 23*, 66–71.
Bacardí, M. (2012). *La traducció catalana sota el franquisme*. Lleida: Punctum.
Bacardí, M., & Godayol, P. (Eds.). (2011). *Diccionari de la traducció catalana*. Vic: Eumo Editorial.
Barral, C. (2001). *Memorias*. Barcelona: Península.
Behiels, L. (2006). La recepción de Sartre en España: el caso de *La nausée" Espéculo. Revista de estudios literarios, 32*, 1–8. Retrieved from: https://pendientedemigracion.ucm.es/info/especulo/numero32/sartrees.html
Castellet, J.M. (1980). El gran emmerdador. *Saber, 1, 3* (May), 68–70.
Castellet, J.M. (1987). Memòries poc formals d'un editor literari. In: *Edicions 62. Vint-i-cinc anys (1962–1987)* (pp. 25–105). Barcelona: Edicions 62.

Castellet, J.M. (2009). *Seductors, il·lustrats i visionaris. Sis personatges en temps adversos*. Barcelona: Edicions 62.
Cisquella, G., Erviti, J.L., & Sorolia, J.A. (1977). *La represión cultural en el franquismo. Diez años de censura de libros durante la Ley de Prensa (1966–1976)*. Barcelona: Anagrama.
Cornellà-Detrell, J. (2010). Traducció i censura en la represa cultural dels anys 1960. *L'Avenç, 359*, 44–51.
Cornellà-Detrell, J. (2013). L'auge de la traducció en llengua catalana als anys 60: el desglaç de la censura, el XVI Congreso Internacional de Editores i el problema dels drets d'autor. *Quaderns. Revista de Traducció, 20*, 47–67. Retrieved from: file:///C:/Users/usuari/Downloads/265452-359501-1-SM.pdf
Corredor J.M. (1980). Comiat a Jean-Paul Sartre. *Avui*, (27 April), 3.
Díaz, C. (1983). Los españoles y Sartre: crónica de un retraso. *Arbor, 114*, 448: 452–462.
Gallofré, M. J. (1991). *L'edició catalana i la censura franquista (1939–1951)*. Barcelona: Publicacions de l'Abadia de Montserrat.
Godayol, P. (2013a). Censure, féminisme et traduction: *Le Deuxième sexe* de Simone de Beauvoir en catalan. *Nouvelles Questions Féministes, 32*(2), 74–88.
Godayol, P. (2013b). Simone de Beauvoir en català. *Bulletin Hispanique, 115*(2), 669–684.
Godayol, P. (2014). Feminism and translation in the 60s: the reception in Catalunya of Betty Friedan's *The Feminine Mystique*. *Translation Studies, 7*(3), 267–283. DOI:10.1080/14781700.2014.921237.
Godayol, P. (in press). Simone de Beauvoir bajo la censura franquista: las traducciones al catalán. Quaderns de Filologia. Estudis Literaris, 20.
Godayol, P. (in press). Las traducciones catalanas de Jean-Paul Sartre. *Bulletin Hispanique*, 120.
Gutiérrez-Lanza, C. (1997). Leyes y criterios de censura en la España Franquista: Traducción y recepción de textos literarios. In Vega, M.-A. & Martín-Gaitero, R. (Ed.). *La palabra vertida. Investigaciones en torno a la Traducción*. (pp. 283–290). Madrid: Editorial Complutense.
Le Figaro. (1965). Malraux interdit à Madrid et publié à Barcelone. *Le Figaro Littéraire* (16 December).
Hurtley, J. (1986). *Josep Janés. El combat per a la cultura*. Barcelona: Curial.
Laprade, D. (2005). *Censura y recepción de Hemingway en España*. Valencia: Universidad de Valencia.
Larraz, F. (2014). *Letricidio español. Censura y novela durante el franquismo*. Gijón: Trea.
Llanas, M. (2006). *L'edició a Catalunya: el segle XX (1939-1975)*. Barcelona: Gremi d'Editors de Catalunya.
Llovet, J. (2005). Autobiografies lletrades. *Avui*, (13 October), 5.
Miralles, M. (2012). Mig segle de llibres. *Presència*, (20–26 April), 6–9.
Merino, R. (2008). *Traducción y censura en España (1939-1985). Estudios sobre corpus TRACE: cine, narrativa, teatro*. Bilbao: Universidad del País Vasco-Universidad de León.
Merino, R. & Rabadán, R. (2002). Censored translations in Franco's Spain: the TRACE Project-Theatre and Fiction (English-Spanish). *TTR, 15*(2), 125–152.
Moret, X. (2002). *Tiempo de editores. Historia de la edición en España, 1939–1975*. Barcelona: Destino.
Munday, J. (2014). Using primary sources to produce a microhistory of translation and translators: theoretical and methodological concerns. The Translator, 20(1), 64-80. http://doi.org/10.1080/13556509.2014.899094.
Pérez, J. (1989). Fascist models and literary subversion: two fictional modes in postwar Spain. *South Central Review, 6*(2), 73–87.
Rabadán, R. (Ed.) (2000). *Traducción y censura inglés-español (1939–1985). Estudio preliminar*. León: Universidad de León.
Roviró, I., García-Duran, X. & Sarrate, C. (2005). El impacto de Sartre en España. *Concordia. International Journal of Philosophy, 48*, 77–102.
Sopena, M. (2009). Intel·lectuals i pensament sota censura. Les traduccions de *Llibres a l'Abast* (1963–1977). In *Actes del catorzè Col·loqui Internacional de Llengua i Literatura catalanes*. (pp. 415–425). Barcelona: Publicacions de l'Abadia de Montserrat.
Sopena, M. (2013). Con vigilante espíritu crítico. Els censors en les traduccions assagístiques d'Edicions 62. *Quaderns. Revista de traducció, 20*, 147–161. Retrieved from: http://www.raco.cat/index.php/QuadernsTraduccio/article/viewFile/265458/353042.
Torrents, R. (1969). Presentació. In J.-P. Sartre, *Baudelaire*. (pp. 7–11). Barcelona: Anagrama.

Triadú, J. (1968). Després d'una generació sense traduccions. *Serra d'Or*, (July), 39–41.
Vall, X. (1990) La literatura catalana de postguerra i l'existencialisme (1945–1968). PHD, Universitat Autónoma de Barcelona, pp. 56–57.
Vallverdú, F. (2004). Testimonis de repressió i censura. In P. Pagès (Ed.), *Franquisme i repressió. La repressió franquista als Països Catalans (1939–1975)* (pp. 81–187). València: Universitat de València.
Vallverdú, F. (2013). La traducció i la censura franquista: la meva experiència a Edicions 62. *Quaderns. Revista de traducció*, *20*, 9–16. Retrieved from: http://www.raco.cat/index.php/QuadernsTraduccio/article/viewFile/265449/353033.
Vandaele, J. (2010). 'It was what it wasn't: translation and Francoism'. In C. Rundle & K. Sturge (Eds.), *Translation under fascism* (pp. 84–116). Basingstoke: Palgrave Macmillan.

Translations of the works by Jean-Paul Sartre into Catalan:

Sartre, J. (1965). *Els mots*. (J.M. Corredor, Trans.). Barcelona: Proa.
Sartre, J. (1966). *La nàusea*. (R. Xuriguera, Trans.). Barcelona: Proa.
Sartre, J. (1967). *Reflexions sobre la questió jueva*. (R. Folch i Camarasa, Trans.). Barcelona: Nova Terra.
Sartre, J. (1968). *Teatre (A porta tancada. Les mosques. Les mans brutes. Morts sense sepulture. Les troianes)*. (M. de Pedrolo, Trans.). Barcelona: Proa.
Sartre, J. (1969a). *Esbós d'una teoria de les emocions*. (M. Adrover, Trans.). Barcelona: Edicions 62.
Sartre, J. (1969b). *Baudelaire*. (B. Vallespinosa, Trans.). Barcelona: Anagrama.
Sartre, J. (1973a). *Qüestions de mètode*. (C. Vilaginés, Trans.). Barcelona: Edicions 62.
Sartre, J. (1973b). *El procés de Burgos*. (L. Creixell, Trans.). Perpinyà: Edicions Esquerra Catalana dels Treballadors.
Sartre, J. (1980). *El mur*. (A. Bartra, Trans.). Barcelona, Proa.
Sartre, J. (1982). *Fenomenologia i existencialisme*. (M.A. Capmany, Trans.). Barcelona: Edicions 62.
Sartre, J. (1985). *Kean: adaptació de l'obra d'Alexandre Dumas*. (C. Serrallonga, Trans.). Barcelona: Edhasa.
Sartre, J. (1993). *Un teatre de situacions*. (J. Melendres, Trans.). Barcelona: Institut del Teatre.
Sartre, J. (1996). *L'imaginari. Psicologia fenomenològica de la imaginació*. (N. Bittoun-Debruyne, Trans.). Lleida: Universitat de Lleida.
Sartre, J. (1999). *L'ésser i el no-res. Assaig d'ontologia fenomenològica: selecció*. (M. Rius, Trans.). Barcelona: Edicions 62.
Sartre, J. (2006a). *Defensa dels intel·lectuals*. (A. Mestres, Trans.). Valencia: Universitat de València.
Sartre, J. (2006b). *Paisatge d'un segle*. (R. Usall & E. Garsaball, Trans.). Lleida: El Jonc.

What is an author, indeed: Michel Foucault in translation

Jeroen Vandaele

> Though the issue of translation occasionally surfaces in Foucault Studies, it remains an area that deserves more attention. To that effect, I briefly introduce some basic concepts of Translation Studies and then compare a chapter from *Surveiller et punir* ('Les moyens du bon dressement') with its English, Spanish, and Norwegian translations. Moving beyond the blatant errors, I argue that these translations are not generally 'the same text in a different language'. Rather, concepts are carved up in translation; or the analysis shifts from the structural to the historical; or syntactic adjustments make Foucault sound like an instruction book writer. Although I have deep respect for the work of the translators, who have brought Foucault to multitudes of new readers, I also argue that Foucault interpretation could profit from a translational turn.

1. Unquotable translations

It does not take a Foucault to explain the appeal of Foucault. For one thing, the French thinker dissects ideology and modern power in all its guises, and 'power', explains Jan Blommaert (2005, p. 1), 'is a concern to many people', it is a thing that never stops being 'the talk of the town'. For another, Foucault's writing style is no less than breathtaking, and I, like Stanley Fish (2011, p. 3), am always 'on the lookout for sentences that take your breath away'. Surrounded by poorly written texts, Foucault's readers find consolation in style; encircled by disciplinary power, his readers find deliverance through deep-cutting analysis. These truisms go a long way toward explaining Foucault's popularity, relevance, and quotability.

These truisms most certainly applied to me when I first read *Surveiller et punir* (Foucault, 1975) as a student of Romance Philology more than 20 years ago. Foucault's graceful and therapeutic text presented itself as a wide-ranging critique of mechanisms I had also seen at work in my strict, Catholic secondary school. Almost 20 years later, when I returned to *Surveiller et punir* – and specifically to the chapter 'Les moyens du bon dressement' – for both a conference talk (to be given in English) and for an MA course on discourse (to be taught in Spanish at the University of Oslo, Norway), I looked up Alan Sheridan's (1979) English translation and Aurelio Garzón del Camino's (1983) Spanish version, yet found that these texts were of limited use for my purposes. The Foucault quotes I needed at the conference were, to confirm the cliché, lost in translation, and my Spanish MA class on discourse in Foucault turned toward a discussion more characteristic of my course on Translation Studies. Finally, and much to my students' surprise, the Norwegian version of *Surveiller et punir* only seemed to complicate interpretive matters further.

Issues of translation occasionally surface in Foucault Studies (including the eponymous journal *Foucault Studies*). Clare O'Farrell's (2005, pp. 7–8) *Michel Foucault* mentions 'the slow work of translation', 'the inevitable errors and omissions', 'the translation of fairly commonplace French terms with esoteric Latinate words in English', and the erroneous 'perceptions of Foucault's male-centeredness' in English that 'help explain the considerable differences in the way Foucault is read in France compared with the English speaking world'. Referring to Neumann, O'Farrell also explains that 'the reception of Foucault's work is further complicated in the non-English language world, for example in Scandinavia, by the fact that his work arrives already filtered by the immense Anglo-Saxon literature' (see also Neumann, in Foucault, 2002). In the journal *Foucault Studies*, several recent essays address aspects of translation, though only in passing remarks (Jordan, 2012; Bussolini, 2010).[1] Specifically, in a recent blog post titled 'Is it time for a new translation of Foucault's *Surveiller et punir*?', Stuart Elden (2014) recently assessed the English translation and translator:

> Sheridan deserves enormous credit for the work he did, translating several of Foucault's books and writing that first, important, study of his work. A good many of his translation choices are undoubtedly correct, and many of his phrasings felicitous. However there are several small errors, strange or unhelpful choices, missing words or phrases, and shifts in register that mar the reading. Additionally the frame within which he read and translated Foucault was the 1970s.[2]

Elden is right. Foucault translation is an area that deserves more attention beyond casual remarks, yet also beyond mere calls for retranslation. Foucault translation will always be of interest. In this essay I will therefore compare 'Les moyens du bon dressement' with its English, Spanish, and Norwegian translations; and I will for the most part address issues of translation beyond the blatant errors, in an attempt to show that the translations are not generally 'the same text in a different language', as non-experts in translation might assume.

2. Questions of translation studies

Translation Studies is an academic field that analyzes the impact of translation on societies and hence stresses the importance of studying translation academically as part of cultural and social analysis. The field is vast and contains numerous subparadigms of research.[3] Thus, the core business of the so-called prescriptive subparadigm in Translation Studies is to criticize and analyze translation errors, look for cases of 'translationese' (unidiomatic language in translations), explain how a proper translation should read, and analyze the mechanisms that lead to idiomatic translation.[4] Such 'prescriptive' research is often carried out by scholars who train translators in vocational programs.

As a response to prescriptivism, scholars working in non-vocational academic settings have pointed out that clear-cut ideas about the proper and the good often reflect norms of a certain social group, if not of the prescriptive scholar's personal preferences.

Universities, so non-prescriptivists might argue, are not places for the blind reproduction of linguistic and other norms but for critical reflection on them. Thus, so-called descriptivist scholars of translation (such as Gideon Toury, 1995) avoid becoming involved in normative debates ('this is good, that is bad') and remain at a scholarly, reflective distance from the cultural and social functions and effects of translations. Descriptivists want to know which original works (often called 'source texts') are – or are not – translated in a given period and culture ('target culture'), and why, how, and to what effect. Or, to frame this research agenda in more Foucauldian terms: Can translations tell us if and how regimes of discourse vary from place to place, period to period, and language to language? Do translators adjust to existing regimes or resist them and even instigate new ones? Do discursive regimes (that exist for translation or for a target language) determine if and how texts are translated? Conversely, do translations inform us about powerful regimes of translation?

While many translation scholars have now turned away from what Hermans (1999, p. 36) calls 'scientific jargon and [Toury's] apparent belief in the possibility of attaining objectivity in cultural and historical research' – a scientism which descriptivism inherited from structuralism – these important research questions are still in place. Thus, translation studies may ask which of Michel Foucault's texts are translated (or not), and into which languages, and when, why, how, and to what effect? And do the textual choices of a translator inform us about the translator's agenda and the norms prevailing in the translating culture? For instance, does Dag Østerberg's (Foucault, 1999) Norwegian translation of *Surveiller et punir* inform us about – or even produce – a Norwegian view on Foucault? If so, what made him produce that view, and to what effect? In Foucauldian terms, did Østerberg apply a normalizing – and for him normal – Norwegian discursive regime to Foucault's text, with possibly important cultural effects? These are important questions that I can only begin to answer in this short essay.

I have used the phrase 'Norwegian view on Foucault' to bring home an important assumption from post-prescriptivist Translation Studies: that translations are facts of the target culture (e.g. Norway), language (e.g. Norwegian), and specific discursive regimes (e.g. Norwegian academic language) rather than just a version of a source text (e.g. *Surveiller et punir*) in another language (e.g. *Discipline and Power*; Toury, 1995, pp. 23–29). To be sure, the phrase 'Norway's view on Foucault' is a sweeping generalization, and translation scholars should not quickly suggest there is one homogeneous Norwegian academic view on Foucault (as Neumann shows; Foucault, 2002). Yet (post)descriptivist research in Translation Studies does intend to move beyond individual texts, to see translations as signs of culture. Hence, translational decisions do instantiate and replicate values ('norms' is Toury's preferred term) circulating in Norway; or they resist norms and attempt to produce new ones; or they strike a balance between domestic and foreign influences on any level (form included). For instance, academic Norwegian may be governed by syntactic rules quite unlike the ones underlying Foucault's sentences, and the translator may be caught between Foucault-oriented syntax and fluent academic Norwegian. Cultural theorists of translation such as Lawrence Venuti will assert that translators can resist culturally domesticating trends, that a translator is more than a position subject to norms and forces in a social field; he or she may have agency, that is, a degree of power to perpetuate or change structures.

Such sweeping concepts are a good way of attracting general attention to translation, yet I believe that Translation Studies may already prove relevant – in a more modest way – by offering a discourse analysis of meaningful shifts in translation, arguing its effects, and speculating on causes (cultural norms, language norms, personal agendas, and so on). Thus, Translation Studies may suggest that the translations of key cultural texts have enduring effects on an entire readership, hence the interpretation and reception of a key author, explaining, for example, to readers of the French Foucault why an Anglophone scholar states as a fact that *Discipline and punish* is 'presented, for the most part, in the form of an historical narrative' (Garland, 1986, p. 848). Before suggesting the possible grounds for this statement, let us turn to the translation of Foucauldian concepts.

3. Power: a carve up

The main concepts of *Surveiller et punir* are expressed by a limited series of words, including the nouns *pouvoir*, *discipline* (or the adjective *disciplinaire*), and *surveillance* (or the verb *surveiller*). It is these words, expressed by these signifiers, that pervade the text and that Foucault's discourse turns into powerful concepts. Foucault uses the terms again and again, avoiding misplaced stylistic variation in basic terminology, avoiding alleged synonyms, hyponyms, or hypernyms.[6] *Pouvoir* is *pouvoir* is *pouvoir*, and it is all over the place.[7] The recurrence of basic terms stands for the recurrence of the phenomena they designate and thus expresses the almost asphyxiating, claustrophobic nature of disciplinary power itself. The textual ubiquity of terms gives the readers a sense of how pervasive Foucault's concepts – and their materializations – are in the mindsets and institutions under analysis.

For this effect to arise, Foucault needs to constantly reconcile conceptual diversity and unity. As for unity, on the one hand, terminological recurrence obliges him to keep his concepts sufficiently broad and abstract; or, more positively put, wide-ranging concepts allow for terminological recurrence along the text. As for diversity, on the other hand, every usage of a term at every moment in the text cumulatively enriches the term. Thus, to understand Foucault's notion of *pouvoir*, one should not look for a ready-made definition (in the book or elsewhere) but gradually become acquainted with Foucault's uses of the term throughout the analysis. Unfortunately, however, terminological abstraction – which may come with a degree of vagueness – is not usually appreciated in discursive regimes of translations. Translations in general – and perhaps even more so from Romance into Germanic languages – tend to disambiguate language, or, as Toury's (1995, p. 270; my emphasis) 'law of translational behavior' formulates it somewhat technically:

> In translation, items tend to be selected on a level which is *lower* than the one where textual relations have been established in the source text.

What this means can be illustrated, first, with Foucault's use of *pouvoir* and its Norwegian 'lower' (that is, more specific) counterparts. On the first four pages of 'Les moyens du bon dressement', Foucault (1975, p. 172) argues that *pouvoir* is a productive force; that is, one that produces, uses, and multiplies disciplined subjects:

> Le pouvoir disciplinaire en effet est un pouvoir qui, au lieu de soutirer et de prélever, a pour fonction majeure de "dresser"; ou sans doute, de dresser pour mieux prélever et soutirer davantage. Il n'enchaîne pas les forces pour les réduire; il cherche à les lier de manière, tout ensemble, à les multiplier et à les utiliser. [...] La discipline "fabrique"

des individus; elle est la technique spécifique d'un <u>pouvoir</u> qui se donne les individus à la fois pour objets et pour instruments de son exercice.

[Disciplinary <u>power</u> is indeed a power that "trains," rather than one that extracts and extorts; or actually, one that trains in order to extort and extract all the more. <u>It</u> does not chain forces so as to reduce them; <u>it</u> seeks to bind them, all together, in order to multiply and use them. [...] Discipline "fabricates" individuals; it is the specific technique of a <u>power</u> that uses individuals both as objects and instruments.][8]

In Foucault's argument, this very *pouvoir* uses the visibility of subjects as a crucial device, as in military camps:

Le camp, c'est le diagramme d'un <u>pouvoir</u> qui agit par l'effet d'une visibilité générale. (Foucault, 1975, p. 174)

[The camp is the diagram of a <u>power</u> that works by way of general visibility.]

And this same *pouvoir* is the result of a machinery that controls, observes, and fabricates disciplined and disciplining subjects via hierarchy, visibility, and gazes:

Les institutions disciplinaires ont sécrété une machinerie de contrôle qui a fonctionné comme un microscope de la conduite; les divisions ténues et analytiques qu'elles ont réalisées ont formé, autour des hommes, un appareil d'observation, d'enregistrement et de dressage. Dans ces machines à observer, comment subdiviser les regards, comment établir entre eux des relais, des communications? Comment faire pour que, de leur multiplicité calculée, résulte un <u>pouvoir</u> homogène et continu? (Foucault, 1975, pp. 175–176)

[The disciplinary institutions have secreted a machinery of control that has worked as a microscope for behavior; the fine, analytic divisions they have produced have formed, around men, an apparatus of observation, recording, and training. In these machines of observation, how to subdivide the gazes? How to establish a relay system between them? How to make them communicate? How to arrange it so that a homogeneous, continuous <u>power</u> would result from their calculated multiplicity? (Foucault, 1979, p. 173)[9]]

In Norwegian, by contrast, the productive *pouvoir* of the first excerpt is not the general *makt* ('power') but *øvrighet* ('the authorities'). It is the authorities who produce, use, and multiply disciplined subjects:

Den disiplinære <u>øvrighet</u> er virkelig en øvrighet som i stedet for å utsuge og skattlegge har som hovedoppgave å "dressere," eller rettere sagt: som dresserer for å kunne utpresse og utsuge enda mer. Denne form for <u>øvrighet</u> legger ikke undersåttene i lenker for å redusere deres krefter, men prøver tvert om å kombinere kreftene slik at de som helhet forøkes og kan tas i bruk. [...] Disiplinen "fabrikkerer" individer. Den er en særskilt metode, hvor individene på samme tid er gjenstand og redskap for <u>øvrighetens maktutøvelse</u>. (Foucault, 1977, p. 151)

[The disciplinary <u>authorities</u> are really authorities whose primary task is to "train" rather than to suck out [i.e. exploit] and tax, or more correctly: that train in order to extort and suck out even more. This form of <u>authority</u> does not put its subjects in chains in order to reduce their forces, but on the contrary tries to combine the forces so that, taken together, they are augmented and can be employed. [...] Discipline "fabricates" individuals. It is a distinct method, in which individuals are at the same time object and instrument of <u>the power exercised by the authorities</u>.]

In other words, Foucault's abstract power concept has been disambiguated – made specific – in strictly political terms. The fact that 'authorities' is really meant in

Norwegian is borne out, first, by the phrase *øvrighetens maktutøvelse* ('exercise of power by the authorities') and, second, by later statements about how the political authorities use 'examination':

> Det tales ofte om den "ideologi" som "vitenskapene" om mennesket stillferdig eller høylytt uttrykker. Men selve deres teknologi—nemlig dette lille skjematiske virkemiddel, denne eksaminering som vi er så fortrolige med og som er så utbredt (fra psykiatrien til pedagogikken, fra diagnostisering til hyring av arbeidskraft)—<u>er den ikke et maktmiddel som gjør det mulig for øvrigheten å bemektige seg en del av samfunnsproduktet og samtidig danne vilkår for en art kunnskap? Politikken påvirker ikke bare bevisstheten, forestillingene og det man tror seg å vite, men også selve vilkårene for kunnskap.</u> (Foucault, 1999, p. 163)

> [Mention is often made of the "ideology" silently or loudly expressed by the human "sciences." But this very technology of theirs—that is, this tiny schematic means, this examination we are so familiar with and that is so widespread (from psychiatry to pedagogy, from diagnosis to the hiring of labor)—<u>is it not an instrument of power that makes it possible for the authorities to appropriate a part of what society produces and simultaneously create the conditions for a sort of knowledge? Politics influences not just consciousness, representations, and what one believes one knows but also the very conditions for knowledge.</u>]

The basic interpretive choice (power = authorities) here leads the translator to give an analysis in strict political terms – the political authorities use examination as an instrument to wield disciplinary power – whereas Foucault does not mention politics in this strictest sense:

> On parle souvent de l'idéologie que portent avec elles, de façon discrète ou bavarde, les "sciences" humaines. Mais leur technologie même, ce petit schéma opératoire qui a une telle diffusion (de la psychiatrie à la pédagogie, du diagnostic des maladies à l'embauche de main-d'œuvre); ce procédé si familier de l'examen, <u>ne met-il pas en œuvre, à l'intérieur d'un mécanisme, des relations de pouvoir, qui permettent de prélever et de constituer du savoir? Ce n'est pas simplement au niveau de la conscience, des représentations et dans ce qu'on croit savoir, mais au niveau de ce qui rend possible un savoir que se fait l'investissement politique.</u> (Foucault, 1975, p. 187)

> [One often speaks of the ideology that the human "sciences," either discreetly or talkatively, carry with them. But their very technology, this tiny operational schema that is so widespread (from psychiatry to pedagogy, from the diagnosis of diseases to the hiring of labor), this so familiar examination method, <u>does it not activate, within one single mechanism, power relations that make it possible to extract and constitute knowledge? It is not simply at the level of consciousness, of representations and in what one thinks one knows, but at the level of what makes knowledge possible that political investment happens.</u> (Foucault, 1979, p. 185)[10]]

Rather than saying that *l'examen* is an instrument of strictly political authorities who intend to seize part of what society produces, Foucault's broad 'political' (or 'ideological') analysis claims that this tiny and omnipresent procedure activates relationships of power *throughout* modern disciplinary society.

Also, where Foucault presented the military camp as a model for disciplinary power in general (given its focus on visibility and surveillance), Dag Østerberg's translation once more presents the camp as a model for the power of authorities, this time using a synonym of *øvrighet*:

> Leiren er diagrammet over en <u>myndighet</u> som håndheves ved virkningene av en allmenn synlighet. (Foucault, 1999, p. 152)

[The camp is the diagram of an authority maintained by the effects of a general visibility.]

In times of digital social networking, it is clear that Østerberg's specification is a reduction. Surveillance cameras are everywhere, and constant and pervasive visibility has become a fact of modern disciplinary life, yet the most damaging uses of pictures and recordings are often made instead by private persons and institutions, entities that do not know, understand, or respect the restrictive and reticent stance of democratic authorities bound (in principle) by legal frameworks. And, in fact, we did not need the arrival of the digital era to understand that Foucault's *pouvoir* was meant as a more general concept than is suggested in the Norwegian translation. Even in his own book, with reference to his own material, Foucault makes it perfectly clear that disciplinary power institutes punitiveness *beyond* the juridical framework. Sometimes he calls such power 'infra-punitive' (*infra-penalité*; Foucault, 1975, p. 180), as when school architecture makes pupils visible and when school rules and codes ('infra-laws', we might say) make them guilty though not criminal. Foucault contends that disciplinary power mechanisms pervade modern societies beyond the strictly political and legal: normalization is discipline's major effect, and normalization is extralegal. In short, if *savoir* ('knowledge') is for 'cutting', as Foucault has argued,[11] it seems *pouvoir* is for cutting too, or, actually, for *being* cut. And the more concepts *are* cut, the less they actually cut.

Østerberg's translation does respect the repetition of another key term, *surveillance*, which he translates – quite literally – as *overvåkning*, yet now it is Sheridan's English translation that partially carves up Foucault's single, multi-purpose concept. The underlined terms below both translate the French *surveillance*:

> In the perfect camp, all power would be exercised solely through exact observation; each gaze would form a part of the overall functioning of power. [...] For a long time this model of the camp or at least its underlying principle was found in urban development in the construction of working-class housing estates, hospitals, asylums, prisons, schools: the spatial "nesting" of hierarchized surveillance. (Foucault, 1979, pp. 171–172)[12]

The stability in Norwegian (*overvåkning*) and the variability in English (*observation, surveillance*) may be related to the respective titles of the translations: *Overvåkning og straff: Det moderne fengsels historie* [*Surveillance and punishment: The history of the modern prison*] and *Discipline and punish: The birth of the prison*. Indeed, translators are bound to pay more attention to a term prominently figuring in their title (such as *overvåkning*) than to one that remains absent from the cover (*surveillance*).

On the other hand, the titular presence of concepts has no absolute predictive value, since the English translation of *surveillance* (absent from the English title) remains less variable than the Norwegian one for *pouvoir* (also conceptually absent from the Norwegian title). Other factors seem to play a role. While Østerberg shows a marked bias toward conceptual specificity, Sheridan exhibits a milder one toward stylistic variation. The latter bias may be a case of what Antoine Berman ironically calls *ennoblement*, the misplaced tendency to make a translation assumedly more elegant than the original, thereby avoiding lexical repetition (Berman, 1985).[13] The trouble with such a stance is repetition's relevance.

4. Structure historicized

Foucault's full title, *Surveiller et punir. Naissance de la prison*, prefigures an ambiguity that runs throughout the whole book, and is therefore also present in the chapter under analysis here. David Garland (1986, p. 848) formulates the ambiguity – to which I have already alluded – as follows:

> Despite being subtitled "the birth of the prison" and presented, for the most part, in the form of an historical narrative, the book is not so much a history of punishment as a structural analysis of power, or, to be more exact, of the peculiarly modern form of exercising power Foucault calls "discipline".

The contrast flagged up by Garland is between historical and structural analysis, and it seems that the latter has generally received a better press than the former. Garland (1986, p. 868) contrasts the reticence of historians with the enthusiasm of those seeking structural analysis:

> Characteristically, while sociologists have tended to generalize from Foucault's work, taking up its concepts, developing its logic, and applying it to other materials, historians have been much more hesitant and circumspect.

Despite the historical inaccuracies in Foucault's text (Garland, 1986, pp. 868–872), many scholars (like me) continue to engage with the text as an analytic toolbox for situations unforeseen – and unforeseeable – by Foucault, such as visibility in an age of digital cameras and archiving. Though Foucault seemed to document the birth of modern power (as the *naissance* of his subtitle signposts), he obviously wanted to make a structural analysis (as suggested by the atemporal infinitives of his main title).

The Norwegian and English translations have noticeably wrestled with this ambiguity (or tension) between history and structure. Notice, for one thing, the Norwegian title change from the first 1977 edition (*Det moderne fengsels historie* [*The history of modern prison*]; Foucault, 1977) to the 1994 and 1999 editions (*Overvåkning og straff: Det moderne fengsels historie* [*Surveillance and punishment: The history of the modern prison*]). For another, close inspection of the English translation shows significant tinkering with verb tenses. In the original, Foucault's interest in structural analysis seems so dominant that he usually employs the present tense to report on history. This use of the historical present allows him to weave a discursive fabric that sounds structural and contemporary to the reader even when its object goes back centuries. Sheridan, by contrast, frequently opts for past tenses. He thus historicizes a statement about school buildings (the French historical presents and English past tenses are underlined):

> L'hôpital—celui qu'on veut aménager dans la seconde moitié du siècle, et pour lequel on a fait tant de projets après le second incendie de l'Hôtel-Dieu—n'est plus simplement le toit où s'abritaient la misère et la mort prochaine; c'est, dans sa matérialité même, un opérateur thérapeutique.
> Comme l'école-bâtiment doit être un opérateur de dressage. C'est une machine pédagogique que Pâris-Duverney avait conçue à l'École militaire. (Foucault, 1975, pp. 174–175)
> The Hospital—which was to be built in the second half of the century and for which so many plans were drawn up after the Hôtel-Dieu was burnt down for the second time—was no longer simply the roof under which penury and imminent death took shelter; it was, in its very materiality, a therapeutic operator.
> Similarly, the school building was to be a mechanism for training. It was as a pedagogical machine that Pâris-Duverney conceived the École Militaire. (Foucault, 1977, p. 172)

Sheridan also fully historicizes Foucault concerning the *regard disciplinaire*, the disciplinary gaze (and I underline again the French historical presents versus the English past tenses):

> Mais le regard disciplinaire a eu, de fait, besoin de relais. [...] Il lui <u>faut</u> décomposer ses instances, mais pour majorer sa fonction productrice. Spécifier la surveillance et la rendre fonctionnelle. <u>C'est</u> le problème des grands ateliers et des usines, où <u>s'organise</u> un nouveau type de surveillance. Il <u>est</u> différent de celui qui dans les régimes des manufactures était assuré de l'extérieur par les inspecteurs, chargés de faire appliquer les règlements; <u>il s'agit</u> maintenant d'un contrôle intense, continu; il <u>court</u> tout le long du processus de travail; il ne <u>porte</u> pas—ou pas seulement—sur la production (nature, quantité de matières premières, type d'instruments utilisés, dimensions et qualités des produits), mais il <u>prend</u> en compte l'activité des hommes, leur savoir-faire, leur manière de s'y prendre, leur promptitude, leur zèle, leur conduite. Mais il <u>est</u> aussi autre chose que le contrôle domestique du maître, présent à côté des ouvriers et des apprentis; car il <u>est</u> effectué par des commis, des surveillants, des contrôleurs et des contremaîtres. A mesure que l'appareil de production <u>devient</u> plus important et plus complexe, à mesure qu'augmentent le nombre des ouvriers et la division du travail, les tâches de contrôle <u>se font</u> plus nécessaires et plus difficiles. Surveiller <u>devient</u> alors une fonction définie, mais qui <u>doit faire</u> partie intégrante du processus de production. (Foucault, 1975, pp. 175–176)

> But, the disciplinary gaze did, in fact, need relays. [...] It <u>had</u> to be broken down into smaller elements, but in order to increase its productive function: specify the surveillance and make it functional. This <u>was</u> the problem of the great workshops and factories, in which a new type of surveillance <u>was</u> organized. It <u>was</u> different from the one practised in the regimes of the manufactories, which <u>had been carried out</u> from the outside by inspectors, entrusted with the task of applying the regulations; what <u>was</u> now needed was an intense, continuous supervision; it <u>ran</u> right through the labour process; it <u>did</u> not bear—or not only—on production (the nature and quantity of raw materials, the type of instruments used, the dimensions and quality of the products); it also <u>took</u> into account the activity of the men, their skill, the way they <u>set</u> about their tasks, their promptness, their zeal, their behaviour. But it <u>was</u> also different from the domestic supervision of the master present beside his workers and apprentices; for it <u>was carried out</u> by clerks, supervisors and foremen. As the machinery of production <u>became</u> larger and more complex, as the number of workers and the division of labour increased, supervision <u>became</u> ever more necessary and more difficult. It <u>became</u> a special function, which <u>had</u> nevertheless to form an integral part of the production process. (Foucault, 1979, p. 174)

Some might object, first, that, despite its present tenses, even the original clearly addresses a situation that can only be read in historical terms; and, second, that the shift from French historical present to English past tense is simply one of adapting the text to the exigencies of idiomatic English.[14] I hasten to disagree with both objections. First, when Foucault so structurally chooses the historical present, although the past tense is also perfectly available in French, he plainly opts for the possibility that his analysis be read as not purely historical. The choice did not miss its effect, certainly not on me as an undergraduate coming to terms with my secondary school. Second, translators continuously have to strike a balance between the rights of the source text and the exigencies of the audience, so (the publisher and copyeditor permitting) they may decide to overrule idiomaticity for the sake of the source text. In this respect, Schleiermacher has famously said that 'either the translator leaves the writer in peace as much as possible and moves the reader toward him; or he leaves the reader in peace as much as possible and moves the writer toward him' (as cited in Venuti, 2004, p. 49). Or, to use Lawrence Venuti's (2008) words, either translators are prepared to use 'foreignizing' strategies (*casu quo*, abundant use of the historical present) or they decide to 'domesticate' the original according to target-culture discursive regimes.

Regarding *Surveiller et punir*, the latter point is not just a matter of principle and interpretation but also of practice. The translation's domesticating decision to comply with an Anglo-Saxon discourse regime – its preference for English idiomaticity over Foucauldian generalizability – is a strategy that runs through the whole translation of this chapter and therefore makes much of 'Les moyens du bon dressement' unquotable for purposes of structural analysis, as I learned when preparing a conference for an international audience. Compare the generality in Foucault's original sentences – which I considered quoting with reference to contemporary situations – to Sheridan's English versions, which are hardly quotable because they are non-general, particularizing, and historical:

L'école <u>devient</u> une sorte d'appareil d'examen ininterrompu qui <u>double</u> sur toute sa longueur l'opération d'enseignement. (Foucault, 1975, p. 188)

[The school <u>became</u> a sort of apparatus of uninterrupted examination that <u>duplicated</u> along its entire length the operation of teaching. (Foucault, 1979, p. 186)]

L'examen <u>porte avec soi</u> tout un mécanisme qui <u>lie</u> à une certaine forme d'exercice du pouvoir un certain type de formation de savoir. (Foucault, 1975, p. 189)

[The examination <u>introduced</u> a whole mechanism that <u>linked</u> to a certain type of the formation of knowledge a certain form of the exercise of power. (Foucault, 1979, p. 187)]

L'examen <u>intervertit</u> l'économie de la visibilité dans l'exercice du pouvoir. (Foucault, 1975, p. 189)

[The examination <u>transformed</u> the economy of visibility into the exercise of power. (Foucault, 1979, p. 187)]

La discipline [...] <u>a</u> son propre type de cérémonie. Ce n'<u>est</u> pas le triomphe, c'<u>est</u> la revue, c'<u>est</u> la "parade," forme fastueuse de l'examen. Les "sujets" y <u>sont offerts</u> comme "objets" à l'observation d'un pouvoir qui ne se <u>manifeste</u> que par son seul regard. (Foucault, 1975, p. 188)

[Discipline [...] <u>had</u> its own type of ceremony. It <u>was</u> not the triumph, but the review, the "parade," an ostentatious form of the examination. In it the "subjects" <u>were presented</u> as "objects" to the observation of a power that <u>was manifested</u> only by its gaze.]

Pendant longtemps [...] la chronique d'un homme, le récit de sa vie, son historiographie rédigée au fil de son existence faisaient partie des rituels de sa puissance. Or les procédés disciplinaires <u>retournent</u> ce rapport, <u>abaissent</u> le seuil de l'individualité descriptible et <u>font</u> de cette description un moyen de contrôle et une méthode de domination. (Foucault, 1975, p. 193)

[For a long time [...] the chronicle of a man, the account of his life, his historiography, written as he lived out his life, formed part of the rituals of his power. The disciplinary methods <u>reversed</u> this relation, <u>lowered</u> the threshold of describable individuality and <u>made</u> of this description a means of control and a method of domination.[15] (Foucault, 1979, p. 191)]

The translations are not just biased and biasing – historicized and historicizing – readings. They are also unquotable texts, to the extent that reversing all tenses (with the requisite square brackets, e.g. 'The school [becomes] a sort of apparatus') would look suspiciously like tinkering with Foucault's original. Alternatively, reversing tenses *without* square brackets while adding 'translation adapted' was also met with suspicion by some.

5. From *syntaxe* to syntax, and power for dummies

Compare, again, Foucault's original with the Spanish, English, and Norwegian translations being discussed here:

> L'exercice de la discipline suppose un dispositif qui contraigne par le jeu du regard. (Foucault, 1975, p. 173)

> El ejercicio de la disciplina supone un dispositivo que coacciona por el juego de la mirada. (Foucault, 1983, p. 175)

> The exercise of discipline presupposes a mechanism that coerces by means of observation. (Foucault, 1979, p. 170)

> For å holde disiplin må man kunne tvinge ved hjelp av blikket. (Foucault, 1999, p. 152)

The constant recurrence of terms as discussed in Section 3 – in this quotation *discipline*, *dispositif*, and *regard* – could turn stylistically awkward in hands less dexterous than Foucault's. Yet it is mostly the syntax of *Surveiller et punir* that makes it rhythmic and quotable, hingeing in part on the strong tendency in French to nominalize; that is, to use nouns rather than verbs.[16] Thus, fluent French will opt for <u>L'exercice</u> de la discipline suppose [The exercise of discipline presupposes [...]] rather than Pour <u>exercer</u> la discipline il faut [In order to exercise discipline one must [...]]. What we find here is an instance of what Vinay and Darbelnet (1977, p. 102, my translation) call the 'predominance of nouns in French', which Foucault exploits to write an elegant, quotable French academic sentence. Since English has no such dominance, according to Vinay and Darbelnet, idiomatic French translations of English texts will often have to 'transpose'; that is, change from one word class to another. According to Vinay and Darbelnet, transpositions from English to French should happen from 'verb to noun', and conversely, they imply, French-to-English translation will have to resort to noun-to-verb transposition. In fact, noun-to-verb transposition (or *denominalization*) generally occurs in translations from Romance languages (e.g. French, Spanish) into Germanic ones (e.g. English, Norwegian, Dutch). So while it was foreseeable that the Spanish translation above would not denominalize the French original, the English version may be thought to actually resist an English call for idiomaticity (i.e. denominalization) or, less favorably, to remain unaware of this call (which happens to infelicitous translators, in Vinay and Darbelnet's prescriptivist logic).

While Vinay and Darbelnet (1995, p. 94) first claim that 'the same meaning can be conveyed by different word classes', they immediately hasten to add that 'the reality facing translators is quite different'. I would agree with the second, qualifying part of their statement only. Just reconsider Østerberg's Norwegian translation, *For å holde disiplin må man kunne tvinge ved hjelp av blikket* (literally, So as to keep discipline one must be able to force by means of the gaze). To be sure, the Norwegian sounds much more idiomatic than my English gloss suggests, but that is exactly the point. Østerberg has apparently listened to a call for idiomaticity coming from the Norwegian discursive regime: Germanic languages tend to denominalize Romance structures, hence Østerberg will denominalize Foucault's sentence. And, to pick up on Vinay and Darbelnet, the denominalized outcome offers far from 'the same meaning' in a 'different word class'. Power for dummies: that is roughly how Foucault's sentence sounds in Norwegian. Call it the introductory how-to guide to disciplinary power: one must train one's gaze as a first step to enforce discipline. The sentence could have been taken out of the very handbooks Foucault is attempting to dissect. What is an author, indeed.

6. Blatant errors are harmless

Of course, there are also plain errors to be noted, which should be corrected in each new edition (especially the Spanish one). In French and Spanish we read, for example, that surveillance, on which disciplinary power hinges, is hierarchically organized. But then compare the specifics of the analysis in French and Spanish (underlined):

> [S]'il est vrai que la surveillance repose sur des individus, son fonctionnement est celui d'un réseau de relations de haut en bas, mais aussi jusqu'à un certain point de bas en haut et latéralement; ce réseau fait "tenir" l'ensemble, et le traverse intégralement d'effets de pouvoir qui prennent appui les uns sur les autres: surveillants perpétuellement surveillés. (Foucault, 1975, p. 179)[17]

> [S]i es cierto que la vigilancia reposa sobre individuos, su funcionamiento es el de un sistema de relaciones de arriba abajo, pero también hasta cierto punto de abajo arriba y lateralmente. Este sistema hace que "resista" el conjunto, y lo atraviesa íntegramente por efectos de poder que se apoyan unos sobre otros: vigilantes perpetuamente vigilados. (Foucault, 1983, p. 183)

In both languages Foucault's imagistic discourse states that the whole of surveillance-based power (*l'ensemble* in French; *el conjunto* in Spanish) has great strength (is 'held together' in French; 'resists' in Spanish), but only the French text explains why this is so: while in French it is the very 'network' (*réseau*) of disciplinary power that holds things together (*fait 'tenir' l'ensemble*), in Spanish it is the 'system' (*sistema*) that somehow 'resists', and we have to read *vigilantes perpetuamente vigilados* [supervisors, perpetually supervised] before we really understand the two preceding sentences. Even so, the French claustrophobic image of an internally regimented and untouchably closed network is replaced in Spanish by the image of a system that is able to hold out against external forces.

Errors also include connectives, which are obviously instrumental to Foucault's reasoning. Compare, again, the underlined parts:

> L'exercice de la discipline suppose un dispositif qui contraigne par le jeu du regard; un appareil où les techniques qui permettent de voir induisent des effets de pouvoir, et où, en retour, les moyens de coercition rendent clairement visibles ceux sur qui ils s'appliquent. (Foucault, 1975, p. 173)

> El ejercicio de la disciplina supone un dispositivo que coacciona por el juego de la mirada; un aparato en el que las técnicas que permiten ver inducen efectos de poder y donde, de rechazo, los medios de coerción hacen claramente visibles aquellos sobre quienes se aplican. (Foucault, 1983, p. 175)

The Spanish translation adheres so closely to the original that a word-for-word comparison is possible. Parallel reading is almost a way for francophones to learn Spanish vocabulary here; except that *en retour* ('in turn', or perhaps 'conversely', as Sheridan writes[18]) does not translate as *de rechazo* [incidentally]. Now this may be a minor issue for absolute beginners of Spanish but not for the current argument: in Foucault's explanation it is *not at all* incidental to disciplinary power that coercion makes subjects visible. Instruments of coercion (e.g. *l'examen*) are an essential part of disciplinary power since they make subjects visible and hence induce in them a feeling of being controlled and have normalizing power over them.

Another excerpt – already quoted above for its narrowly politicized Norwegian translation, where *pouvoir* was translated not as 'power' but as 'the authorities' – is also partly incomprehensible in its English version. In the original, Foucault insisted that the politics of knowledge, its ideology, occurs 'not simply at the level of consciousness, of representations and in what one thinks one knows', but that 'political investment' also happens 'at the level of what makes knowledge possible' (my translation). In other words, the politics or ideology of knowledge refers not only to the knowledge that is produced but also, crucially, to the conditions and ways of knowledge production:

> Ce n'est pas simplement au niveau de la conscience, des représentations et dans ce qu'on croit savoir, mais au niveau de ce qui rend possible un savoir que se fait l'investissement politique. (Foucault, 1975, p. 187).

This idea is impossible to infer from Sheridan's translation:

> It is not simply at the level of consciousness, of representations and in what one thinks one knows, but at the level of what makes possible the knowledge that is transformed into political investment. (Foucault, 1979, p. 185)

It bears repeating: the original's syntax is for advanced learners. Yet Foucault's syntactic riddles do have a solution, while Sheridan leaves us in linguistic limbo.

Errors can of course be even more blatant; as in the Norwegian version, when the subsection numbers on page 159 inexplicably jump from 2 to 5. Such plain errors in important books by recognized publishers (Penguin, Siglo XXI, Gyldendal) may astonish readers. Importantly, however, such errors are often less influential than consistent biases in translation. Blatant errors will be noted and signaled by readers, missing punctuation can be added by each individual reader, and awkward syntax will not be quoted or remembered, and may even be publicly corrected by expert readers.[19] By contrast, Translation Studies has shown in a variety of discourse domains that coherently biased translations will often remain unquestioned, thus perhaps 'reproducing culture' (i.e. its own) under the guise of 'reproducing knowledge' (i.e. another's).

7. *Merci* to mercy

Translators, many of my readers may now object, generally play a constructive role in society since they are agents of intercultural dialogue who render a service to communities and individuals that could otherwise not converse. My argument, it seems, has cast translators in a quite negative role, perhaps as agents who have willfully domesticated the original text, adapting it to homegrown standards and values, producing the self under the guise of reproducing the other. However, the argument I intend to make here is more complicated, in at least two ways.

First, while there are obviously many cases in which translators serve domesticating agendas (see, for instance, Rundle & Sturge, 2010; Vandaele, 2015), there can be no doubt that the overall purpose of the Foucault translators under analysis was to render their respective linguistic communities an academic service. They made an iconic scholarly French text available to non-francophone readerships, to potentially millions of readers. And while serving those readers, translators continuously have to choose between fidelity (to the original) and acceptability (for the new readers). They make hundreds of thousands of choices for each text, and by and large they serve both their readers and the original. While I can easily allow myself to propose stylistically awkward academic 'glosses' of Foucault's text (that is, faithful literal translations that do not necessarily sound elegant), the translators of a commercial publication will usually run a much greater risk with such a strategy. Thus, the *traduttore traditore* cliché expresses a real threat to them: translators run risks with every choice.

Consider the potential conflict between style and concept. From a stylistic viewpoint, some readers might criticize Sheridan, Østerberg, and Garzón del Camino for having delivered 'awkward', 'translationese', 'unnatural', or 'unidiomatic' sentences and phrases. Thus, one Norwegian MA student commented in class that the sentence *Disiplinen 'fabrikkerer' individer* [Discipline 'fabricates' individuals] (Foucault, 1999, p. 151)[21] sounded artificial in Norwegian, because *fabrikkerer* sounded 'odd', and that she preferred Sheridan's 'Discipline "makes" individuals' (Foucault, 1979, p. 170). From a conceptual viewpoint, on the other hand, Sheridan might be criticized for *not* having chosen 'fabricates', especially since Foucault already used quotation marks that mitigated the strangeness of the French term in the present context. It is a Catch 22: whatever one decides, there will always be an angle from which to criticize a translation, since choosing one option means *not* choosing another option; the one that others may prefer. Regarding Foucault, specifically, how to choose at all between style and concept, beauty and fidelity? How to find a gracious style that would remain conceptually faithful? Foucault translators often have to choose between the ugly faithful translation or the *belle infidèle*, as when they find wordplay without perfect equivalents in their languages. An example here is Foucault's play on *objet* and *sujet*, which only Sheridan could reproduce:

> [L'examen] manifeste l'assujettissement de ceux qui sont perçus comme des objets et l'objectivation de ceux qui sont assujettis. (Foucault, 1975, p. 187)

> [The examination] manifests the subjection of those who are perceived as objects and the objectification of those who are subjected. (Foucault, 1979, pp. 184–185)

> [El examen] manifiesta el sometimiento de aquellos que se persiguen como objetos y la objetivación de aquellos que están sometidos. (Foucault, 1983, p. 189)

> [Eksaminasjon] manifesterer underkuelsen av dem som oppfattes som objekter, og objektgjøringen av dem som underkues. (Foucault, 1999, p. 162)

When a translation is unquestionably bona fide, the task of Translation Studies is not to attack the translator but to show that the translation was only one interpretation, show which other interpretations are therefore abandoned, indicate the possible consequences of this choice and abandonment, speculate about its causes, and spark a debate about partial or total retranslation; not necessarily better but new and different. In our case, re-translators could follow Neumann's lead (Foucault, 2002) and use paratexts to inform readers about the roads they could or did not take, though Foucault possibly took them.

Second, and also going against easy accusations, it is important to distinguish between the translator's intentions and the translational effects (carved up concepts, shifts from the structural to the historical and to instruction book style, etc.). As I argued, translation research may prove relevant in a modest way by arguing the effects of key translations even if one can only speculate on the causes (e.g. personal agendas) of these effects. A translator may intend to remain faithful to the spirit of Foucault yet produce a translation that needs to be read critically. Of Dag Østerberg, for instance, we know that he was Norway's leading left-wing ('radical'; Kalleberg, 2009, February 13) sociologist from the 1960s until the end of the twentieth century, and it may have made sense for him, perhaps even from an empathic Foucauldian position, to translate *pouvoir* as 'authorities' rather than 'power' and to clarify Foucauldian language. After all, Foucault saw his work as toolboxes (*boîtes à outils*) for others to use and so break up systems of power (Foucault, 1994, p. 720). Yet this should not blind us to the fact that Dag Østerberg's much-praised 'clarity of writing' (Kalleberg 2009) – a compelling regime of discourse in intellectual Norway since the 1968 generation (Foucault, 2002, p. 27) – could push Foucault into the corner of instruction-book style while also diminishing the conceptual range, and hence power, of *pouvoir*. Similarly, Elden (2014) notes the many virtues of Sheridan's work yet rhetorically asks: 'Is it time for a new translation of Foucault's *Surveiller et punir*?' The more significant the original, the more a translation, however admirable, will call for what seems a foe but is a fellow: a new translation, a fresh interpretation.

Acknowledgements

I received valuable feedback from this journal's anonymous referees as well as from Christian Refsum, Kristiina Taivalkoski, Mieke Neyens, Jon Roglien, Dina Roll-Hansen, Cecilia Alvstad, Stig Oppedal, and Susan Bassnett (who encouraged me to aim at a readership beyond Translation Studies). I also wish to thank the European Humanities Research Center (University of Oxford) for inviting me to present and publish this paper. This research is financed by the project Voices of Translation (Research Council of Norway and the University of Oslo; project 213246).

Disclosure statement

No potential conflict of interest was reported by the author.

Notes

1. For occasional remarks on a number of Foucault translations, see also http://www.michel-foucault.com/trans/
2. Elden's blog entry was posted after I first delivered my paper. I should thank an anonymous referee of *Perspectives* for alerting me to this text.
3. One of the most accessible and stimulating overviews is Anthony Pym's (2010) *Exploring translation theories*. Incidentally, while Pym was preparing his doctoral thesis in sociology at the Parisian École des Hautes Études en Sciences Sociales in the early 1980s, he also took the chance to attend some of Foucault's last lectures (personal communication, March 26, 2009.). A valuable one-stop introduction to the field is Baker and Saldanha (2008).
4. A classic example of prescriptivism I will use below is Vinay and Darbelnet (1995), originally published in French in 1958.
6. Hyponymy is 'the relation which holds between a more specific, or subordinate, lexeme, as exemplified by such pairs as "cow" : "animal", "rose" : "flower." […] Let us say then that "cow" is a hyponym of "animal"' (Lyons, 1977, p. 291). Thus, we might say that since 'authority' is a specific form of 'power', then 'authority' is the hyponym (the 'under-word') and 'power' is the hypernym (the 'over-word') of the other term.

7. As Clare O'Farrell (2005, p. 96) writes, 'Foucault's name is linked most famously with the notion of power'. While the notion is omnipresent in *Surveiller and punir* and stays prominent in later work, Foucault's views on power obviously evolved: from discursive power and power-knowledge (*savoir-pouvoir*), through disciplinary power, to 'biopower', Foucault's term for 'the techniques of managing the life and death of populations' (O'Farrell, 2005, p. 105).
8. All translation glosses between square brackets are mine.
9. This gloss is adapted from Foucault (1979, p. 173); that is, Sheridan's translation.
10. Again, my gloss is adapted from Foucault (1979, p. 185). Note also that Foucault, unlike Østerberg, does not put quotation marks around the word *idéologie*.
11. 'C'est que le savoir n'est pas fait pour comprendre, il est fait pour trancher', Foucault (1971, p. 160) famously wrote in his 'Nietzsche, la généalogie, l'histoire'.
12. The original goes as follows: 'Dans le camp parfait, tout le pouvoir s'exercerait par le seul jeu d'une <u>surveillance</u> exacte; et chaque regard serait une pièce dans le fonctionnement global du pouvoir. [...] Longtemps on retrouvera dans l'urbanisme, dans la construction des cités ouvrières, des hôpitaux, des asiles, des prisons, des maisons d'éducation, ce modèle du camp ou du moins le principe qui le sous-tend: l'emboîtement spatial des <u>sur-veillances</u> hiérarchisées' (Foucault, 1975, p. 173).
13. For an English translation, see Venuti (2004).
14. In regard to idiomaticity, translation scholars Vinay and Darbelnet refer to Hillaire Belloc, who describes the historical present 'as a form which is alien to the nature of English', and conclude that 'though the *présent historique* occurs in English, it is much less frequent in English than in French. Translators must therefore use their discretion' (Vinay & Darbelnet, 1995, p. 134). The book dates from 1958, but one can find similar statements from more recent studies on Romance languages. In Spanish, for instance, 'the present tense is used much more than in English to refer to the past [...] This device is usually restricted to popular English' (Butt & Benjamin, 2011, p. 204). In recent times, Susan Bassnett informs me, the historical present seems to become a more fashionable – though still controversial – stylistic device, as in Mantel (2009) [personal communication, October 1, 2013].
15. Notice also, in the third quotation, the error of translating *intervertir* [to invert] as 'to transform'.
16. Foucault can start with a noun – say *le pouvoir disciplinaire* – and continue at will with its pronominal substitute: 'Il n'enchaîne pas, [...] il cherche, [...] il sépare, analyse, différencie, pousse. [...] Il "dresse"' (Foucault, 1975, p. 172).
17. Sheridan's translation is accurate: 'although surveillance rests on individuals, its functioning is that of a network of relations from top to bottom, but also to a certain extent from bottom to top and laterally; this network "holds" the whole together and traverses it in its entirety with effects of power that derive from one another: supervisors, perpetually supervised' (Foucault, 1979, p. 179).
18. 'The exercise of discipline presupposes a mechanism that coerces by means of observation; an apparatus in which the techniques that make it possible to see induce effects of power, and in which, <u>conversely</u>, the means of coercion make those on whom they are applied clearly visible' (Foucault, 1979, p. 171).
19. See, for instance, http://www.michel-foucault.com/trans/dp.html for the following correction of Sheridan's above-mentioned translation from Foucault, *Surveiller et punir*, p. 187: 'It is not simply at the level of consciousness, of representations and in what one thinks one knows, but at the level of that which makes a knowledge possible that political investment occurs'. Interestingly, I discovered this correction after detecting the error myself, which demonstrates its visibility and hence its relative harmlessness.
21. It is Østerberg's translation of Foucault's (1975, p. 172) 'La discipline "fabrique" des individus'.

References

Baker, M., & Saldanha, G. (Eds.). (2008). *Routledge encyclopedia of translation studies* (2nd ed.). London: Routledge.
Berman, A. (1985). La traduction comme épreuve de l'étranger. *Texte, 4*, 67–81.
Blommaert, J. (2005). *Discourse: A critical introduction*. Cambridge: Cambridge University Press.
Bussolini, J. (2010). What is a dispositive? *Foucault Studies, 10*, 85–107.
Butt, J., & Benjamin, C. (2011). *A new reference grammar of modern Spanish* (5th ed.). London: Hodder Education.
Elden, S. (2014). Beyond 'Discipline and Punish': Is it time for a new translation of Foucault's 'Surveiller et punir'? Retrieved from http://progressivegeographies.com/2014/01/22/beyond-discipline-and-punish-is-it-time-for-a-new-translation-of-foucaults-surveiller-et-punir/
Fish, S. (2011). *How to write a sentence: And how to read one*. New York, NY: HarperCollins.
Foucault, M. (1971). Nietzsche, la généalogie, l'histoire. In S. Bachelard, G. Canguilhem, & F. Dagognet (Eds.), *Hommage à Jean Hyppolite* (pp. 145–172). Paris: Presses Universitaires de France.
Foucault, M. (1975). *Surveiller et punir. Naissance de la prison*. Paris: Gallimard.
Foucault, M. (1977). *Det moderne fengsels historie* (D. Østerberg, Trans.). Oslo: Gyldendal.
Foucault, M. (1979). *Discipline and punish: The birth of the prison* (A. Sheridan, Trans.). London: Peregrine Books.
Foucault, M. (1983). *Vigilar y castigar: Nacimiento de la prisión* (A. Garzón del Camino, Trans.) México DF: Siglo XXI.
Foucault, M. (1994). Des supplices aux cellules [From public executions to prison cells]. In D. Defert, F. Ewald, & J. Lagrange (Eds.), *Dits et écrits 1954–1988* [Sayings and writings 1954–1988] (Vol. 2) 716–720. Paris: Gallimard.
Foucault, M. (1999). *Overvåkning og straff: Det moderne fengsels historie* (D. Østerberg, Trans.). Oslo: Gyldendal.
Foucault, M. (2002). *Forelesninger om regjering og styringskunst* (I. B. Neumann, Trans.). Oslo: Cappelen akademisk.
Garland, D. (1986). Foucault's discipline and punish: An exposition and critique. *Law & Social Inquiry, 11*, 847–880. doi:10.1111/j.1747-4469.1986.tb00270.x
Hermans, T. (1999). *Translation in systems: Descriptive and systemic approaches explained*. Manchester: St. Jerome.
Jordan, M. D. (2012). Foucault's ironies and the important earnestness of theory. *Foucault Studies 14*, 7–19.
Kalleberg, R. (2009, February 13). Dag Østerberg. In *Norsk biografisk leksikon. Store norske leksikon*. Retrieved November 29, 2013, from http://nbl.snl.no/Dag_%C3%98sterberg
Lyons, J. (1977). *Semantics*. Cambridge: Cambridge University Press.
Mantel, H. (2009). *Wolf Hall*. London: Fourth Estate.
O'Farrell, C. (1997). Translation: Discipline and punish. Retrieved from http://www.michel-foucault.com/trans/dp.html
O'Farrell, C. (2005). *Michel Foucault*. London: Sage.
Pym, A. (2010). *Exploring translation theories*. London: Routledge.
Rundle, C., & Sturge, K. (Eds.). (2010). *Translation under fascism*. Basingstoke: Palgrave-MacMillan.
Toury, G. (1995). *Descriptive translation studies and beyond*. Amsterdam: Benjamins.
Vandaele, J. (2015). *Estados de Gracia. Billy Wilder y la censura franquista (1946–1975)* [States of Grace. Billy Wilder and Francoist censorship (1946–1975)]. Leyden & Boston: Brill-Rodopi.
Venuti, L. (2004). *The translation studies reader*. New York, NY: Routledge.
Venuti, L. (2008). *The translator's invisibility: A history of translation*. London: Routledge.
Vinay, J.-P., & Darbelnet, J. (1977). *Stylistique comparée du français et de l'anglais: méthode de traduction*. Paris: Didier.
Vinay, J.-P., & Darbelnet, J. (1995). *Comparative stylistics of French and English: A methodology for translation*. Amsterdam: John Benjamins.

Censoring Lolita's sense of humor: when translation affects the audience's perception

Patrick Zabalbeascoa

There are numerous reasons for taking an academic interest in both Nabokov's (1955/2000) novel, *Lolita*, and Kubrick's (1962) film adaptation. Not least of these is their work *per se*, its quality (in both senses of the word) despite any controversy due to the theme chosen. Both works are growing in prestige. These artists have a knack for provocation, wittingly or unwittingly is beside the point, but provocation alone is surely not enough for them to emerge as giants of literature and filmmaking. The point of interest for the present study is the humorous nature of their work, and how that relates back to the nature of humor, and how all of this is relevant to translation studies, as illustrated in a handful of examples. A useful measure for this quest is Adrian Lyne's (1997) film, claiming as it does to be a more faithful rendering of the book than Kubrick's. Kubrick and Lyne coincide in much of Nabokov's novel, but only Kubrick's is (classified as) comedy. All other things being equal, by and large, this provides insight into the nature of humor (in comedy) and the benefits of translating it comically, to fit the genre of comedy, and as an element of other texts. We also find that sex and taboo are alluded to by Kubrick in words and images, whereas Lyne is more visually explicit. The aim is to show a case study of how censorship, taboo and ideological misconceptions of an author's work can affect its perception by the public, so that it becomes unclear whether popular images of Lolita as a fictional character are a cause or a consequence of certain translations and new film versions such as Adrian Lyne's.

In Woody Allen's *Bananas*, in the scene in the porn shop, he says, 'I'm doing a sociological study on perversion. I'm up to advanced child-molesting.' This has been changed [in the German version] to: I'm up to sexual offenses to mules. (Ebert, 1997, p. 78)

1. Introduction

Stanley Kubrick's (1962) *Lolita* has long been considered something of a critical failure (Duckett, 2014, p. 528). Duckett's opening sentence is argued against throughout her paper all the way to the conclusion, where she says, among other things, 'I would argue that we are also implicated as senseless critics' (2014, p. 539). There are numerous reasons for taking an academic interest in both Vladimir Nabokov's (1955) novel, *Lolita*, and Stanley Kubrick's film adaptation. Not least of these, above and beyond any morbid controversy, is the interest *per se* of their work and its quality (in both senses of the word). *Lolita* is included, for instance, in *Time's* (Grossman & Lacayo, 2005) List of the 100 Best Novels in the English language since 1923 (when *Time* started). Both artists have a knack for provocation, wittingly or unwittingly is beside the point, but provocation alone is surely not enough for them to emerge as giants of literature and filmmaking. The points of interest for the present study are: (i) the humorous nature of their work, how this informs the nature of humor; and (ii) the importance of its relevance to translation studies, as illustrated below in a handful of representative examples. A useful measure for this methodological venture is Adrian Lyne's (1997) film, claiming as it does to be a more faithful rendering of the book than Kubrick's. Kubrick and Lyne coincide in much of Nabokov's novel, but only Kubrick's is (classified as) comedy. Schuman (1978) points out 'Kubrick's quite wild and often grotesque dark humor' (p. 198), hopefully illustrated in the examples analysed here. I am not claiming to have discovered Kubrick's comic intent; I am just stating its importance (or not, as may be the case for some translators) from the point of view of translation, and how and why it might appear and disappear in certain translations. All other things being equal, by and large, this provides insight into the nature of humor (at least in comedy) and the benefits of translating it with a sense of humor, either to fit the genre of comedy or as a key feature of other text types. Viewers also find that sex and taboo are only alluded to by Kubrick, whereas Lyne is more visually and verbally explicit. *Lolita* 1962 is used here to refer to Kubrick's adaptation, and *Lolita* 1997 to Adrian Lyne's. The aim of this study is to present an example of how taboo and misconceptions of an author's work can affect its perception by the public, so that it is not clear whether popular images of Lolita as a fictional character are a cause or a consequence of certain translations and new film versions such as Adrian Lyne's. The following quote supports the methodology used in analysing the examples and the claim that there is something worthwhile in *Lolita* 1962[1], especially when compared to *Lolita* 1997.

> In many respects *Lolita* [1962] might be considered an essential movie in the establishment of Kubrick's reputation as a provocative filmmaker, as well as making him aware of the subtleties of censorship. The movie [...] underlined the limits imposed to filmmakers who tried to tackle controversial issues [...] Interestingly, in recent years, critics and scholars are more inclined to reject a hard judgment on the miscarried adaptation [by Kubrick] and on the negative impact of censorship, especially when compared to Adrian Lyne's more faithful *Lolita* adaptation in 1997. (Biltereyst, 2015, p. 140)

The analysis is done within the theoretical framework of audiovisual translation, i.e. the translation of audiovisual texts, including films (Delabastita, 1989; Zabalbeascoa, 2001–2008, among others), assuming that its verbal, nonverbal, audio and visual elements are all textual constituents. The following quote shows how scholars of literary adaptation to film agree with an audiovisual approach to gain insight into audiovisual texts and audiovisual translation alike.

> If we begin the task and start with the screen itself – that is, if we allow ourselves to have visual as well as literary depth – then we might finally have the freedom to let *Lolita* [1962] laugh. (Duckett, 2014, p. 539)

From this point of view of translation within audiovisual semiotics (Chaume, 2001), and the specific language of film as an integral part of audiovisual text composition, any meaningful analysis of audiovisual text and audiovisual translation must take into account the whole range of relationships that can be established between the various textual constituents through different semiotic codes, as Chaume (2001) maintains, including words, paralinguistics, music, photography, and film narrative, as well as camera movements, shots and angles. Zabalbeascoa (2008) proposes (in a way that is perfectly compatible with Chaume, 2001) the relationships that can be established between the (verbal and nonverbal, in any combination) constituent elements of audiovisual texts (complementarity, redundancy, contradiction, incoherence, separability, and aesthetic quality) used to compose any audiovisual text. The second analytical tool is that of humor studies from an interdisciplinary theoretical approach, such as Attardo's (2001) general theory of verbal humor (GTVH) – without going into an explicit account of this theory for lack of space – and its application within translation studies (Attardo, 2002; Chiaro, 1992; Zabalbeascoa, 2005). The goal here is not to make any strong claims about the quality of humor translation in subtitles, based on a substantial corpus of instances, but to raise awareness of how a relatively large number of important issues and factors (humor, translation, sensitive issues, literary film adaptations) converge and interplay in very specific small instances of interlingual subtitles, in a case study of important scenes within *Lolita* 1962. If there is a claim to be made it is that the examples of important scenes and their analysis are interesting enough in their own right, both for purely theoretical thinking and for applied studies (Holmes, 1972), regardless of their statistical relevance.

2. Kubrick and Lyne: films, styles, themes

Before we even go into a textual analysis of this case study, which can hardly escape from the subjectivity of textual interpretation (Richards, 2012; Duckett, 2014; Biltereyst, 2015), we can see that there are some aspects of Kubrick and Lyne that seem to support the claims of this study. One remarkable fact is Nabokov's involvement in Kubrick's film and his ultimate approval of the final result, notwithstanding all the constraints of prejudice and censorship at the time (Biltereyst, 2015). Another one is drawn from a quick comparison of the two directors' filmographies. *Lolita* 1997 is part of Lyne's 'sex sells' commercial strategy, with the addendum that sex combined with scandal sells even more. Lyne's titles are great feats of synthesis of this strategy. Furthermore, Lyne's female characters often carry some blame for their tribulations. *Flashdance* (1983) depicts a bright 18 year-old girl with a welding job who supplements her day job by doing erotic dancing by night. *Fatal Attraction* (1987) shows a woman involved in adultery which develops into stalking, obsession and crime. His *9 1/2 Weeks* (1986) deals with female masochism. *Indecent Proposal* (1993) is about both members of a married couple consenting to hire out the wife's sexual services for a night if the price is right. *Lolita* 1997 was Lyne's next film. And after that, *Unfaithful* (2002) adds to Lyne's recurrent theme of shady sex in domestic settings with highly dubious moral standards: most frequently, adultery or sex for money. *Lolita* 1997 could be said to fit into this pattern because it features adultery compounded with crimes of child abduction, incest and paedophilia, but it also seems to be consistent with Lyne's tendency to 'blame' his female characters somewhat.

Lyne's Lolita is an underage seductress, a slutty nymphet, very much in line with popular imagery of a Lolita stereotype, and Humbert Humbert's definition of nymphets. This is not Nabokov's (1955) Lolita, however, who remains blameless throughout the book. Humbert Humbert is the sick perverted criminal character of the novel.

The interest and fascination of the character lies essentially in the literary point of view. The book is written as a first-person confession, and it is only natural for the fictional writer to wish to justify to some extent his behaviour, or at least raise some sympathy from the reader. Nabokov's technique of letting the character try to account for his past behaviour is very similar in that respect to other novels; for example, Kazuo Ishiguro's (1989) butler in *The Remain's of the Day*. The difference between the acceptability of the two novels is that nobody would accuse Ishiguro of actually defending his character or being like him, despite the similarities in the books of psychological analysis through the first-person point of view and the ultimate ugliness of the portrayal, clearly showing how the author, in both novels, distances himself from his fictional 'I', largely through irony.

Kubrick tends to draw inspiration from novelists and most of his films (*Paths of Glory*, 1957; *Spartacus*, 1960; *Dr. Strangelove*, 1964; *2001: A Space Odyssey*, 1968; *A Clockwork Orange*, 1971; *Barry Lyndon*, 1975; *The Shining*, 1980; *Full Metal Jacket*, 1987; *Eyes Wide Shut*, 1999) share two common traits that are of interest to the present study and distinguish him quite clearly from Lyne, bringing him closer in these features to Nabokov's *Lolita* in terms of artistic quality: they are among the best films of all time or are highly regarded in some way, and they also show traits of humor, which are clearly present though not always obvious to everyone. Kubrick may not be laden with Academy Awards and box-office triumphs but his films grow in prestige over time; appreciation and praise often appear years later, and never decline. Lyne deliberately seeks controversy and provocation as a commercial strategy, no matter how short-lived. Kubrick shares with Nabokov the curse of controversy and public outrage or incomprehension as a delaying factor in achieving full-deserved acknowledgement for the value of their art. Kubrick and Nabokov agreed to turn the 1962 film into a farce as a reaction to censorship, although pathos runs throughout the film, too. Burke (2003, p. 19) stresses Kubrick's inclination towards 'playfulness and pathos rather than eroticism', no doubt due to the constraints of censorship. This is not to say that Lyne was unconstrained by censorship, simply that each author had to undergo different censorship constraints, which leads one to expect that the same would be the case for each translator:

> There is no doubt that Kubrick and Harris would have made a different picture if there had been no external, institutionalised forms of censorship. The impact of these forces is evident on nearly every level of the film art, including the elaboration of the story line, very concrete actions, on character development, casting, the use (and absence) of very particular words and expressions, or on themes, as well as how very concrete scenes are filmed and edited. (Burke, 2003, p. 17)

3. Sex, crime and taboo. How does humor come into the picture?

The academic challenge of a detached, non-judgmental study of cases like *Lolita* (any version) includes a number of thorny issues, such as the author's humorous treatment of paedophilia or statutory rape (e.g. without attenuating the seriousness of the crime and/or without offending when the intention is not to offend). Related to this is the question of how to portray the characters and their behaviour (e.g. regarding the readership's empathy and sympathy), and how interpretation is affected – for the purposes of translation and taboo – by the fact that in some countries there are arranged marriages and commitments between families affecting extremely young girls or by the observation that the law and the notion of age of consent and women's rights vary across time in the same place as well as across national and cultural borders. A long-standing debate in translation studies is the notion of translatability (i.e. which items and texts, if any, are untranslatable?). Similarly, one might ask if there are topics which cannot be used as material for humor, and how 'offensive' humor is dealt with (and translated), and who decides what can or cannot be used for humor and whether and how it can be translated. Even if we agree that rape is not an appropriate topic to joke about, we can see that what actually constitutes rape is too often culturally bound. Further, jokes about rape can vary considerably according to who is targeted as the butt of the joke, namely the rape victim, the rapist, or third parties who may have some degree of responsibility, such as social groups or institutions. So, just by saying that rape, for example, is a no-go area is not necessarily doing rape victims a favor, but merely turning it into a taboo. One might even say that in dealing with such a topic, Nabokov alerts his readers to the dangers of apparently decent men who are actually monsters in disguise, and how certain social factors (including social taboos, prejudice and hypocrisy) may make women and children more vulnerable and exposed to sexual predators.

Apart from these general theoretical and research questions regarding humor and its translation, there are specific considerations for the *Lolita* versions. In the book there is no real romance, no actual 'healthy' love. This crucial element of the novel is clearer in Kubrick's adaptation because Lyne's decontextualises quotes from the book of the first person narrator (the sick paedophile) mentioning love and the fact that Lolita feels very fond of the lodger who later becomes her stepfather. Tragicomical humor in Nabokov's book and Kubrick's film is carefully couched in a wealth of evidence that the story and its ending are quite sad. In this sense, Kubrick brings the final chapter of the book to the beginning of the film, so there is no doubt that we are being shown the story of a tragic crime, with noone else to blame but the two paedophile characters, Humbert and Quilty, who both prey on a poor hapless girl and ruin her life forever.

What is there in *Lolita* that is worthwhile adapting to film and translating? For Adrian Lyne, the answer seems to be restricted to smuttiness and scandal, mistakenly – according to my reading of Nabokov's novel – based on the theme that child-temptresses can lure men to their doom through sexual provocation (so-called Lolitas, or nymphets), like sirens, really exist. Crucially, the very word 'Lolita', as a noun or an adjective, has taken on a very distinct meaning since Nabokov wrote his famous novel from that which it had before then, and he is only partly to blame for this; the rest of the blame lies in Lyne-like myths created almost as soon as the book came out. Lyne misses, by choice or by oversight, Nabokov's insistence on Lolita's innocence and right to be considered as a tragic victim. Any shortcomings in her personality are carefully explained as being either a normal trait of her age, or very likely the result of some fault of her mother's, the early loss of her real father, and (most definitely) partly a reaction to Humbert's criminal acts towards her. Of course, there is some social criticism, too. However, Nabokov's greatest achievement does not lie in his choice of paedophilia as a topic, but in his fascination for the English language and literary style and figures of speech, including alliteration, parody, wordplay and irony for the purpose of humor (Torres-Nuñez, 2005; Wepler, 2011; Duckett, 2014). Similarly, Kubrick is mostly interested in the art of filmmaking and innovation in film language (Biltereyst, 2015) and modes of expression, including the various possibilities of audiovisual irony.

Both Nabokov and Kubrick are obsessed with detail and perfection in composition, one literary, the other, audiovisual (Duckett, 2014). Nabokov was undoubtedly interested in film as much as Kubrick was keen on literature, so they were both aware that books and film are different modes of expression and require different storytelling strategies. The fact that Lyne follows the narrative structure of the book more closely and includes more direct quotes, then, is probably not enough to make the film necessarily more faithful to the novel, nor (more importantly) a better film, as the Biltereyst quote above points out, even though he has the benefit of being able to draw inspiration from Nabokov and Kubrick, as well as the passage of time, and a more permissive censorship system. It might be said that for Kubrick's project humor becomes a substitute for a more explicit display of images, language, and treatment of topic, especially if compared to Lyne's approach. Compared to the book, Kubrick's audiovisual humor is probably more readily accessible to a wider public. It could be a filmmaking strategy of compensation for a more subtly elaborated kind of humor that works in written literature but requires 'adapting' as the very term film adaptation indicates. These could be important considerations for understanding aspects of Lolita's (1962) dubbed and subtitled versions. It cannot be ruled out that any omissions or changes in the humor of Kubrick's film may be due to ideological or cultural forces or censorship. An alternative or complementary factor could be the translators' grasp of the text and/or their self-appointed duty towards the target-text viewers (moral or aesthetic or whatever). Kubrick certainly uses humor as a substitute for censored explicit images and language (turning it all into a joke since he feels he cannot deal with these issues openly and frankly, not even within artistic fiction). Interpretation and appreciation (by audiences and translators) of Kubrick's *Lolita* no doubt have a lot to do with censorship, culture and ideology.

Also of paramount importance is the realisation that the myth that there are real-life Lolita-nymphets misses the literary 'point of view' that it is a fiction of a sick man's mind. What one cannot know (unless by direct interrogation and unquestioning belief in the answers returned) is what is going on in the translator's mind when confronted with a variety of possible interpretations, with the additional complication that by 'translator' we are often actually referring to anyone and everyone who had any responsibility in the job or who could have edited, censored or supervised the translated text. The translation could be influenced somehow by a preconception or prejudice as regards the whole Lolita concept. Certain shifts and renderings could be a manifestation of incompetence, oversight, personal interpretation, a particular translating ethics or deliberate manipulation. A translation commission could be deliberately assigned to someone who could be expected either not to spoil a popular though possibly mistaken view of what Nabokov and Kubrick were trying to do or to intervene proactively to censor censorable lines and scenes by means of translation 'errors'. In other words, researching such issues and possible motivations, linked to ethics and censorship, is an attempt to frame the difficulty of providing an explanation of how and why humor can be affected in an audiovisual translation where a potentially taboo theme of paedophilia (with the aggravating circumstances of incest, technically speaking) or a smutty theme of pre-teen temptresses may overshadow the comic side of the film to favour a darker side.

4. The targets of Kubrick's jokes. Examples of verbal and audiovisual humor

Humbert is a pathetic, laughable figure who cannot fool anyone except Lolita's mother, and even she sees through him eventually. He is entirely to blame for his crime towards Lolita, just as Quilty is, his antagonist and alter ego, for trying to get her into pornographic films. Lolita's mother, Charlotte, is only guilty of being vain, blind, and 'not smart', but she is also a very lonely widow. Charlotte's friends are caricatured by insinuating extramarital sex, just as in the book several minor characters personify Nabokov's social criticism. Kubrick reserves one of the funniest scenes for Mr. Swine, the hotel night manager, who displays a very particular sense of humor, in one of the clearest illustrations of the difference between the two film versions (examples 5 and 6). The young girl (1962) is not the butt of any joke and Kubrick does not make fun of statutory rape or child molestation victims. Actually, many of the jokes about sex deal with adult (extra)marital sex (e.g. Charlotte's friends' hints), or goings-on in the hotel as narrated by Swine. By contrast, Lyne sees and portrays Lolita as a nymphet, and his Humbert has a certain sad romantic quality about him.

The purpose of the examples that follow is to illustrate the humorous quality of *Lolita* 1962 and how it may fare if its translators do not treat it as an important factor, either inadvertently or as part of a (censoring?) strategy. Bold type is used in the examples to show oral stress or emphasis as performed on screen. Each example includes the synchronised subtitles in German and Spanish (in Appendix 1) from the DVD distributed by Warner Home Video (2001). The film was not dubbed in Spain until 1982 (eldoblaje.com). A 20-year time lapse due to the workings of censorship seems like a feasible hypothesis.

> Example 1. Humbert suddenly agrees to rent a room from Charlotte.
>
> Charlotte – What was the decisive factor? My **garden**?
> Humbert – I think it was your **cherry pies**.

Example 1 is part of a scene that is one of the high moments of the film, as it is love-at-first sight for Humbert, and the first time Lolita is shown (spectacularly) to the audience. Following Chaume (2001) and Zabalbeascoa (2008), there is a meaningful relationship of complementarity between the words spoken, and the nonverbal cues offered by the image (camera shots). Thus, 'cherry pies' seems to refer to Lolita's virginity as Humbert echoes Charlotte's mention of one of the attractions of becoming her lodger, 'I can offer you a comfortable home ... a sunny garden ... a congenial atmosphere ... my cherry pies' (17:01). The camera (nonverbal elements) focuses squarely on Lolita immediately after Humbert's line. The Spanish subtitle is a translation of the literal meaning only, and consequently does not render Humbert's private joke (Charlotte is not meant to grasp it). It does not even carry over the parallel possessives very well (my cherry pies, my garden, your cherry pies). The German subtitles spoil the joke by translating cherry pies with two different renderings: literally, *Kirschkuchen* (17:01) and *Plätzchen* (17:47), German Christmas biscuits. Two audio-visual details support the humoristic interpretation of these words. One is the fact that the camera lingers on Lolita as Humbert says 'your cherry pies'; the other is how both 'my cherry pies' (Charlotte) and 'your cherry pies' (Humbert) are said with noticeable pauses at either end, which makes them stand out verbally and mix in semiotically with Lolita's onscreen beauty and Humbert's irrepressible staring (in what might constitute another, non-verbal visual joke, a travesty of love at first sight). Always important for audiovisual translation is to know whether there are visual restrictions such as a camera shot of the cherry pies, for instance. In this particular case they are not visible at any point, thus providing the translator with an opportunity to explore alternatives that could fit in with the apparent requirement of something like a word to do with attractions for lodgers and a homophone meaning loss of virginity or something so outrageously paedophilic that it would be natural for Lolita's mother not even to contemplate such a rude interpretation, even though the joke would remain accessible to the audience.

> Example 2. Charlotte and Humbert are playing chess. She is struggling, he is bored to tears.
>
> Charlotte – You're going to take my **queen**? (Lolita comes into view, and quietly walks up to lean on Humbert's shoulder)
> Humbert – That was my intention, certainly. (Lolita leaves after saying goodnight to both) [...]
> Humbert – Well, that wasn't very clever of you. (smugly)
> Charlotte – Oh, dear. Oh dear. Ooh! (desperate, as Humbert takes her queen)
> Humbert – It had to happen sometime. (suddenly less bored)

Example 2 is also one of verbal wordplay reinforced by the camera's point of view (fitting the theoretical proposal that camera shots constitute a semiotic code), bringing Lolita into the spectator's view just on cue (complementarity between the word 'queen' and the image of Lolita), as she walks up to Humbert. Charlotte is not clever enough for chess, nor is she capable of seeing Humbert's move to take her other queen, Lolita. The German subtitles use 'attack' rather than 'take/take away' (*meine Königin nehmen/ wegnehmen?*), and the Spanish uses 'eat', quite colloquial for chess, instead of the more technical 'take' (*tomar* or *capturar*), which potentially could have a rude (funny?) interpretation of its own, unlike *attackieren*. In both of these examples, humor is underlined by the background music. This scene can be interpreted as foreshadowing Humbert 'taking' Lolita. The tune becomes a humorous theme in a number of scenes throughout *Lolita* 1962, signalling that a joke is on the way, even when the characters themselves are suffering, and the victim of this kind of humor is nearly always Humbert Humbert. All of the main characters are pathetic figures, Lolita and her mother as victims, and Humbert, as any debased criminal would be, if we were inclined to follow the ethics of 'hate the crime and pity the criminal'.

Even though Humbert is fundamentally pathetic, especially as the story develops, Kubrick forces us to acknowledge his intellectual superiority over Charlotte, and even his barefaced cynicism, just as many villains often have certain attractive, even admirable qualities that make them likeable, and certainly more interesting characters in fiction than flat goody-goody characters, the epitome of this being John Milton's (1667) Satan (Rosenfeld, 2008). The Spanish version translates, 'that was my intention' as 'that was not my intention' (*no era esa mi intención*), which would be more polite and expected and less cynical but also less fitting with the nature of the game of chess unless the player is more worried about being gentlemanly than winning the game. In this case, although the translation states the exact opposite of the utterance in the 1962 source text it could still work as a humoristic element, to be understood as irony rather than barefaced sarcasm which helps to develop Charlotte's potrayal as being blind to the threat posed by Humbert. Charlotte cannot see Humbert for what he is and she cannot even see she is being insulted. The cynical and foreboding quality is obviously enhanced by the nonchalant words 'It had to happen sometime' and a brilliant accompanying performance by James Mason. Of course, the insult of 'that wasn't very clever of you', thus calling her stupid to her face is downplayed in Spanish, making it a much more impersonal reference to a wrong move, limited to the scope of chess (literally, that was not a very smart move). Kubrick's script seems carefully worded so the whole exchange can also refer to HH's taking Lolita from under Charlotte's nose, surely a feature that would be desirable to keep in uncensored translation.

> Example 3. Lolita is counting the number of times she can get a hula hoop to spin around her hips. Humbert is sitting close to her, holding a book. He does not reply to Charlotte's observation.
>
> Lolita – 31, 32, 33, 34, 35, 36, 37, 38, 39, 40, 41, 42, 43, 44, 45, 46, 47, 48, 49, 50, 51, 52, 53 (interrupted by her mother's presence)
> Charlotte – See how **relaxed** you're **getting!** (to Humbert)

Example 3 is another case of audiovisual irony (the relationship of contradiction between the word 'relaxed' and the nonverbal element of the look on his face and his tight jaw), Charlotte's mistaken impression that Humbert is relaxed is ludicrous as the camera shows him to be pretending only, and quite unsuccessfully, too. The German and Spanish subtitles miss an opportunity to render this joke effectively by keeping close to its literal meaning; 'relaxed' is important but so is 'getting' for the ironic humor to work to its full potential. Lolita's counting gives the idea of progressiveness which is supported by the gerund; the implication is that the pervert is more and more excited by the girl's hip movements, as he sits strategically a few feet away, wearing something akin to a bath robe, with his legs crossed but showing his naked knees and shins. The Spanish version uses 'See how relaxed you are' instead of 'you're getting relaxed', which could have provided various possibilities for innuendo (e.g. *se pone/se va poniendo*). The German version uses 'absorbed' instead of relaxed, missing the importance of the relaxed/excited opposition. A closer alternative to the humoristic value (and the words) of this line might have been *Sehen Sie, wie entspannt Sie sind* or *Sehen Sie, wie gut Sie hier entspannen können?*

A visual component of this joke which is very important for understanding the relationship between these three characters is how it shows that Charlotte only has eyes for Humbert, completely blind to her daughter's needs and any harm she might come to, though she is not a particularly bad mother, either. The audience can also see how Lolita is Humbert's obsession and his vision is focused entirely on her, while she remains oblivious of both adults, and certainly ignorant of their darker feelings and intentions. This blindness is the main cause of the downfall for each of them (albeit in different ways). Crucially, it is also used for comic purposes. My claim here is that a good audiovisual translator should have analytical tools to decipher these semiotically coded messages (Chaume, 2001). When they are overlooked or otherwise interpreted and rendered (especially after ignoring a profusion of clues and repetitions, which is the case of the examples provided here) it can either be because the translator (as defined above) deliberately chooses to ignore the clues, in some sort of censoring strategy, or that in a different sort of censoring strategy the employer has wilfully chosen a translator who is not up to the job or is under highly problematic working conditions (e.g. a tight deadline). Or there is a woeful lack of literary, cinematic and translational sensitivity and/or training.

In one of the jokes shared by all three (1955, 1962 and 1997) versions, Lolita is sent by her mother to Camp Climax (!) for young girls in order to get her out of the way, so the grownups can develop their romance together. Although Camp Climax is not translated in either the Spanish or the German version, it is mentioned once orally and appears several times in writing on the screen. It is transparent enough in all likelihood for large sections of both audiences, certainly among the younger generations. The name Swine would be a similar case for German audiences. The novel displays a rich variety of wordplay involving names and a fraction of that humor is picked up and reflected in Kubrick's film. Surely no one can deny the tongue-in-cheek humoristic intentionality of this particular name, which, in turn, should alert the translator to the presence of humor there, and potentially elsewhere as part of a stylistic pattern; additionally, guided by the clue that the happy theme tune on the soundtrack becomes louder when Camp Climax comes into view. If ever any music could be defined as ironic it has to be this jazzy piece (Chaume's, 2001, musical semiotic code), especially the way it is used by Kubrick. When Charlotte is accidentally run over and killed, Humbert rushes to Camp Climax to 'take' Lolita, as foreshadowed in the chess scene (example 2). His behaviour at the camp is pathetically funny, trying to act as a respectable stepfather, and example 4 is part of the conversation he has with Lolita as they drive off towards The Enchanted Hunters Lodge to spend the night.

Example 4. Humbert is trying to change the topic of conversation.

Humbert – Did you have a **marvellous** summer?
Lolita – Yeah, I guess so.
Humbert – Were you sorry to leave?
Lolita – Not exactly.
Humbert – You know, I've **missed** you terribly.
Lolita – I haven't missed **you**. In fact, I've been **revoltingly** unfaithful to you. But it doesn't matter a bit, because you've **stopped caring** anyway.
Humbert – What makes you say I've **stopped caring** for you?
Lolita – You **haven't even kissed** me yet, have you?

In example 4, 'terribly' is already suspect and could be rendered carefully in translation so that it is coherent with what is to follow. The Spanish subtitle plays down 'marvellous' as 'good', which does not help to build up the string of hyperboles as they appear in English (marvellous, terribly, revoltingly). Spanish norms for good style recommend that a writer steer away from the copresence of adverbs ending in *–mente* (the Spanish equivalent of *–ly* ending for adverb formation in English). Despite the unidiomatic (and uncharacteristic for Lolita) *horriblemente* for 'revoltingly', the subtitle resorts quite skilfully to a slight shift for 'terribly' to 'you don't know how [much] I've missed you'. What seems most out of place in the source-text script, compared to what one would normally expect from a father and daughter's conversation in similar circumstances, is Lolita saying 'revoltingly unfaithful', leading up to what could easily be regarded as the punchline of the joke, i.e. the way she says 'kissed me'. Actually, from a semiotic point of view the punch line is the visual effect of the car revving up and shooting down the road just after Lolita utters these words, in a clear audiovisual metaphor of Humbert getting all excited (Chaume's, 2001, semiotic code of camera shots and angles), and also a clear hint that censorship would not allow anything more explicit than that in 1962. This technique of the car shooting down the road as a metaphor of sexual excitement is repeated as a follow-up to the so-called 'seduction scene' which starts with example 8.

The whole car scene can be straightforwardly compared to Lyne's film, most probably inspired by the 1962 scene, and it is quite obvious that Lyne plays the card of an erotic scene with partial nudity and on-screen kissing as an alternative approach to Kubrick's metaphor, visual ellipsis and humor. In 1962, the girl is only slightly provocative, mostly through some of the things she says (example 4); in 1997, by contrast, she literally jumps on top of her stepfather and kisses him quite hard. Just as Lolita (1997) teases Humbert, Lyne teases his audience by creating a false expectation of more explicit sex scenes under the cover of supposedly faithfully adapting Nabokov's book, while actually being faithful to his own filmography, as we have already seen. The Spanish and German versions of this scene seem to disregard the importance of a double discourse that could be (i) a father-daughter exchange or (ii) an argument between lovers, through carefully planted words pointing one way or the other (e.g. miss, care and kiss). 'Not exactly' is rendered as *Nein, gar nicht* (not at all); but more mysterious is the translator's decision to make Lolita address Humbert as *junger Mann* (young man) as if she were older than him. The important repetition of the word 'caring' is kept in Spanish but absent in the German subtitles, just as it was for 'cherry pies'. A small but important detail can be found in the Spanish rendering of 'kissed me' as 'give me a kiss', because of the difference between giving someone a kiss (as one would give one's daughter) or kissing them (more fitting with sexual activity, foreplay or petting). Nor is there anything for 'yet', or 'have you', which help the provocative tone.

One of the funniest scenes in the film features Peter Sellers in the role of Quilty, Humbert's nemesis, talking to the night manager, Mr. Swine (partly transcribed as example 5). The conversation is bizarre in many ways, the kind of verbal incoherence (at least in appearance) that tends to disarm translators, so often formally trained to look for and keep 'the sense' of a text. Nonsense humor and surrealism can be just as problematic if not more so than symbolism, irony and metaphor. This is why a translator would do well to read the textual warning signs, in order to have a firmer ground on which to make decisions and come up with purposeful solutions. In this respect, there are several nonverbal, visual clues. One is the body language of all three characters, including Quilty's female partner. She mysteriously never utters a word out loud, and seems like some sort of dominatrix (Richards, 2012), in her appearance and general demeanour, in stark contrast to Lolita, who appears in the next scene.

Example 5. Quilty has been talking to Swine, amiably, almost flirtatiously.

Swine – ... What do **you** do with **your** excess energy?
Quilty – Well, **we** do a lot of things with **my** excess energy. One of the things we do a lot of is **judo**. Did you **ever** hear about that?
Swine – Judo! Yes, I've heard about it. You do judo **with the lady**?
Quilty – Yes, she's a yellow belt, I'm a green belt, that's **the way nature made** it. **What happens is** she throws me all over the place.
Swine – **She** throws **you**?
Quilty – What she does, she gets me in a sort of thing called a sweeping-ankle throw. She sweeps my ankles from under me. **I go down** with one hell of a **bang**.
Swine – Doesn't it **hurt**?
Quilty – I lay there **in pain but I love it**. I really love it. I lay hovering between **consciousness** and **unconsciousness**. It's the **greatest**.

Example 5 belongs to a scene of key importance in the film as it depicts the atmosphere of the place where Humbert will make his first criminal sexual assault on Lolita, presumably, as this is not shown explicitly. Example 5 is an instance of Seller's considerable contribution to the humor of Lolita 1962. The absurd conversation is sexually charged and is supported by both actors' delivery of the lines, in their intonation and looks, and how closely all three lean towards each other, their foreheads almost touching. Swine talks about Quilty's 'lady' almost as if she were not inches away. Two points are essential for translating the humor here. First, a rendering of double-entendre through idiomatic language to go beyond the apparent nonsense; second, the parallel scene that comes immediately after it, involving Humbert (with Lolita) and Swine, which is funny because of how differently it plays out. Humbert's antagonising clumsiness (e.g. he stands stiffly away from his interlocutor) puts him at the mercy of the shrewd night manager, and the audience knows that Humbert is fooling nobody but himself. Certain changes or decisions in any translation can either convey all of this or spoil the effect. In particular, a scene of Humbert with Swine is also present in Lolita 1997, but it is turned into a very sombre, sinister situation, because the 1997 villain is Quilty, with Humbert and Lolita just having an ill-fated romance, downplaying the paedophilia somewhat. Even the music for these scenes is quite different from one adaptation to the other (underscoring comedy or suspense, respectively). The carefully crafted script (example 5) tellingly makes Swine refer to Quilty's partner as 'the lady' and the effect of this choice of wording is picked up in the German dubbing as *gnädige Frau* in a display of exaggerated, false respect, interestingly repeated this time for 'she throws you?' (unlike 'caring' and 'cherry pies' before) even though it is not repeated in English.

Whatever sexual allusion there may be in 'do judo' as a code word is also attempted in the phrase *Treiben Sie*, which could mean do judo or (*es treiben*) have sex (do it). The outrageous logic of 'that's the way nature made it' is dubbed as *und Sie versteht es!* ('she knows how to do it!', literally, 'she understands it') and is simply omitted from the subtitles although there is enough time to fit in an extra subtitle. In Spanish, a near-literal translation is blurred by expressing it as 'that's the way nature wished for it', which in Spanish sounds like an almost pious (or blasphemous) echoing of the phrase 'God willing'. The calculated ambiguity of 'all over the place' becomes a more specific *vielleicht über das Parkett*. The double meaning and innuendo of 'bang' is missed in the German dubbed rendering ... *ich fliege auf die Erde* (I fall down on the ground), and again not even attempted in the subtitles. The Spanish translation is quite similar in abandoning any attempt to portray the double meaning of 'bang', and matters are made worse by choosing words which might just as well have come straight out of a Spanish nun's mouth, but definitely not something one would hear from a man-of-the-world playwright. The German translation of Quilty's last turn in example 5 adds two features from the translator's own initiative: one is that the utterance stops as if unfinished and the other is the inclusion of the word 'sport'. The Spanish rendering is bizarre grammatically and idiomatically, but not comically bizarre, just the opposite of the English words which are grammatical but full of comic sexual allusion. This is noteworthy as there seems to be no obstacle in the way of an effective literal translation.

> Example 6. Quilty leaves the reception desk as Humbert arrives with Lolita, in the scene immediately following example 5, to book two rooms or twin beds for the night. Swine tells Humbert the hotel is full, except for a room with a double bed.
>
> Humbert – Well, perhaps you could find a **folding** bed or a **camp** bed.
> Swine – **Potts**, do we have any **cots**? (...) I'm sure you'll find **one** room satisfactory. Our double beds are really **triple**. One night we had **three ladies** sleeping in one.

'Cot' is used repeatedly in Lolita 1962, including comments by several characters and synonymous alternatives, as in example 6, encouraging the viewer to see the connection with babies and paedophilia, and it becomes a theme within the film and a metonym of the paedophilic assault. This connection is harder to see in the Spanish and German translations, which use words that are restricted to equivalences of folding bed or camp bed (e.g. *Klappbett*, *Feldbett*, or even *Couch*, as used in the dubbing), but not to a word like cot, which so effectively helps to visualise the crime. Accordingly, the joke relies on how Humbert avoids the word and (pathetically) flinches as Swine insists on repeating it out loud (paralinguistic code, following Chaume, 2001), quite amused, as if he were in the know. It is developed further when the cot is brought to the room in a comic scene that is reminiscent of silent-film slapstick. The Spanish language offers the possibility of *catre*; it is a literal translation of camp bed or folding bed and often used idiomatically as a vulgar metonym for fornication.

Swine never refers to Lolita as anything but 'the girl', while referring to adult females (examples 5 and 6) as 'ladies' rather than women or other synonyms, sounding vaguely offensive or vulgar in doing so. In the German subtitles and dubbed version there is a remarkable change from 'ladies' to 'men', spending the night in one bed. It is not clear whether this is a typo (the dubbed version also uses 'men') or an attempt to clean up the dialogue … or to make it dirtier! Who knows!

Example 7. The bellhop and Humbert manage to unfold the bed not without considerable effort, in a hilarious silent scene that further develops the 'cot' theme.

Bellhop – We **did it**, Sir!

Example 7 includes the expression 'do it', which can be interpreted as 'to be successful', but also 'to have sex'. This interpretation is not very far-fetched, at least jokingly, since they have been literally rolling around together on the bed trying to get the cot to unfold and stay open. The Spanish subtitle definitely misses an easy opportunity to translate the pun almost literally, with only a slight change to keep it just as idiomatic. The double meaning of 'do it', can be replicated in Spanish with *hacerlo*, but the subtitle has opted for a less literal translation (*conseguir*) which explains only one of the meanings, the less naughty one. The problem in the German subtitle seems to be of a technical nature, with words that belong to a different subtitle, with no correspondence in the English version, producing audiovisual incoherence (Zabalbeascoa, 2008).

Example 8. Daybreak. Humbert is lying in the cot, which is lying on the floor. Lolita has slept in the double bed.

Lolita – By the way, what happened to your bed? It looks a lot lower.
Humbert – Well, the bed collapsed. It's a collapsible bed.

Example 8 is also a pun but unlike example 7 the speaker is punning deliberately. It also closes the cot theme after many minutes of verbal and nonverbal play. The German subtitle opts for words with similar pronunciations rather than double meaning (*zusammenlegbar* and *zusammenbrechbar*) to say that the bed is not 'foldable', it is 'collapsible' thus implying that it is low because it has broken and collapsed, establishing complementarity between the two words in a different way. The Spanish subtitle is incoherent with the nonverbal image (Zabalbeascoa, 2008), strictly speaking, because it states that the bed has folded up, meaning to close like a book, which is how it was brought into the room. But the scene shows the bed completely unfolded, flat on the floor. If the Spanish subtitles had really aimed for some sort of joke they could have done something similar to the German version (*no es una cama desplegable, es desmoronable*) to say the bed is not one that folds, but a bed that crumbles. It is clear in these examples that the whole cot theme is of paramount importance in the film; it is the focal point of sexual tension and paedophilia reduced to ridicule and farce.

Another key feature of *Lolita* 1962 is the character called Quilty, who also preys on Lolita. Quilty takes on different disguises, the most unlikely one being that of some sort of German psychiatrist. We assume he is German as he speaks non-native English with stereotypical traits of what is often taken for Germans failing to speak English properly. The foreign-sounding speech is the only item of his disguise along with a pair of thick glasses, so it is an important element to render in translation, apart from being very funny, because Humbert has spoken to Quilty before and could easily recognize him otherwise. The stereotypical German flavor of his English can be heard in the accent, in the choice of words and in quirky grammar, as can be seen in example 9. He repeats Humbert's name several times, but always mispronouncing it badly to sound like 'Humbert's', stretching out the 's' sound at the end.

> Example 9. Quilty is disguised as Dr. Zemph, the psychiatrist, speaking in an improbable German accent, as part of his disguise; the other is a thick pair of glasses.
>
> Quilty – Dr. Humbert (pronounced 'Humbertssss'), would you mind if I am putting to you the blunt question?

In a way, all of this foreignness, as both Humbert and the fake psychiatrist are not originally from the USA, sets up the joke in example 10.

> Example 10. Dr. Zemph is interviewing Humbert, compared to a much earlier scene with Quilty speaking to Humbert in a different guise.
>
> Zemph – We Americans ... [referring to himself and Humbert] ...
> Quilty –You are either Australian ... or a German refugee.

Zemph's remark is extraordinary (audiovisual contradiction), coming from someone posing as a German speaking to an English character who stands out wherever he goes in America, even if we grant that both might wish to become naturalized US citizens. It is a funny self-description coming from someone with such a thick accent. However, neither the Spanish nor the German subtitles show any foreignness or linguistic variation at all. This has two effects, one is that Quilty's disguise depends entirely on his glasses (visual code) with no accent (paralinguistic and verbal code), and the other is that any joke like the one illustrated in example 10 is completely invisible to the Spanish and German viewers. The rationale for the German case is revealed in how it renders 'Australian or German refugee' as 'a gangster or a dissolute tramp'. This means that any mention of anything German is as much of a taboo, at least, as paedophilic sex. The relationship between the audiovisual elements as established by the German subtitles for example 10 are not contradictory (i.e. incongruous) and hence not funny, as all mention of foreignness and German origin have been deleted, coherently and humorlessly. The Spanish subtitles, unlike the German ones, translate all the nationality words faithfully (Australian, German, American) thus creating an unfunny relationship of incoherence between the audiovisual text elements (verbal and nonverbal) because there is no accompanying accent or clue to justify the explicit comments on national origin.

5. Conclusions

I hope to have shown that humor, as a main feature of *Lolita* 1962, especially if compared to *Lolita* 1997, needs to be addressed in any dubbed or subtitled version, unless it is deliberately omitted or impoverished. Omission of humor may be because the translator has missed it or disregarded it, believing the film to be (more) about a taboo crime of paedophilia, or because humor would either distract from a morbid approach, or somehow endorse child abuse. *Lolita* (any version) is often referred to as 'controversial', almost as an inevitable prefix: controversial *Lolita*. Eventually, it is taken for granted that *Lolita* must be controversial *per se*, with no analysis needed to support or explain the claim. Nabokov's book was initially labelled as pornographic also with the implication that no further analysis was needed. Leaving aside morbid controversy, Nabokov's (1955) and Kubrick's (1962) *Lolita* can be regarded as works of art that are about much more than a story of paedophilia. More importantly, they provide great insight into literary and cinematic composition, respectively. The examples presented here and the analysis of their translations is intended to support the idea that maybe (just maybe) a translation with apparent shortcomings and errors could constitute a form of censorship, no longer requiring the presence of active censorship, by making the final result one of poorer quality and diminished interest.

The analysis illustrates a variety of translation problems. In some examples there is an avoidance of a straightforward solution that could be achieved through literal translation ('ladies' translated as 'men', example 6) or by respecting the repetition of a key word ('cherry pies', example 1). Sometimes there is a challenge for the translator ('cot', example 6) that does not seem insurmountable but is nevertheless hardly even attempted, possibly through a lack of sufficient interest (e.g. maybe because of a taboo helping to diminish such an interest). There is an obvious comic purpose in many of the names: Camp Climax, Swine, Potts, and others that do not appear in the examples (e.g. Captain Love, Enchanted Hunters, Dr. Cudler). Another kind of problem is the comical nature of innuendo and double discourse, analysed in examples 4 and 5. In example 4, the dialogue can be interpreted as being spoken by a father and his daughter, but also by two lovers talking about missing each other and being faithful or otherwise. Example 5 is a conversation about judo that is clearly not about judo, but about masochistic sex between consenting adults.

Lolita 1997 is supposed to be a faithful adaptation because it follows the structure of the 1955 novel more closely than Kubrick does, and includes more direct quotes from the novel. But Adrian Lyne's humor is lamer and scarcer than Kubrick's, and even Nabokov realised that film is a different medium and requires a different approach. Casting and performance are basic aspects of filmmaking and *Lolita* 1962 is better and more humorous than *Lolita* 1997 partly because of Kubrick's choice of cast and their performances. Proof of this is synthesised in each one of the 10 examples provided here, some because they are replicated in 1997 (example 4) and are easy to compare, and others (examples 5, 9, 10) because they are absent, so that the absence of a humorous scene or the way it is dealt with is telling of authorial intent and resulting effect. Ultimately, both Kubrick and Nabokov, and critics and scholars long after them (Burke, 2003, Richards, 2012, Duckett, 2014, Biltereyst, 2015) understood that artistic quality (literary or audiovisual) is a more worthwhile goal than likeness, almost in the vein of *belles infidèles*, so well known in translation studies. This view of translation could be applied to film adaptation as translation (Cattrysse, 1992), and to the translation of humor, when comic effect is a high priority (Zabalbeascoa, 2005).

Acknowledgements

My sincere thanks to Elena Voellmer and Blanca Arias-Badia for their help with the German examples, and Javier Muñoz for his encouragement and advice.

Disclosure statement

No potential conflict of interest was reported by the author.

Note

1. *Lolita* 1962 is used throughout to refer to Kubrick's adaptation, and *Lolita* 1997 to Adrian Lyne's.

ORCID

Patrick Zabalbeascoa http://orcid.org/0000-0002-4027-5178

References

Attardo, S. (2001). *Humorous texts: A semantic and pragmatic analysis*. Berlin: Mouton de Gruyter.
Attardo, S. (2002). Translation and humor. *The Translator*, 8(2). Special issue: Translating humor, 173–194.
Biltereyst, D. (2015). A constructive form of censorship: Disciplining Lolita. In T. Ljujić, P. Krämer, & R. Daniels (Eds.), *Stanley Kubrick: new perspectives* (pp. 139–151). London: Black Dog Publishing.
Burke, K. (2003). Novel to film, frame to windows: The case of Lolita as text and image. *Pacific Coast Philology*, 38, 16–24.
Cattrysse, P. (1992). Film (adaptation) as translation: Some methodological proposals. *Target*, 4(1), 53–70.
Chaume, F. (2001). Los códigos de significación del lenguaje cinematográfico y su incidencia en traducción [Codes of meaning of cinematic language and their effect on translation]. In J. Sanderson (Ed.), *¡Doble o nada! Actas de las I y II Jornadas de doblaje y subtitulación* (pp. 45–57). Alicante: Universitat d'Alacant.
Chiaro, D. (1992). *The language of jokes. Analysing verbal play*. London: Routledge.
Delabastita, D. (1989). Translation and mass-communication: Film and T.V. translation as evidence of cultural dynamics. *Babel*, 35(4), 193–218.
Duckett, V. (2014). Letting Lolita Laugh. *Literature-Film Quarterly 07/2014*, 42(3), 528–540.
Ebert, R. (1997). Questions for the movie answer man: Andrew McMeel Publishing.
Eldoblaje.com (website).
Grossman, L., & Richard Lacayo, R. (2005). All-Time 100 Novels. Retrieved from http://entertainment.time.com/2005/10/16/all-time-100-novels/slide/lolita-1955-by-vladimir-nabokov/
Holmes, J. S. (1972/1988). The name and nature of translation studies. In J. S. Holmes (Eds.), *Translated!* papers on literary translation and translation studies. (pp. 67–80). Amsterdam: Rodopi.
Ishiguro, K. (1989). *The Remains of the Day*. United Kingdom: Faber and Faber.

Milton, J. (1667). *Paradise Lost* (1st ed.). London, UK: Samuel Simons.
Nabokov, V. (1955). Lolita. Edition used: Penguin Modern Classics (2000) ebook.
Richards, E. (2012). 'I get sort of carried away, being so normal and everything': The oscillating sexuality of Clare Quilty and Humbert Humbert in the works of Nabokov, Kubrick and Lyne. Alphaville: Journal of Film and Screen Media 4 (Winter 2012). Retrieved from http://www.alphavillejournal.com/Issue%204/HTML/ArticleRichards.html
Rosenfeld, N. (2008). *The human Satan in seventeenth-century English literature from Milton to Rochester.* London: Ashgate.
Schuman, S. (1978). 'Lolita': Novel and screenplay. *College Literature: A Journal of Critical Literary Studies,* 5(3), 195–204.
Torres-Nuñez, J. (Ed.). *Estudios de literatura norteamericana: Nabokov y otros autores contemporáneos.* Almería: Universidad de Almería.
Wepler, R. (2011). Nabokov's nomadic humor: Lolita. *College Literature: A Journal of Critical Literary Studies,* 38(4), 76–97.
Zabalbeascoa, P. (2001). El texto audiovisual: factores semióticos y traducción [The audiovisual text: semiotic factors and translation]. In J. Sanderson (Ed.), *¡Doble o nada! Actas de las I y II Jornadas de doblaje y subtitulación* (pp. 45–57). Alicante: Universitat d'Alacant.
Zabalbeascoa, P. (2005). Humor and translation: an interdiscipline. *Humor,* 18(2), 185–207.
Zabalbeascoa, P. (2008). The nature of the audiovisual text and its parameters. In J. Díaz-Cintas, (Ed.), *The Didactics of Audiovisual Translation* (pp. 21–37). Amsterdam: John Benjamins Films.
Kubrick, S. (1957). *Paths of Glory.* USA: Bryna Productions.
Kubrick, S. (1960). *Spartacus.* USA: Bryna Productions.
Kubrick, S. (1962). *Lolita.* USA: Seven Arts production Company. Warner Home Video DVD (2001).
Kubrick, S. (1964). *Dr. Strangelove.* UK: Hawk Films.
Kubrick, S. (1968). *2001: A Space Odyssey.* USA: Metro-Goldwyn-Mayer.
Kubrick, S. (1971). *A Clockwork Orange.* USA: Polaris Productions.
Kubrick, S. (1975). *Barry Lyndon.* UK: Peregrine Productions.
Kubrick, S. (1980). *The Shining.* UK: Hawk Films.
Kubrick, S. (1987). *Full Metal Jacket.* USA: Harrier Films.
Kubrick, S. (1999). *Eyes Wide Shut.* USA: Pole Star.
Lyne, A. (1983). *Flashdance.* USA: PolyGram Filmed Entertainment.
Lyne, A. (1986). *9 1/2 Weeks.* USA: Producers Sales Organization.
Lyne, A. (1987). *Fatal Attraction.* USA: Paramount Pictures.
Lyne, A. (1993). *Indecent Proposal.* USA: Paramount Pictures.
Lyne, A. (1997). *Lolita.* France: Pathé Production Company. Fox Home Entertainment DVD (1997).
Lyne, A. (2002). *Unfaithful.* USA: Regency Enterprises.

Appendix 1. Spanish and German subtitles for each example above, with time codes.

1.	00:17:42:21 - 00:17:45:18	¿Cuál ha sido el factor decisivo? ¿El jardín? What was the decisive factor? The garden?
	00:17:47:20 - 00:17:49:19	Creo que sus pasteles de cerezas. I think it was your cherry cakes.
	00:17:42:21 - 00:17:46:00	Was hat Ihren Entschluß am meisten bestärkt? Mein Garten? What has strengthened your resolve most? My garden?
	00:17:47:10 - 00:17:49:19	Nein, ich, glaube, es waren wohl ... Ihre Plätzchen. No, I think it was probably ... your biscuits.
2.	00:18:42:02 - 00:18:44:00	¿Va a comerse mi reina? Are you going to eat my Queen?
	00:18:44:08 - 00:18:46:11	No era esa mi intención. [...] That was not my intention. [...]
	00:19:07:13 - 00:19:09:19	No ha sido una jugada muy inteligente. That was not a very smart move.
	-	(no subtitle for "Don't! No! Oh!")
	00:19:14:09 00:19:15:21	Alguna vez tenía que suceder. It had to happen sometime.
	00:18:42:02 - 00:18:44:06	Wollten Sie meine Königin attackieren? Did you want to attack my Queen?
	00:18:44:08 - 00:18:46:11	Ja, das wollte ich allerdings. Yes, I wanted to, indeed.
	00:19:07:13 - 00:19:10:00	Ah! Das war aber nicht sehr überlegt von Ihnen. Ah! But this was not very careful of you.
	00:19:10:02 - 00:19:11:23	Nicht doch! Nicht doch! Och! Don't! No! Oh!
	00:19:14:09 - 00:19:15:21	Das mußte dochmal passieren. It just had to happen.
3.	00:19:14:09 - 00:19:15:21	... 31, 32, 33 ...
	00:19:32:22 - 00:19:34:21	¿Ve lo relajado que está? You see how relaxed you are?
	00:19:16:06 - 00:19:17:21	... 31, 32, 33, 34 ...
	00:19:32:22 - 00:19:34:21	Sie saßen eben ganz versunken da! You were sitting just completely absorbed.
4.	01:09:30:19 - 01:09:33:02	¿Has pasado un buen verano? Did you have a nice summer?
	01:09:34:13 - 01:09:35:22	Sí, creo que sí. Yes, I think so.
	01:09:36:01 - 01:09:37:18	¿Te ha dado pena marcharte? Were you sad to leave?
	01:09:37:21 - 01:09:39:03	No exactamente. Not exactly.

IDEOLOGY, CENSORSHIP AND TRANSLATION

	01:09:50:11 - 01:09:52:14	No sabes cuánto te he echado de menos. You don't know how much I've missed you.
	01:09:53:15 - 01:09:57:12	Yo a ti, no. La verdad es que te he sido horriblemente infiel. I haven't missed you. The truth is I've been horribly unfaithful to you.
	01:09:58:08 - 01:10:01:23	Pero da lo mismo, porque ya no te importo. But it doesn't matter, because you no longer care about me.
	01:10:02:17 - 01:10:05:08	¿Qué te hace decir que ya no me importas? What makes you say I no longer care about you?
	01:10:06:16 - 01:10:08:16	Ni siquiera me has dado un beso. You have not even given me a kiss.
	01:09:30:19 - 01:09:33:16	Ah, hast du ... hast du einen schönen Sommer gehabt? Ah, Did you ... did you have a nice summer?
	01:09:34:13 - 01:09:35:22	Ja, es ging. Yes, it was.
	01:09:36:01 - 01:09:37:19	Hat es dir leid getan, fortzugehen? Were you sorry to leave?
	01:09:37:21 - 01:09:39:03	Nein, gar nicht. No, not at all.
	01:09:50:11 - 01:09:52:14	Nebenbei habe ich dich sehr vermißt. By the way, I missed you very much.
	01:09:53:15 - 01:09:57:19	Ich dich dafür gar nicht. Im Gegenteil, ich war dir geradezu empörend untreu. I did not miss you at all. On the contrary, I was downright outrageously unfaithful to you.
	01:09:58:08 - 01:10:02:02	Aber das ist dir ja gleich, du magst mich ja nicht mehr, junger Mann. But to you it is all the same, you do not like me any more, young man.
	01:10:02:17 - 01:10:05:08	Wie kommst du denn darauf? What makes you think that?
	01:10:06:16 - 01:10:08:16	Du hast mich noch nicht einmal geküßt. You have not even kissed me yet.
5.	01:10:02:17 - 01:10:05:08	¿Qué hace usted con su exceso de energía? What do you do with your excess energy?
	01:11:19:07 - 01:11:22:00	Hacemos muchas cosas con mi exceso de energía. We do a lot of things with my excess energy.
	01:11:22:03 - 01:11:24:07	Una de las cosas que hacemos es judo. One of the things we do is judo.
	01:11:24:09 - 01:11:26:13	-¿Ha oído hablar del judo? Have you heard about judo? - ¡Judo! Judo.
	01:11:26:15 - 01:11:28:08	Sí, he oído hablar de eso. Yes, I've heard about it.

01:11:28:23 - 01:11:30:13	¿Practica el judo con la señora? Yes, I've heard about it. You practice judo with the lady?
01:11:30:15 - 01:11:34:19	Sí, ella es cinturón amarillo y yo, verde, así lo quiso la naturaleza. Yes, she's a yellow belt and I'm a green one, that's how nature wished for it to be.
01:11:34:21 - 01:11:37:09	Lo que ocurre es que siempre me tira por los suelos. What happens is she always throws me on the floor!
01:11:37:13 - 01:11:38:17	¿Ella a usted? She [throws] you?
01:11:38:19 - 01:11:42:21	Lo que hace es cogerme en una especie de llave que llaman barrido de tobillo. What she does is catch me in a sort of technique they call an ankle sweep.
01:11:44:13 - 01:11:47:01	- Y me pego un batacazo de aúpa. I take a jolly almighty fall. - ¿No se hace daño? Don't you hurt yourself?
01:11:47:03 - 01:11:49:19	Me quedo un poco dolorido, pero me encanta, de verdad. It hurts a little bit, but I love it, really.
01:11:49:21 - 01:11:54:00	Estar echado en un estado de semiinconsciencia es lo mejor que hay. To lie there in a state of semiunconsciousness is the best there is.
01:11:16:00 - 01:11:18:19	Und was machen Sie mit der überschüssigen Energie? And what do you do with the excess energy?
01:11:22:03 - 01:11:24:07	Wenn wir zu Haus sind, machen wir meist Judo. When we are at home, we usually do judo.
01:11:24:09 - 01:11:26:13	- Haben Sie schon mal davon gehört? Have you ever heard of it? - So, Judo. Why yes, judo.
01:11:26:15 - 01:11:28:12	Hab' schon viel davon gehört. I've heard a lot about it.
01:11:28:23 - 01:11:30:13	Treiben Sie Judo mit der Dame? You do it, the judo, with the lady?
01:11:30:15 - 01:11:34:19	Ja, sie hat einen gelben Gürtel und ich einen grünen. Yes, she's a yellow belt and I'm a green one.
01:11:34:21 - 01:11:37:09	Sie wirft mich vielleicht über das Parkett! She throws me all over the floor!
01:11:37:13 - 01:11:38:17	Die Dame wirft Sie? The lady throws you?
01:11:38:19 - 01:11:42:21	Ja, wie sie das anstellt, ich weiß es nicht. Yes, how she does that, I do not know.

	01:11:44:13 - 01:11:47:01	- Sie hat so ihre Tricks. She has her tricks. - Tut das nicht weh? Doesn't it hurt?
	01:11:47:03 - 01:11:49:19	Und wie! Aber je mehr es wehtut, umso mehr Spaß macht's. And how! But the more it hurts, the more fun it is.
	01:11:49:21 - 01:11:54:00	Und wenn der Partner der Richtige ist, dass ist diese Sportart … And if the partner is the right one, it's that kind of sport.
6.	01:12:43:02 - 01:12:46:22	Tal vez podamos arreglarnos con una cama plegable. Maybe we can make do with a folding bed.
	01:12:47:02 - 01:12:48:20	Potts, ¿tenemos camas plegables Potts, do we have any folding beds?
	01:12:50:21 - 01:12:54:18	Creo que con una habitación les bastará. Nuestras camas dobles son triples. I think that with one room you'll have enough. Our double beds are triple.
	01:12:54:20 - 01:12:56:23	Una noche durmieron tres señoras en una. One night three ladies slept in one of them.
	01:12:43:02 - 01:12:46:22	Hätten Sie noch ein Klappbett? Would you have a folding bed?
	01:12:47:02 - 01:12:48:17	Haben wir ein Feldbett frei? Do we have a free camp bed?
	01:12:50:23 - 01:12:54:18	Trotzdem wird das Zimmer ausreichen. Unsere Doppelbetten sind so groß, Nevertheless, the room is sufficient. Our double beds are large,
	01:12:54:20 - 01:12:56:23	neulich haben 3 Herren in einem übernachtet. recently we had 3 men spending the night in one.
7.	01:22:27:14 - 01:22:29:01	Lo conseguimos, señor. We achieved it, sir.
	01:22:27:14 - 01:22:30:11	Idiot! Passen Sie doch auf! Go carefully, you fool! Ja! So, jetzt steht es. Yes! Now that's it.
8.	01:25:25:24 - 01:25:29:10	Por cierto, ¿qué le ha pasado a tu cama? Parece mucho más baja. By the way. What happened to your bed? It looks a lot lower.
	01:25:29:15 - 01:25:33:06	Se ha plegado. Es una cama plegable. It's folded up. It's a folding bed.
	01:25:26:00 - 01:25:29:10	Was hast du mit dem Bett gemacht? Es ist so niedrig. By the way, what happened to your bed? It is so low.
	01:25:29:15 - 01:25:33:06	Das Bett ist nicht zusammenlegbar, es ist zusammenbrechbar. The bed is not a folding bed, it is a collapsible bed.

9.	01:40:42:15 - 01:40:47:11	Dr. Humbert, ¿le importa que le haga una pregunta directa? Dr. Humbert, do you mind if I ask you a direct question?
	01:40:42:15 - 01:40:47:11	Dr. Humbert, sind Sie böse, wenn ich eine etwas heikle Frage an Sie richte? Dr. Humbert, do you mind if I ask you a slightly tricky question?
10.	01:43:11:22 - 01:43:13:06	Nosotros, los americanos, We Americans,
	00:07:17:12 - 00:07:19:23	Usted es australiano ... You are Australian ...
	00:07:20:17 - 00:07:22:08	o un refugiado alemán. or a German refugee.
	01:43:11:22 - 01:43:13:06	Wir Amerikaner ... We Americans
	00:07:17:12 - 00:07:19:23	So, entweder sind Sie ein Gangster ... So, you're either a ganster
	00:07:20:17 - 00:07:22:15	oder ein verkommener Vagabund. or a dissolute tramp.

The crooked timber of self-reflexivity: translation and ideology in the end times

Stefan Baumgarten

> We need to start looking at translational phenomena from an intensely self-reflexive and ethical-ideological viewpoint. We are caught in a (post-)neoliberal world order in which capitalist values become an ever more deeply engrained and unquestioned standard, an order of discourse the structures of domination and hegemony of which define global power relations, just as they permeate scholarly discourses. Promising research exists that questions the cultural hegemony of Anglophone value systems and their underlying positivist epistemologies. Important inroads have been made to uncover the intellectual roots of the epistemic threat which Anglophone discourse poses towards alternative forms of knowledge. These efforts question the epistemological and colonial roots of Anglophone supremacism, yet they do not venture into a more combative anti-neoliberal, in fact anti-imperialist, mode of reasoning. The missing piece in the jigsaw may be found in some strands of critical theory that question the socio-economic consequences of the Enlightenment in conjunction with a post-anarchist epistemology. In view of current geopolitical realities, this paper attempts to inject the notion of 'hegemonic non-translation' into the discourse of translation theory by stressing the significance of enhanced 'self-reflexivity' and a 'critical economics' for future research.

1. Ideology and history in the end times

'Out of the crooked timber of humanity, no straight thing was ever made' (Kant, 1784/1963).

Ideology and history are intertwined and inextricably linked to human communication. Just as we cannot escape the normative presuppositions of ideology, we cannot escape the teleological assumptions of history. All scholarship, therefore, needs to be as conscious of its own ideological presumptions as of the asymmetries of power which shape any act of translation. Without the possibility of surrendering our social subjectivity, the least we can do is to base our scholarship on a strongly self-reflexive and critical historiography which places the notion of human suffering at the centre of its attention (Benjamin, 1940/1989). If, indeed, 'history is what hurts', if Jameson's (1988, p. 164) widely cited aphorism is to be taken at face value, then the only thing we can do is to work as hard as we can to be as self-reflexive as humanly possible.

And if ideology is everywhere, self-reflexivity, too, should be omnipresent. Slavoj Žižek's insights on ideology are significant in this respect, since for him ideology is working on *both* our innermost sense of self and reality, just as on our knowledge of and assumptions about the world we inhabit. According to Žižek (1989, p. 15), the Marxian principle that sees ideology mainly as a form of 'wrong thinking' needs to be ontologically grounded, since 'ideology is not simply a "false consciousness", an illusory representation of reality, it is rather this reality itself which is already to be conceived as "ideological"'. Be that as it may, if we conceive of ideology as a quasi-universal cognitive cobweb, then we run the risk of rendering the concept meaningless, as it is not inconceivable to consider some communicative practices – let's say baby talk – as non-ideological.

It is, however, significant to move away from apolitical conceptions of ideology – as I will do in the following pages – in order to place a spotlight on our current ideological subjection to the logic of capitalist exchange principles. However, overall it is clear that ideology can never be just a good or a bad thing; it is an abstract concept, regardless of the horrendous repercussions of ideological regimes on the global political stage. After all, only people can be good or bad, not abstract concepts. But still, whilst most dominant ideologies are standing in the way of living in a juster and better world, some good people, let's call them 'good ideologists', are genuinely trying to improve our lives (Critchley, 2008; Graeber, 2013). They are working towards a world not defined by massive power inequalities, in which millions of people in poor countries continue to live inside huge garbage dumps. The debate in academic and public discourse on the historical origins and structural causes of global inequality and its cures is beset by fierce ideological struggles, a fact which is echoed in the ideological discourses besetting translation theory. Indeed, ideology is more than just a bunch of ideas that make me think, say, or write certain things against my conscious control, or a distortion of my class consciousness that makes me, a middle-aged white middle-class academic located in one of the richer parts of the world, dance to the tunes of those who hold power over me, be that my employer or my bank manager.

This article will outline how we may theoretically unravel the unethical practice of what I shall call hegemonic non-translation, and it will attempt to sketch the philosophical and political contours of activist scholarship. If we understand hegemonic non-translation as based on a supremacist worldview coupled with an arrogant disregard for otherness, we can appreciate the work of Karen Bennett and other (theoretical) activists such as Mona Baker (2009) and Maria Tymoczko (2010) as exemplary. However, since they only rely on the history of ideas, in other words on 'traditional' rather than on 'critical' theory (Horkheimer, 2011), it can be argued that our practical-theoretical work needs to become even more sophisticated and biting when it comes to unravelling the structures of domination and hegemony to which we are all subjected to. José Lambert (1991/2006, p. 74) rightly noted more than 20 years ago that '[p]art of the moral of my tale is directed against the widespread belief that individual researchers have their own priorities and need not worry too much about larger responsibilities'. Surely many other colleagues share his concern. But it may be asked where are the activists in translation studies who don't duck away from real political responsibilities and their implications? There are still many people in the world who seem to believe that their thoughts can be ideology-free, just like a Disney movie can be free of adult content. But they are tragically mistaken, since, to evoke our baby example again, only a toddler does not have an ideology. A baby cannot think ideologically (though cognitive science might beg to differ); any other human brain thinks ideologically (at least if we believe in the Žižekian postulate). For us beyond toddler age, ideology is everywhere; everywhere we communicate, by means of language, sign language, hand signs, or whatever else we might use to signal our intentions. And because – at least during our current age of advanced consumer capitalism – everything is ideological, we cannot escape it.

As academics, especially as translation scholars, we have a huge responsibility to help improve the world. Yet academic conformism, deeply engrained ideologies of institutionalised elitism, and, perhaps most importantly, our emotional enslavement to social hierarchies are standing in the way of genuine progress. Ideological attachments like these are genuine obstacles for the few critical and progressive translation scholars amongst us. In the remaining three sections, I will critically reflect on the role of self-reflexivity in translation studies research (Baker, 2001) against the backdrop of (capitalist) globalization, and it will be argued that new critical-normative notions such as hegemonic non-translation and the postulate of a critical economics may inject some fresh blood into the discourse of translation theory. In an attempt to propagate an ethics of commitment (Critchley, 2008), the overall discussion draws on (meta-)critical discourses in the social sciences and philosophy (e.g. Chomsky, 2003; Graeber, 2013). I will attempt to unravel some knotty issues from the wide field of critical theory which so far, unfortunately, have found little coinage in the work of translation scholars (but see the recently published article by Dizdar, 2014). In highlighting the absence of questions of critical economic significance in translation research, and by stressing the continuous relevance of notions such as instrumental reason and reification, I will argue for a more normatively defined body of a yet non-existent 'post-anarchist translation theory'. Right from the start, I would also like to suggest that the concept of censorship, being largely over-theorized in our field, might be best suited to the study of discursive practices and texts that explicitly deal with political content or social inequality. By and large, the notion of hegemonic non-translation serves as the *Leitmotif* for the overall argument, because it undergirds, at least in my view, the phenomenological tyranny of Western (especially Anglophone) cultural supremacy. After all, the entire architecture of Žižek's (2010, p. x) epochal *Living in the End Times* is built around the simple premise that 'the global capitalist system is approaching an apocalyptic zero-point'; an assertion that rings less and less polemic as the days go by.

In the absence of an empirically verified and 'objectively' sanctified 'truth' about the world's unequal economic relations, a truth that translation studies, like any discipline, will most possibly never unravel, I might be able to achieve 'true' self-reflexivity by envisioning my ideological subjection along the three major lines of *phenomenological* experience. In *ontological* terms, I therefore position myself on the side of those I perceive to be the good guys, on the side of those who, for instance, describe rampant global inequalities as 'the outcomes of neoliberal policies' (Pieterse, 2004, p. 71), a phenomenological move that allows me to demand that the *foundations of our manifold experiences* in our interconnected world become established as an equal playing field (though possibly only in 2083, after the next war). Likewise, in view of the power politics of knowledge, or *epistemology*, I want the *foundations of our manifold perceptions* – that is, the way our embodied cognitions construct assumptions about the world – to attain genuine self-reflexivity, an objective we are far from achieving in the current neoliberal climate, especially in the commodified higher education systems that mushroom everywhere in the Western world. A politicization of these two phenomenological dimensions might be one step towards heightened self-knowledge, as much as the neo-rationalists and staunch objectivists, the traditionalists or conservatives, let alone the indifferent and career-minded, would beg to differ. But no one can deny the sell-out and intellectual implosion of the postmodern orthodoxy, or wish away the inescapable fragmentation of the unequal academic playing field into a game between *Fachidioten* (a conventional German academic term literally meaning 'subject idiots') and genuinely concerned (post)humanists. Consequently, modern translation studies also needs to thoroughly reconsider its practical and thus *ethical* concerns. In modern translation studies, to the detriment of liberationist reform and despite a seemingly established consensus about non-essentialist principles, there is still too much literary scholarship, too much focus on identity politics, too much nit-picking over correct ways to translate; in short, too much conformity and ingratiation towards institutional hierarchies, national political biases, and the techno-scientific *Zeitgeist*. Mind you, these are my own ideological concerns, based on my belief that the neoliberal world order, i.e. the inescapable logic of global capitalism, permeates our thoughts and actions much more than most of us would care to admit.

2. Hegemonic non-translation under advanced capitalism

Translation studies has produced much promising research that questions the global hegemony of Anglophone value systems and their underlying positivist epistemologies (Arrojo, 1998; Bassnett & Trivedi, 1999; Niranjana, 1992; Venuti, 1995, 1998). Important inroads have been made to lay bare the epistemic threat which Anglophone discourse poses towards alternative forms of knowledge. Karen Bennett (2006, 2007), for instance, has highlighted the ways in which English academic discourse in translation mainly serves to eliminate alternative ways of perceiving the world. For her, *epistemicide* by translation is invested with the power to cause the gradual erasure of entire worldviews. From an Anglophone perspective, different worldviews are encoded in any discursive Other that is less infused with positivist-rationalist values. The coinage 'epistemicide' goes back to the Portuguese activist scholar Boaventura de Sousa Santos (2006), referring to the way alternative modes of *being in* and *knowing about* the world are subject to the dizzying pull of dominant discourse norms, especially when coming into intercultural contact with Western hegemonic, i.e. instrumentalized, discourse. As one of the key intellectuals behind the World Social Forum, Santos (2006, p. 13) circumscribes the ethical tenets of the alternative globalization movement as having 'their origin in very distinct epistemological assumptions (what counts as knowledge) and ontological universes (what it means to be human)'. Whilst Venuti and Bennett largely look at *actual* translational products, it is time to acknowledge much more thoroughly what the Anglophone empire deems *not* worthy of translating, with the non-translation – i.e. erasue – of Portuguese discourse norms, once they travel into the Anglophone world, just one case in point. Modern translation scholars are thus well advised to investigate 'epistemicide by ignorance', which furthermore entails a subconscious desire to engage in (self-)censorship. Emily Apter, for instance, suggests that it is not unreasonable to ponder on the extent to which '"foreign" writers of ambition [just like Portuguese academics] are consciously or unconsciously writing for international markets; building translatability into their textuality' (Apter, 2001, p. 101; cf. Tymoczko, 2005).

The international book trade's *modus vivendi* is entrenched within the neoliberal marketplace, driven by the accumulation of profit, with the Anglophone world being its main beneficiary (Venuti, 1998). What is more, the Anglophone world has a huge problem with a claim to moral and cultural superiority. The ideology of Anglophone supremacism has become truly hegemonic. Anglophone supremacists, apart from staunchly worshipping free market liberalism and positivist science, believe in the selfish accumulation of economic, cultural, symbolic, and social resources, to evoke Pierre Bourdieu's (1977) theory of power relations. And of course they largely don't even know it! After all, any genuine self-awareness about their own spoils in the hegemony game is veiled through durative ideological dispositions in the form of a dominant *habitus* (Bourdieu, 1991) that is inculcated through individual socialization as well as elitist and state-controlled education systems. This largely invisible matrix of power relations and ideological (dis)positions is decisively structured along the blind acceptance of capitalist ontologies such as profit-based commodity exchange or the epistemological illusion of free trade amongst nations. Within the realm of textual politics, we could therefore say that hegemonic non-translation constitutes the dominant (seldom consciously reflected) habitus of the Anglophone supremacist.

Such theoretical musings surely need some practical explanation. We need to link the notion of hegemonic non-translation to the world of sensual experience and empirical reality. In this context, Santos' (2006, p. 15) 'sociology of absences' might serve as a useful analytical device, since it constitutes 'an inquiry that aims to explain that what does not exist is in fact actively produced as non-existent, that is – as a non-credible alternative to what exists'. The Anglophone and English-speaking world of commerce, for instance, 'actively produces' illusory assumptions of cultural supremacy, which in turn foster the systemic discrediting of any alternative ways of experiencing, knowing, and shaping the world. Consequently, such manifestations of phenomenological ignorance may be analytically accounted for through the notion of *absence*. The US literary translator Edith Grossman reports that a mere 2–3% of all books published in the USA and the UK are translations. In the meantime, a whopping 50% of all literary works worldwide appear to be translated out of English (Grossman, 2010, pp. 27, 52; cf. Apter, 2001, p. 101). According to Grossman, 'the recalcitrance of the English-language publishing industry seems unshakeable and immutable', whilst, almost customarily, 'translations are actively discouraged' despite occasional commercial success:

> They can be commercially successful (think of the cachet enjoyed in this country by *The Name of the Rose*; *Beowulf*; *Don Quixote*; anything by Roberto Bolaño), and still the majority of American and British publishers resist the very idea of translation and persistently hold the line against the presence of too many translated works in their catalogues. Some years ago, to my most profound consternation, I was told by a senior editor at a prestigious house that he could not even consider taking on another translation since he already had two on his list. (Grossman, 2010, p. 28)

Blissful ignorance at home, fervent oversupply abroad? Well, it is of course far too simplistic to make Anglophone supremacism solely responsible for this general resistance to literary translation and in turn for rampant quantitative imbalances. Power is never only imposed from a purportedly stronger position, to throw one of Foucault's (1972) more useful innovations into the mix, given that the struggle over power resources occurs within differentiated fields of social influence (Bourdieu, 1977; for a more pessimistic account of global power relations, see Baudrillard, 2010).

The phenomenon of systemic *quantitative* non-translation is paralleled by a *qualitative* eliminationist tendency. In his discussion of the translator's invisibility, Venuti (1995, p. 17) puts it somewhat more politely, likening this parallel development to a 'complacent' cultural attitude towards otherness, which, however, in the end, reflects a dominant habitus that is 'imperialistic abroad and xenophobic at home' (see also Pym, 1999). According to Venuti (1995), translations into English keep eradicating the foreign flavour of their source texts through a domesticating translation strategy due to the almost inescapable pull of global (market) forces, yet translations out of English into most other languages tend to maintain Anglophone socio-cultural specificities through a foreignizing translation strategy. An Anglo–German example may further illustrate the phenomenological multidimensionality of hegemonic non-translation under advanced capitalism. When scientific positivism was at its peak early in the twentieth century, its orthodox grip played a decisive role in the production of English translations of Sigmund Freud's work. Driven by the conviction that the scientific credibility of Freudian psychoanalysis needed serious enhancement, his ideas were 'regimented into a so-called classical method as well as into some sharply defined "metapsychological" theories' (Ornston, 1992, p. 211; also Hall, 2005). The fact that still today the English-speaking Freud employs highly scientific phraseology, whereas his German idiom was deliberatively crafted in a colloquial tone, is an example of positivistic appropriation, and thus a form of hegemonic non-translation on the level of knowledge politics. According to Venuti (1995, p. 27), the English standard translation 'sought to assimilate Freud's texts to the dominance of positivism in Anglo-American culture so as to facilitate the institutionalization of psychoanalysis in the medical profession and in academic psychology'. Yes, when seen in the context of historically-rooted frameworks of knowledge, it is perfectly understandable to blame 'the entrenchment of a positivistic reading of Freud in the Anglo-American psychoanalytic establishment' (Venuti, 1995, p. 28) for ideologically skewed translations, yet again it also seems reasonable to ask why, apart from the epistemic annihilation of an idealistic philosophical tradition, we should not more rigorously interrogate the rifts and contradictions in the global political economy. Of course, speaking of 'ideologically skewed' translations evokes the notion of censorship, but this notion, defined by Billiani (2007, p. 3) as 'a form of manipulative rewriting of discourses by one agent or structure over another agent or structure' falls slightly short of giving us at least an inkling of an increasingly commodified marketplace of translational exchange, with an Anglophone commercial empire calling the shots. The misrecognition of other cultural traditions obviously relates to knowledge politics and institutional power play, but most decisively to those guys, practically speaking, who command the biggest cash flow, this is where the power lies. The hegemony of non-translation perhaps manifests itself most visibly in the fields of international commerce, where Anglophone cultural products find their ways largely 'unfiltered' into the consciousness of a global non-Anglophone audience, for instance when brand names and advertising slogans are either non-translated or foreignised (Cronin, 2003, p. 97), or when we consider again the pulling power of the hegemonic Anglophone culture industry:

> This drive toward a transnationally translatable monoculture is supported by the fact that linguistic superpowers increasingly call the shots and turn once formidable competitors (European languages) into gladiators fighting among themselves for international market share. In French bookstores, for example, translations or even *un*translated

books in English have acquired more and more space on the shelves. (Apter, 2001, p. 99, emphasis in original)

The notion of non-translation itself is, of course, not new. Arguing from a polysystemic perspective, Lambert (1995/2006, p. 98) describes it as 'the import of non-translated discourse, which obliges given populations to adapt themselves to the idiom and the rules of the visitors', and van Doorslaer (2009, p. 90) says that in the modern news media factors such as 'languages and (the absence of) translation seem to be important framing and agenda-setting factors'. Moreover, in terms of English as a lingua franca, IT education in countries such as Germany is increasingly held in English, thus further adding to the symbolic value of English and its economic standing. And let us not forget that the worldwide promotion of English as a foreign language is almost entirely incentivized through economic objectives, a fact that is perfectly encapsulated in the claim that 'Britain's real black gold is not North Sea Oil but the English language' (former head of the British Council Sir Richard Francis, quoted in Phillipson, 1992, pp. 48–49). Within the more localised context of South African multilingualism, Marais (2014, p. 167) points to the non-translation of development documentation in English, stating that despite constitutional guarantees for linguistic multiplicity non-translation has become established as 'a de facto translation policy'. Significantly, the fact that development documents only 'reach communities in one language, foreign to most of them', enshrines a 'dominating, hegemonic perspective' which, in the end, excludes large swathes of the South African population from having a stake in local and regional decision-making processes. Consequently, and apart from all those tricky questions surrounding Anglophone (and other manifestations of) supremacism, we are in desperate need of critical and systematic investigations of the socioeconomic origins and functions pertaining to translational exchange across and within national boundaries. So would it not be an idea to much more sharply scrutinize the major causes and effects of non-translation in advanced capitalist 'Anglophonia'? Additional studies would need to look at why the Anglo-American mainstream is so desperately ignorant of everything foreign, and why it keeps isolating itself so fervently from the vast and fertile grounds of alternative modes of experience, knowledge, and ethical practice. One significant answer to these questions, I believe, lies in the economic and material foundations apparent in the current neoliberal world order.

3. Does translation studies need a critical economics?

We should expend all conceivable efforts to render visible Anglophone hegemonic non-translation. Paradoxically, however, it appears an impossible task, given the global levelling already achieved through the adjustment of international trade legislation according to the dictates of the financial elites. There are, nevertheless, millions who see through the unsustainability and absurdity of a planet rigidly divided along access to resources, opting instead for modest lifestyles with a concern for the preservation of humanitarian, ecological, and epistemological pluralities. Thomas Piketty's (2014) recent influential thesis that the structural basis of the capitalist system, essentially the fact that money is endlessly generated through interest and thus will never enable the working classes to level up with the rich, or the less powerful with the power-spoilt, has produced huge waves of discussion. Whilst the phenomenological basis of this hugely imbalanced system, of course, rests on property and ownership, his conclusion is relevant to my suggestion that thinking about translation along the lines of hegemonic ignorance or, to put it more neutrally, along a sociology of absence, might be another activist step forward:

> [A] market economy based on private property, if left to itself, contains powerful forces of convergence, associated in particular with the diffusion of knowledge and skills; but it also contains powerful forces of divergence, which are potentially threatening to democratic societies and to the values of social justice on which they are based [...] The consequences for the long-term dynamics of the wealth distribution are potentially terrifying. (Piketty, 2014, p. 571)

To the detriment of a strongly self-reflexive ethos of capitalist critique, the academic discourse on translation is littered with the problematization of notions with only random liberationist significance, evidenced in an abundance of debates on 'authorship', 'intercultural space', or 'multilingualism', but so far no one has looked at translation from the much more daring perspective of property and ownership, an angle which for critical scholars of an anarchist persuasion represents humanity's Achilles heel. Similarly, post-structuralism's infatuation with Michel Foucault's theory of power points to nothing else than our ongoing and indeed 'odd blind spot for economics' (Graeber, 2013, p. 120), a situation that is deeply obvious in modern translation studies (but see also Milton, 2008). This also applies to current debates on censorship in translation. If we merely regard censorship as a discursive phenomenon along Foucauldian lines, then we relegate its socioeconomic significance to something at the bottom of our list to investigate. Here, Billiani's (2007, p. 2) conception of censorship is indicative when she conceives of censorship 'as one of the discourses [...] expressed either through repressive cultural, aesthetic and linguistic measures or through economic means'. There is surely nothing wrong with this definition, but an engaged 'critical economic' approach along post-Marxist principles, paired with an anarchist ethos that prefigures non-hierarchical decision-making practices, might perhaps help to institute a reversal of analytical priorities.

As a scientific discipline, economics itself has a notorious blind spot towards questions of human equality, power politics, and institutionalized ideologies (cf. Backhouse, 2010). Indeed, it has become increasingly obvious that most of modern economics, especially its educational wing, is a massive fraud (cf. Chakrabartty, 2013): it is replete with abstract mathematical models, and these models are being propagated worldwide to the detriment of real people, and to the benefit of an internationally mobile and cash-rich elite. This process is referred to by Graeber (2013, p. 117) as the 'manufacture of intellectual authority', in which 'real political debate becomes increasingly difficult, because those who hold different positions live in completely different realities'. Chomsky (2003, pp. 254–255, emphasis in original) says that no international trade agreement, for instance the ones instituted by the World Trade Organisation, has any relationship whatsoever with reality:

> Nothing in these abstract economic models actually *works* in the real world. It doesn't matter how many footnotes they put in, or how many ways they tinker around the edges. The whole enterprise is totally rotten at the core: it has no relation to reality anymore – and furthermore, it never did.

It seems odd to quote scathing attacks on the economic system at length in a translation studies journal, but I would like to suggest that a reluctance to engage with phenomenological questions that involve our relationship with private property and the resulting rationalization and normalization of economic exploitation and social domination are a major blind spot in our very own efforts to become ever more self-reflexive. Hence, in addition to the sad spectacle surrounding the conformity and docility of academic economics comes the global fragmentation into 'knowledge tribes', which will become ever more bewildering without scholarly attention to the most fundamental questions of *property* (instead of innocuous authorship), *planetary elites* (rather than toothless literary theory), and *phenomenological disparities* (rather than lame cross-cultural discourse analysis; see Baumgarten & Gruber, 2014; also Baumgarten, 2015). Without grappling seriously with the dubious role of economics and the related issue of access to intellectual and material resources, how can one willingly subscribe to any 'community of practice' (Wenger, 1998) or any comparable initiatives, given that the wealth distribution across the globe is so profoundly unequal? I am a utopian realist, tending towards the pessimistic, but I am also a realist dreamer, and of course I am condemned to care about 'larger responsibilities' (as evoked by José Lambert), not only in my position as someone who gets paid for thinking about translation. It would therefore be a welcome development to see activist scholars, at the very least, question the fragmentation of knowledge to the detriment of the real issues at stake, or to condemn today's practices in universities, which, as Chomsky (2003, p. 239) nicely puts it, 'encourage people to occupy themselves with irrelevant and innocuous work'; and here he does refer only to research! In the same vein, it would be nice to see activist scholars adopting a highly critical stance towards universalizing narratives such as polysystemic explanations of translated literature, narratives the sweeping reach of which principally serves to occlude systemic economic and social injustices. Systems approaches, to be sure, are pedagogically viable in that they offer a range of diagnostic and explanatory devices to students of literature, especially concerning the study of the interconnected power relations and ideological positions in our globalized world, but, then again, they brush aside the really urgent questions concerning staggering economic inequalities throughout the globe.

Even though John Milton (2008, p. 163) suggests that economic factors have 'been almost totally ignored' in translation studies, the question still remains as to precisely *what kind of economics* has been ignored? In today's lukewarm climate of academic shadow boxing, some will regard it heretical to suggest more committed investigations of the political economy along post-Marxist lines, but why not move this methodology centre stage? Indeed, why not complement a broadly historical materialist approach with a commitment to an epistemological pluralism that is linked to an anarchist ethos that directly questions the alienating forces of advanced consumer capitalism? And whilst there is nothing to be said against the application of vaguely defined concepts such as ideology, power, discourse, etc., for they circumscribe important areas of investigation (at least when it comes to using the 'appropriate' terminology when applying for research funding!), it is inexcusable to apply these concepts in the service of apparently impartial research. Similarly, why spend so much time grappling with a mystical 'remainder' in translation, or with 'in-between spaces' of intercultural mediation, when the really urgent questions relate to the economic plight of real people who produce, consume, and disseminate (or they do not!) translations under the current neoliberal regime. Tang and Gentzler (2009, p. 179) say that today, '[i]n this globalised age, an initiator of a translation project often has to balance economic, political and ideological concerns so as to decide which text will be translated'; fine, but for them, like for almost everyone in our field, the economy is only one of many factors determining the fate of translation, while it appears to be most of the time *the only* truly meaningful analytical factor. As always, of course, there are numerous exceptions, for instance when activist subtitlers in Greece initiate their translations themselves, give up their time for free and upload the subtitles for free on *YouTube*, they mainly translate to spread their version of the crisis in Greece (Delistathi, in progress). But, then again, at the bottom line, these translators are deeply affected by the devastating economic restrictions imposed on Greece by undemocratic transnational institutions such as the European Union, international banking cartels, and especially the International Monetary Fund, which enforce measures of austerity which, as David Harvey (2014, p. 235) puts it, amount to nothing less than 'a geographical version of the redistributions of wealth occurring between rich and poor'. In analogy, hegemonic non-translation, by cultivating the absence of non-Anglophone identities in translation, also has its fair share in the unequal distribution of textual and other resources between the Anglophone empire and the rest. And in translation studies itself, a still pending 'critical economic' debate surely would need to continuously reflect on its very own political and ideological origins and positions.

4. Towards a normative ethics of commitment for modern translation studies

In an intriguing paper entitled 'The Pragmatics of Cross-Cultural Contact and some False Dichotomies in Translation Studies', Mona Baker (2001, pp. 10–11, emphasis added) claimed that there was increasing 'evidence of genuine *self-reflexivity*', with the potential to encourage 'contextualised critical assessments of our own theoretical literature', citing Theo Hermans' excellent *Translation in Systems* (1999) as a prime example of this development. Agreed. In her conclusion, however, Baker (2001, p. 18) seems to suggest that we should question 'normative approaches' to the benefit of an 'increased attention to human agency'. I am aware that Baker here largely refers to the normativity of a large bulk of approaches before descriptive translation studies and the cultural turn ignited the institutional success of the discipline; normative tendencies that still insisted on telling people the best ways to translate, including other birth pangs besetting an emerging field of power/knowledge (to employ the best-known Foucauldianism). Yet, normativity, unfortunately, is the very *raison d'être* of our institutionalized existence, and if we cannot escape it, why should we not celebrate it? It might at least make some of us feel better about ourselves. And yes, elucidating human agency is at the core of all our research endeavours, but considering the unfortunate occasion of only toddlers displaying little to no ideological inklings, the only existential way out of this quandary is to embrace normativity, a tactical charade for those of us who (at least pretend to) display genuine ambitions to grapple with the world's suffering. If we take a deep and honest look at ourselves, then we must admit our own collusion within the capitalist power game. And trying to disentangle our conformism, docility, and complicities from our research is an unappetizing business, a still pending business of unravelling that remains far beyond the remit of this paper. Let us just presuppose that our own collusion with the dominant powers, most obviously with the machinery of the state, unveils some unpleasant truths because it compels us to critically interrogate our privately-held ontological beliefs, our attitudes to the production and dissemination of knowledge, and our desires and moral intentions. We might start at a genuine self-reflexive analytics of power by recourse to critical theory, moving concepts such as instrumental reason and reification into the midst of our analytical matrix. One main objective of this special issue concerns 'a re-examination of the role of the historian, the ideologist or the censor' in translation studies, but let us first see how our suffering in history, our ideological complicities, and our constant subjections to self-censorship are shining in the light of the reified principles of commodity rule and techno-scientific rationality.

Advanced capitalism rests on a knowledge system diagnosed in critical theory as an epistemology of *instrumental reason* that perpetuates itself through the evolutionary dynamics of *reification*, a process understood as a commodified form of (cultural) forgetting (Adorno & Horkheimer, 2002; Horkheimer, 2012; Lukács, 1971). Fuelled by the fast-paced commodification of our world, this near-universal instrumental rationality has become parasitic upon our cognitive faculties (Bewes, 2002). The implications for intellectual and, especially, everyday life are stark, though they tend to be mainly self-consciously reflected by scholars, placing an even stronger charge on them to cut through the social domination exercised by instrumental reason, but, as I have argued, they need to keep a cold eye on the structurally tilted and essentially exploitative economic foundations inherent in the current world order. Within this context, hegemonic non-translation, as I would like to suggest, rests on the evolutionary interplay of instrumentally rationalized thinking; a pattern of thought that, at least at the current historical junction, is strongly affected by powerful economic forces in the international political economy. Once we begin looking at translational phenomena from a normative position that takes suffering, for instance in the form of exploitation in the commodified marketplace, as the *terminus a quo*, we begin to understand that social domination manifests itself through the reified processes of capital accumulation, and only *peripherally* through social realities such as mono- or multiculturalism (Žižek, 2000), or interculturality for that matter. In the sense that the capitalist logic permeates most forms of translation, it is totalitarian, and in the sense that hegemonic non-translation might be diagnosed as endemic in the neoliberal world order, we begin to understand that Toury's (1995) norm concept can only be the starting point for socially meaningful research (cf. Pym's [1998, p. 111] critique of norm theory). To take a second example from the history of Anglo–German intellectual relations: the translation of some works of German critical theory was heavily bent towards Anglophone norms and value systems, at least until postmodern relativism noisily asserted itself on the international academic scene towards the end of the twentieth century. Theodor Adorno's critical thought suffered profoundly in English translation. Ironically, whilst his life's mission was to mitigate and debunk the worst excesses of the positivist *Weltanschauung*, early translations of some of his major works, many of which are still in wide circulation, severely destabilize the fragmentary and speculative character of his philosophy (Adorno, 1984, 1997; Hullot-Kentor, 1985). The philosophical dislocations and textual destabilizations evident in Adorno's early English mirror image ironically invalidate an idealistic metaphysics that sought to expose the 'identitarian thinking' that bolsters the capitalist world project. Instrumental reason attempts to grasp the world according to the cold logic of computational algorithms, and in doing so it gradually purges the world of its infinite range of intellectual and biological resources; indeed, it purges it of its mysteries. To be sure, these hegemonic non-translations of Adorno's oeuvre, large numbers of which are still being read, cited, and consumed in English, remain under the spell of the reified principles of advanced consumer capitalism.

In concluding this normative narrative about the fate of translation in the global political economy, let me now put forward a tentative sketch of the philosophical and political implications for activist translation scholarship. Given our current historical predicament, the blind spots of an idealized self-reflexivity can be elucidated along ontological, epistemological, and ethical dimensions. Firstly, if scholars clarify for themselves the ways in which they purport to experience, know, and shape the world, these could function as the Archimedean points of departure towards an ethics of commitment for modern translation studies. Under the current regime of advanced capitalism, we have internalized an *ontology* of 'profitable exchange' which intensely alienates us from nature and from ourselves. If commodified experience is an ideological entrapment for most of the world's population, then this also rings true for us as translation scholars. Secondly, and on the *epistemological* plane, hegemonic non-translation constitutes an outgrowth of 'instrumental reason' that goes against the idea of ecologically sustainable coexistence. Paradoxically, hegemonic non-translation also constitutes a *visible* strategic move; its visibility, however, remains defined through absence, through the absence of any consideration for the infinite plurality of life. For Santos (2006, p. 18), the most conspicuous epistemological absence in our postmodern human condition is a profound 'lack of social experience' that urgently needs to be recuperated into a 'waste of social experience'. Hence, and by means of analogy, hegemonic non-translation is always at pains to contain, indeed extinguish, the anarchic multitude of voices, this endless stream of intersubjective consciousness that gives our planet its colourful tint. Santos' (2006, p. 27) sociology of absences also pursues an ethical agenda that 'consists in recuperating and valorising alternative systems of production, popular economic organizations, workers' cooperatives, self-managed enterprises, solidary production, etc., which have been hidden or discredited by the capitalist orthodoxy of productivity'. It is clear that any translational production outside these sparsely dispersed alternative centres of production, dissemination, and consumption only keeps the wheels of the neoliberal empire in motion.

This last point leads me to the *ethical* dimension of an expressly normative self-reflexivity for translation scholars, a new ethical stance that presupposes the desire for a world which is not primarily geared towards the benefit of an internationally mobile and cash-rich elite. How many of us translation scholars are part of this elite? Are we sufficiently self-reflexive about this question? To take an extreme example, if you can afford to work as an independent scholar in Prague, Madrid, or elsewhere, because you happen to be a London landlord who exploits working-class tenants, can you ever be honestly self-reflexive? Whilst Zygmunt Baumann (1998) in his well-known *Globalization: The Human Consequences* describes this phenomenon as 'absentee landlordism', we might find more answers to such questions in the newly revived modern anarchist movement, 'which is less about seizing state power than about exposing, delegitimizing and dismantling mechanisms of rule while winning ever larger spaces of autonomy from it' (Graeber, 2002, p. 68); ever larger spaces of autonomy from the stifling hierarchies of the educational sector, from the cultural politics of the pro-capitalist funding establishment, especially in countries like the USA and the UK, and from the pretentiousness of a professorial class that survives on the remnants of ancient and authoritarian regimes of knowledge control. Moreover, and by analogy, a normative-ethical attitude towards scholarly and political practice which takes account of absences induced by hegemonic power relations – such as those inscribed in hegemonic non-translation – may not only 'transform impossible into possible objects' (Santos, 2006, p. 15), but, above all, such an attitude may pave the way for 'the construction of counter-hegemonic globalization' (Santos, 2006, p. 12). Let me therefore conclude, in support of Simon Critchley's (2008, p. 3) seminal call for engaged scholar- and citizenship, with a call for an 'ethics of commitment for modern translation workers and theorists'. Such a committed ethical stance aims to elaborate 'normative principles that might enable us to face and face down the present political situation'. Such a form of commitment does not, of course, call for the immediate abolition of the state, as traditional anarchism did, but for an 'anarchic meta-politics', which might lead 'from an ethics of infinitely demanding commitment to a politics of resistance' (Critchley, 2008, p. 89; cf. Graeber, 2002). And, in an attempt to weaken the harmful ideological divisions across the authoritarian spectrum of Marxism and the professed ethos of horizontal decision making in progressive anarchist circles, we could then conceivably ponder genuine practical issues, for instance why we should not envisage a division of labour between a historical materialist, i.e. an economics-centred, and a post-anarchist phenomenology of translation research, 'in which Marxists critique the political economy, but stay out of organising, and anarchists handle the day-to-day organising, but defer to questions of abstract theory' (Graeber, 2004, p. 331)? That would be something to work towards; but, hey, it's just a daydream of an incorrigible utopian.

Acknowledgments
I would like to thank Chantal Gagnon and Christina Delistathi, and the anonymous reviewers for their constructive feedback and comments on earlier versions of this paper.

Disclosure statement
No potential conflict of interest was reported by the author.

References
Adorno, T. W., & Horkheimer, M. (2002). *Dialectic of enlightenment – Philosophical fragments*, translated by Edmund Jephcott. Stanford: Stanford University Press.
Adorno, T. W. (1984). *Aesthetic theory*, translated by Christopher Lenhardt. London: Routledge and Kegan Paul.
Adorno, T. W. (1997). *Aesthetic theory*, translated by Robert Hullot-Kentor. London: Continuum.
Apter, E. (2001). On translation in a global market. *Public Culture, 13*(1), 1–12. doi:10.1215/08992363-13-1-1
Arrojo, R. (1998). The revision of the traditional gap between theory and practice and the empowerment of translation in postmodern times. *The Translator, 4*(1), 25–48. doi: 10.1080/13556509.1998.10799005
Backhouse, R. E. (2010). *The puzzle of modern economics: Science or ideology?* Cambridge: Cambridge University Press.
Bassnett, S., & Trivedi, H. (Eds.). (1999). *Post-colonial translation: Theory and practice*. London: Routledge.

Baudrillard, J. (2010). *The agony of power*, with an introduction by S. Lotringer. (A. Hodges, Trans.). Los Angeles: Semiotext(e).
Baker, M. (2001). The pragmatics of cross-cultural contact and some false dichotomies in translation studies. *CTIS Occasional Papers, 1*, 7–20.
Baker, M. (2009). Resisting state terror: Theorizing communities of activist translators and interpreters. In E. Bielsa & C.W. Hughes (Eds.), *Globalization, political violence and translation* (pp. 222–242). Basingstoke: Palgrave Macmillan.
Baumann, Z. (1998). *Globalization: The human consequences*. Cambridge: Polity Press.
Baumgarten, S., & Gruber, E. (2014). Phenomenological asymmetries in Welsh translation history. In C. Rundle (Ed.), Theories and methodologies of translation history. Special issue of *The Translator, 20*(1), 26–43. doi:10.1080/13556509.2014.899092
Baumgarten, S. (2015). Language, translation, and imperialism. In I. Ness & Z. Cope (Eds.), *The Palgrave encyclopedia of imperialism and anti-imperialism* (pp. 507–513). Basingstoke: Palgrave Macmillan.
Benjamin, W. (1940/1989). Theses on the philosophy of history. In S. E. Bronner & D. MacKay Kellner (Eds.), *Critical theory and society – A reader* (pp. 255–263). London: Routledge.
Bennett, K. (2006). Critical language study and translation – The case of academic discourse. In J. Ferreira Duarte, A. Assis Rosa, & T. Seruya (Eds.), *Translation studies at the interface of disciplines* (pp. 111–127). Amsterdam: John Benjamins.
Bennett, K. (2007). Epistemicide! The tale of a predatory discourse. *The Translator, 13*(2), 151–169. doi:10.1080/13556509.2007.10799236
Bewes, T. (2002). *Reification or the anxiety of late capitalism*. London: Verso.
Billiani, F. (2007). Assessing boundaries – Censorship and translation. An introduction. In F. Billiani (Ed.), *Modes of censorship and translation* (pp. 1–25). Manchester: St. Jerome.
Bourdieu, P. (1977). The economics of linguistic exchanges. *Social Science Information, 16*(6), 645–668. doi:10.1177/053901847701600601
Bourdieu, P. (1991). *Language and symbolic power*. Cambridge: Polity Press.
Chakrabartty, A. (2013, October 28). Mainstream economics is in denial: The world has changed. *The Guardian*. Retrieved from http://www.theguardian.com
Chomsky, N. (2003). Intellectuals and social change. In P. R. Mitchell & J. Schoeffel (Eds.), *Understanding power – The indispensable Chomsky* (pp. 224–266). London: Vintage Books.
Critchley, S. (2008). *Infinitely demanding: Ethics of commitment, politics of resistance*. London: Verso.
Cronin, M. (2003). *Translation and globalization*. London: Routledge.
Delistathi, C. (in progress). 'Activist subtitlers and the Greek crisis'.
Dizdar, D. (2014). Instrumental thinking in translation studies. *Target, 26*(2), 206–223. doi:10.1075/target.26.2.03diz
van Doorslaer, L. (2009). How language and (non-)translation impact on media newsrooms: The case of newspapers in Belgium. *Perspectives: Studies in Translatology, 17*(2), 83–92. doi:10.1080/09076760903125051
Foucault, M. (1972). *The archeology of knowledge* (A.M.S. Smith, Trans.). London: Tavistock Publications.
Graeber, D. (2002). The new anarchists. *New Left Review, 13*, 61–73.
Graeber, D. (2004). The twilight of vanguardism. In J. Sen, A. Anand, A. Escobar, & P. Waterman (Eds.), *World Social Forum – Challenging empires* (pp. 329–335). New Delhi: The Viveka Foundation.
Graeber, D. (2013). *The democracy project – A history. A crisis. A movement*. London: Allen Lane.
Grossman, E. (2010). *Why translation matters*. New Haven and London: Yale University Press.
Hall, K. (2005). Where 'id' was, there 'it' or 'es' shall be: Reflections on translating Freud. *Target, 17*(2), 349–361. doi:10.1075/target.17.2.08hal
Harvey, D. (2014). *Seventeen contradictions and the end of capitalism*. London: Profile Books.
Hermans, T. (1999). *Translation in systems: Descriptive and systemic approaches explained*. Manchester: St. Jerome.
Horkheimer, M. (2011). *Traditionelle und kritische Theorie – Fünf Aufsätze*. Frankfurt: Fischer Verlag.
Horkheimer, M. (2012). *Critique of instrumental reason* (Matthew J. O'Connell, & others, Trans.). London: Verso.

Hullot-Kentor, R. (1985). Adorno's aesthetic theory: The translation. *Telos, 65*, 143–147.
Jameson, F. (1988). *The ideologies of theory: Essays 1971–86*, 2 vols. London: Routledge.
Kant, I. (1784/1963). Idea for a universal history from a cosmopolitan point of view, translated by Lewis W. Beck. Retrieved from https://www.marxists.org.
Lambert, J. (1991/2006). In quest of literary world maps. In D. Delabastita, L. D'hulst, & R. Meylaerts (Eds.), *Functional approaches to culture and translation –Selected papers by José Lambert* (pp. 63–74). Amsterdam: John Benjamins.
Lambert, J. (1995/2006). Literatures, translation and (de)colonization. In D. Delabastita, L. D'hulst, & R. Meylaerts (Eds.), *Functional approaches to culture and translation – Selected papers by José Lambert* (pp. 87–103). Amsterdam: John Benjamins.
Lukács, G. (1971). *History and class consciousness* (R. Livingstone, Trans). Cambridge, MA: MIT Press.
Marais, K. (2014). *Translation theory and development studies: A complexity theory approach.* London & New York: Routledge.
Milton, J. (2008). The importance of economic factors in translation publication: An example from Brazil. In A. Pym, M. Shlesinger, & D. Simeoni (Eds.), *Beyond descriptive translation studies – Investigations in homage to Gideon Toury* (pp. 163–173). Amsterdam: John Benjamins.
Niranjana, T. (1992). *Siting translation – History, post-structuralism, and the colonial context.* Berkeley: University of California Press.
Ornston, D. G. (1992). Improving Strachey's Freud. In D. G. Ornston (Ed.), *Translating freud* (pp. 191–222). New Haven, CT: Yale University Press.
Phillipson, R. (1992). *Linguistic imperialism.* Oxford: Oxford University Press.
Pieterse, J. N. (2004). *Globalization or empire?* London: Routledge.
Piketty, T. (2014). *Capital in the twenty-first century* (A. Goldhammer, Trans.). Cambridge, MA: Harvard University Press.
Pym, A. (1998). *Method in translation history.* Manchester: St. Jerome.
Pym, A. (1999). Two principles, one probable paradox and a humble suggestion, all concerning percentages of translation and non-translation into various languages, particularly English. Retrieved from: http://usuaris.tinet.cat/apym/on-line/translation/rates/rates.html
Santos, B. de S. (2006). *The rise of the global left – The world social forum and beyond.* London: Zed Books.
Tang, J., & Gentzler, E. (2009). Globalisation, networks and translation: A Chinese perspective. *Perspectives: Studies in Translatology, 16*(3–4), 169–182. doi:10.1080/09076760802707918
Toury, G. (1995). *Descriptive translation studies – and beyond.* Amsterdam: John Benjamins.
Tymoczko, M. (2005). Censorship and self-censorship in translation: Ethics and ideology, resistance and collusion. In E. Ni Chuilleana, C. O Cuilleanáin, & D. Parris (Eds.), *Translation and censorship: Patterns of communication and interference* (pp. 24–45). Papers from a conference on translation and censorship held in Trinity College Dublin.
Tymoczko, M., (Ed.). (2010). *Translation, resistance, activism.* Amherst, MA: University of Massachusetts Press.
Venuti, L. (1995). *The translator's invisibility: A history of translation.* London and New York: Routledge.
Venuti, L. (1998). *The scandals of translation – Towards an ethics of difference.* London: Routledge.
Wenger, E. (1998). *Communities of practice: Learning, meaning, and identity.* Cambridge: Cambridge University Press.
Žižek, S. (1989). *The sublime object of ideology.* London: Verso.
Žižek, S. (2000). Holding the place. In J. Butler, E. Laclau, & S. Žižek (Eds.), *Contingency, hegemony, universality: Contemporary dialogues on the left* (pp. 308–326). London: Verso.
Žižek, S. (2010). *Living in the end times.* London: Verso.

Index

Note: **Bold** page numbers refer to tables and page numbers followed by "n" denote endnotes.

Abramson, Adelina 24–26
Abramson, Paulina 24–26
Acuña-Partal, Carmen 2
Adorno, Theodor 125
Albee, Edward 3; *Who's afraid of Virginia Woolf?* 39–43; *The Zoo Story* 43n2
Allen, Woody: *Bananas* 93
Álvarez Turienzo, Saturnino 66–68, 71
Anglophone supremacism 118–121
Animal Farm (Orwell) 1
Apter, Emily 118
Arias Salgado, Gabriel 61
assumed translators 39
Attardo, S. 95
audience's perception and translation: audiovisual semiotics 94–95; humor 95; Kubrick vs. Lyne films 95–96; problems in *Lolita* 107; translatability of humor in *Lolita* 96–98; verbal vs. audiovisual humor 98–106, 110–114
Aymà (publishing company) 63–68

Bacardí, Montserrat 63
Bacon, E. 49
Baker, M. 22
Baker, Mona 124
Bananas (Allen) 93
Baquero, Arcadio 44n9
Barea, Arturo: *The Forging of a Rebel* 28, 33n3
Bartra, Agustí 67
Baudelaire (Sartre) 70
Baumgarten, Stefan 4
Beauvoir, Simone de 63, 64, 66
Beevor, A. 23, 24
Bennett, Karen 116, 118
Berzin, Yan K. 24
Billiani, F. 120, 122
Blium, Arlen 50
Blommaert, Jan 76
Bourdieu, Pierre 119
Brezhnev period and translation: attention paid to national writers, decrease in 54; *Novyi mir* 51–52, **53**, 55; publication of Western literature 50–51; Soviet literature and stagnation 48–49; Tvardovskii and Kosolapov editorships 56–57; Western writers *vs.* republics 54–55
Britanishskii, Vladimir 57
Bronn, Heinrich Georg 8–9, 12
Browne, J. 11, 15

Carus, Julius Victor 12
Castellet, Josep Maria 65, 69, 72
Catalan translation, Sartre's works: censorship and Francoist dictatorship 60–61; circumstances for entrance into Spain 70–72, 73n17, 73n18; institutional censorship 59–60; publishing permits and dossiers 63–65; translations between 1965–1973 61–63; *see also* censorship and Catalan translation of Sartre
Cendrós, Joan Baptista 63, 64, 72n1
censorship and Catalan translation of Sartre: *Baudelaire* 70; dossiers 63–65; *Esquisse d'une théorie des émotions* 70; Francoist dictatorship 60–61; institutional censorship 59–60; *La nausée* 65–67; *Le mur* 67; *Les mots* 67; *Questions de méthode* 69; *Réflexions sur la question juive* 67–68; *Teatre* 68–69
Chaume, F. 99
Chesterman, A. 8
Chomsky, N. 123
Chukovskaia, Lidiia 50
Civil War 36, 60; *see also* Spanish Civil War translators
Claparède, Edouard 10–11
Clarke, Arthur C. 51
Cold War 48
The Complaisant Lover (Greene) 38
Corredor, Josep M. 61, 63, 71

Darbelnet, P. 86, 91n14
Darwin, Charles 2, 7–18; authorizing new European translations 11–15; disappointed

expectations on translations 8–11; *[On] The Origin of Species* 2, 7–18
Darwin, Francis 12
Delgado, M. 37
Die Bücherei 16
Duckett, V. 93

Elden, Stuart 77
El Diario Regional 41
Esquisse d'une théorie des émotions 70

Falcón, Irene 27
Fatal Attraction (Lyne) 95
Le Figaro 70
Fischer, Louis 28
Flashdance (Lyne) 95
The Forging of a Rebel (Barea) 28, 33n3
Fortus, Maria 24–26
Foucault, Michel 4, 76–91; domesticating trends, translators 88–89; historical inaccuracies 82–85; issues in translations 76–77; Norwegian view 78; plain errors 87–88; power, conceptual use of 79–82; power for dummies 86–87; sructural analysis 82–85; syntax 86
Foucault Studies 77
Francoist dictatorship 59–61
Fr. Artola 40
Les Fruits d'or (Sarraute) 55–56

García Escudero, J. M. 41–42
Garland, David 83
Garzón del Camino, Aurelio 76
General Administration Archive (AGA) 36
General Archive of the Administration (AGA) 3, 60, 63
general theory of verbal humor (GTVH) 95
Gies, D. T. 37
Glavlit 50, 53
Godayol, Pilar 3
Goriaeva, T. M. 50
Graeber, D. 122
Gray, Asa 10
Greene, Graham: *The Complaisant Lover* 38
Groff, C. 8
Grossman, Edith 119

Harding, S. A. 22
Harvey, David 124
hegemonic non-translation 4, 117–121
Hermans, T. 78
Herrera, José Méndez 38
Hjermitslev, H. 16
Hooker, J. D. 9
hyponymy 90n6

ideology: apolitical conceptions 116; history 115–118; translation scholars 117
Indecent Proposal (Lyne) 95
Inghilleri, M. 22, 23
Inostrannaia literatura 51–52, 57
Iribarne, Manuel Fraga 61
Ishiguro, Kazuo: *The Remain's of the Day* 96

Jameson, K. 115
Juventud Socialista Unificada (JSU) 26–27

Koestler, Arthur 51
Kovalesky, V. O. 13
Kowalsky, D. 24
Kubrick, Stanley 4; *Lolita* (1962) 93–108; *2001: A Space Odyssey* 51
Kuznetsov, Anatolii 50

Lambert, José 116
Levi, Giovanni 60
Living in the End Times (Žižek) 117
Llovet, Jordi 61
Lolita (1955, Nabokov) 93–108
Lolita (1962, Kubrick) 93–108
Los girasoles ciegos (Méndez) 39
Lygo, Emily 3
Lyne, Adrian 93–108; *Fatal Attraction* 95; *Flashdance* 95; *Indecent Proposal* 95; *9 1/2 Weeks* 95

Magris, Claudio 8
Maier, C. 23
Mauriac, François 56
Méndez, Alberto 39
Merino-Álvarez, Raquel 3
microhistory 59–60, 70
Milton, John 123
Ministerio de Información y Turismo (MIT) 60, 61, 65–70
Morán, Borges 68
Les mots (Gallimard) 59–60, 67
Moulinié, J. J. 13
Mozhaev, Boris 50
Mr. Baquero 40
Mr. Mostaza 40
Munday, Jeremy 59–60, 70
Le mur 63, 64, 67, 68
Murray, John 8

Nabokov, Vladimir 93
La nausée 61, 63–67
9 1/2 Weeks (Lyne) 95
normative ethics of commitment 124–127
Nosotros 27
Novyi mir 3, 51–52, **53,** 55–58

INDEX

O'Farrell, Clare 77, 91n7
O'Farrell, Neumann 77
[On] The Origin of Species (Darwin) 2, 7–18
'open' censorship policy 38
Orwell, George: *Animal Farm* 1
Østerberg, Dag 78
Osuna, José 41

Palmer 23
Peckham, M. 7, 15
Pomerantsev, Peter 2
post-anarchist translation theory 117
Prum, Michel 18
Pui, Manuel 68–69
Pym, A. 8, 90n3

Questions de méthode 69

Rayfield, D. 16
Réflexions sur la question juive 67–68
The Remain's of the Day (Ishiguro) 96
Rodríguez-Espinosa, Marcos 3
Royer, ClemenceAuguste 10
Rupp-Eisenreich, B. 9
Russia Today 2

Salama-Carr, M. 22
Salinger, J. D. 52
Sandle, M. 49
Santos, Boaventura de Sousa 118, 119
Sarraute, Nathalie: *Les Fruits d'or* 55–56
Sartre, Jean-Paul 3–4, 59–73; *Baudelaire* 70; *Teatre* 68–69
scholars translation 117; self-reflexivity 126
Schuman, S. 94
Serra d'Or 63
Sheridan, Alan 76
Sherry, Samantha 51, 57
"Social Darwinism" 10
Solzhenitsyn, Aleksandr 50
Sopena, Mireia 66, 71
Spanish Civil War 3
Spanish Civil War translators: Abramson 24–26; civilian translators 26–29; exiles 29–31; Fortus 24–26; military translators 24–26; shortage of military translators 23; traitors 29–31; Trotskyists 29–31; war chroniclers 31–33
Spanish theatre translations: censors of *Who's afraid of Virginia Woolf?* 39–43; under Franco's rule 37–38; Herrera's works 39; historical accounts 36–37; role of professional translators 38–39
stagnation 48
Streetcar named Desire (Williams) 38, 39
Surveiller et punir 4, 76–90

Teatre (Sartre) 68–69
Thomas, H. 23
translation: *vs.* adaptation 38–39, 43n2; audience's perception (*see* audience's perception and translation); audiovisual semiotics 94–95; Catalan translation, Sartre's works (*see* Catalan translation, Sartre's works); censorship in USSR 51; European translations, Darwin 11–15; historical accounts 1; issues in Foucault's works 76–77; microhistory 59–60, 70; scholars 91n14, 117; *Surveiller et punir* (*see* Foucault, Michel); technological advancements 2; *[On] The Origin of Species* (*see* Darwin, Charles); in USSR (*see* Brezhnev period and translation); *see also* Spanish theatre translations
'translationese' 77
TRAnslations CEnsored (TRACE) project 37–38
translation studies 77; economic factors 122–123; normative ethics of commitment 124–127
translator: assumed 39; civilian translators 26–29; domesticating trends 78, 88–89; epistolary exchange 8; ethical and ideological implication 2; exiles 29–31; military translators 24–26; Soviet censorship 50; traitors 29–31; Trotskyists 29–31; *vs.* adaptor 38–39, 43n2; war chroniclers 31–33
Triadú, Joan 63
Trotskyists 29–31
2001: A Space Odyssey (Kubrick) 51

Ukrainian government 2

Vallverdú, Francesc 60, 63, 70
Vandaele, Jeroen 4
Venuti, L. 78, 118, 120
Vilaginés, Carme 63
Vinay, J.-P. 86, 91n14
Volodarsky, B. 24

war chroniclers 31–33
Who's afraid of Virginia Woolf? (Albee) 39–43
Williams, Tennessee 3, 38; *Streetcar named Desire* 38, 39

Xuriguera, Ramon 63, 66

Zabalbeascoa, P. 95, 99
Zabalbeascoa, Patrick 4
Zanotti, S. 8
Žižek, Slavoj 116
The Zoo Story (Albee) 43n2